Moving Beyond Your Past

TIM SLEDGE

LifeWay Press
Nashville, Tennessee

ACKNOWLEDGEMENTS

LifeWay Press books are published by LifeWay Christian Resources, 127 Ninth Avenue, North, Nashville, Tennessee 37234

ISBN 0-8054-9927-X
Dewey Decimal Number 615.8
Subject Heading: Church Work with the Hurting / / Dysfunctional Families

Sources for definitions in *Moving Beyond Your Past*:
By permission. From Merriam-*Webster's Collegiate Dictionary, Tenth Edition* ©1993 by Merriam-Webster Inc., publisher of the Merriam-Webster® dictionaries

Unless otherwise indicated, biblical quotations are from the Holy Bible, *New International Version*, copyright © 1973, 1978, 1984 by International Bible Society (NIV). Other versions used: the *New American Standard Bible.* © The Lockman Foundation, 1960, 1962, 1963, 1968, 1971, 1972, 1973, 1975, 1977. Used by permission; the *King James Version* (KJV).

To order additional copies of this resource: WRITE LifeWay Church Resources Customer Service; 127 Ninth Avenue, North; Nashville, TN 37234-0113; FAX order to (615) 251-5933; PHONE 1-800-458-2772; EMAIL to CustomerService@lifeway.com; or visit the LifeWay Christian Store serving you.

Printed in the United States of America

LifeWay.

As God works through us, we will help people and churches know Jesus Christ and seek His kingdom by providing biblical solutions that spiritually transform individuals and cultures.

Table of Contents

About the Author

Tim Sledge is a native Texan, having been born in Austin. In 1976 he earned the doctor of ministry degree from Southwestern Baptist Theological Seminary. He is the pastor of Kingsland Baptist Church in Katy, Texas. Writing is one of Tim's many gifts, and he uses that gift to write for various Southern Baptist agencies. He and his wife, Linda, have two sons, Jonathan and David.

Tim's experience with an alcoholic father led him to seek help in resolving personal, emotional, and spiritual issues growing from his past. He developed *Making Peace with Your Past*, and now this sequel, *Moving Beyond Your Past*, to assist people in his church and community who came from dysfunctional families. Tim and others in his church have led more than 48 groups through these two courses. So many people have responded that Kingsland Baptist has developed a major emphasis on ministry to adults from dysfunctional families. A number of people travel great distances to participate. Because of this ministry, a strong prayer ministry, and aggressive outreach ministries, worship attendance increased over a four-year period from around 350 to around 1,000, and baptisms average over 100 a year. A significant number of these persons were reached through the church's ministry to dysfunctional families.

LIFE® Support Group Series Editorial Team
Kay Moore, Design Editor
Dale McCleskey, Editor
Kenny Adams, Manuscript Assistant

David Walley, Team Leader/LIFE® Support Group Series Specialist

Graphics by Lori Putnam
Cover Design by Edward Crawford

Preparing to Move Beyond

SHUNNED AND HUMILIATED

Beth believed her idea to hold her office's annual picnic at a new location this year was a smart move that the other employees would enjoy. She could hardly wait for the next staff meeting to present her social committee's plan to her co-workers. Her presentation turned out to be a flop, however. One employee publicly criticized Beth's plan. She said she believed the picnic would be poorly attended if Beth insisted on the new choice of sites. After the staff meeting several people approached Beth and accused her of being insensitive and pushy. Beth reacted to the incident by compulsive overeating to mask her pain. On her way home from work she stopped by the grocery and bought two giant packages of cream-filled chocolate cookies and ate them all in one sitting. Then she became ill and had to miss the next two days of work because of the effects of the eating spree. Beth felt shunned and humiliated.

Many of us have been in situations like Beth in which we felt embarrassed because of someone's critical remarks. Because she had experienced a painful childhood, however, the situation about the office picnic prompted Beth to have an unhealthy reaction that could harm her physically or eventually cause her to lose her job.

In *Making Peace with Your Past*, you learned about growing up in a family in which the presence of an emotionally needy family member kept you from developing healthy behaviors and relationships. The course helped you understand feelings and problems related to your childhood experiences. In your Face-to-Face support group you learned to face painful childhood experiences and to feel the emotional pain resulting from those experiences. You began to understand how those experiences affect you today.

When she studied *Making Peace with Your Past*, Beth realized that the powerful feeling she experienced after the employees criticized her was the feeling of shame. Because she grew up in a home with an alcoholic parent, she grew up feeling that something was basically wrong with her. In *Making Peace with Your Past* she studied about how she learned to feel this kind of shame.

Moving Beyond Your Past would help Beth focus on changing present behaviors which grow out of those painful childhood experiences. In this study we will continue to look into the past when appropriate, but our focus is on present-tense change.

In *Moving Beyond Your Past* you will take these steps to change present behavior:
- Learn to alert yourself when a painful childhood experience causes you to react in an unhealthy way to a given situation.

- Begin to make new choices about how you respond to situations rather than simply react according to childhood hurts.
- Learn some new ways of responding to people and to situations.
- Go through an intense time of confronting these issues, which results in significant changes in your life. You continue to make new discoveries about yourself that cause you to go through the healing process again, but on a smaller scale.

For example, when someone criticizes a decision she makes, Beth could identify the powerful feeling she has and would know to call it shame. She would remember how she learned to feel that kind of shame. Then as she felt shame coming over her, she could decide to say no to it. She could address the compulsion of overeating that she falls into whenever shame comes over her, and she could choose a different reaction. When she feels a shame attack about to occur, she could reflect on the fact that Christ loves and accepts her and the fact that she respects herself. She could choose some Christ-honoring ways of responding: she could talk privately with the co-workers who criticized her to try to enlist their support of her plan, or she could seek the advice of a trusted friend to help her deal with the situation in her workplace.

This study is built on the concept that emotional recovery occurs in cycles. People who have worked on emotional recovery for a while often say they feel like they are "back to square one"—right back where they started—in their emotional healing. In truth, though, what feels like a return to "square one" probably is a need to start another cycle of recovery.

On the inside back cover you will find an illustration of the cycles of pain and recovery, which you will study in *Moving Beyond Your Past*. This illustration will help you visualize where we are going on this journey. Throughout this study you also will encounter nine Turning Points. At each Turning Point we ask you to make a decision which will be crucial to your recovery process. On page 224 you will see a drawing that illustrates the cycles of recovery with the nine turning points.

Moving Beyond Your Past is part of the LIFE® Support Group Series, an educational system of discovery-group and support-group resources for providing Christian ministry and emotional support to individuals in areas of social, emotional, and physical need. These resources deal with such life issues as chemical dependency, codependency, abuse recovery, eating disorders, divorce, and grieving life's losses. Individuals using LIFE® Support Group Series courses will be led through recovery to discipleship and ministry.

Moving Beyond Your Past is a support-group course designed to be basic to any church's support-group ministry. A support group studies dysfunctional family issues and other sensitive emotional issues that individuals might face. A carefully selected group facilitator guides discussion of the topics and helps group members process what they have learned during their study. This group is not a therapy group. Rather, this is a self-help group, in which group members help one another by talking in a safe, loving environment.

Moving Beyond Your Past is an integrated course of study. To achieve the full benefit of the educational design, prepare your individual assignments, share your moral inventory with your sponsor (you'll read more about this in unit 1), and participate in the group sessions.

How to study the book

Study Tips. Five days a week (which compose a unit) you will be expected to study a segment of content material. You may need from 30 to 60 minutes of study time each day. Even if you find that you can study the material in less time, spread out the study over five days. This will give you more time to apply the truths to your life. Study at your own pace. This book has been written as a tutorial text. Study it as if Tim Sledge is sitting at your side helping you learn. When the book asks you a question or gives you an assignment, respond immediately. Each assignment is indented and appears in **boldface type**. When we ask you to respond in writing, a pencil appears beside the assignment. For example, an assignment will look like this:

✎ **Read Psalm 139:13. Write what the verse tells about God's care for you.**

Of course, in an actual activity, a line would appear here and below each assignment. You would write your answer on this line. Then, when we ask you to respond in a nonwriting manner—for example, by thinking about or praying about a matter—an arrow appears beside the assignment. This type of assignment will look like this:

➤ **Stop and pray, thanking God for someone who affirms you regularly.**

In most cases your "personal tutor" will give you some feedback about your response—for example, a suggestion about what you might have written. This process is designed to help you learn the material more effectively.

Set a definite time and select a quiet place where you can study with little interruption. Keep a Bible handy for times when the material asks you to look up Scripture. Memorizing Scripture is an important part of your work. In the margin make notes of problems, questions, or concerns that arise as you study. You will discuss many of these during your support-group sessions.

Support-Group Session. Once each week, attend a *Moving Beyond Your Past* support-group session designed to help members discuss the content they studied the previous week and share personal responses to issues and problems. These groups provide a safe and loving environment for personal and spiritual healing, growth, and recovery. This group studying *Moving Beyond Your Past* is called a Heart-to-Heart support group. During this 13 weeks the members of your group will share on a Heart-to-Heart level as they discuss brokenness, surrender, and recovery.

Getting the most from the course

The support group adds a needed dimension to your learning. If you have started a study of *Moving Beyond Your Past* and you are not involved in a group study, try to enlist some friends or associates who have been through *Making Peace with Your Past* and who will work through this course with you. Approach your church leaders about beginning such a group. *Moving Beyond Your Past Facilitator's Guide* provides guidance and learning activities for these sessions. (For orders WRITE LifeWay Church Resources Customer Service; 127 Ninth Avenue, North; Nashville, TN 37234-0113; FAX order to (615) 251-5933; PHONE 1-800-458-2772; EMAIL to CustomerService@lifeway.com; or visit the LifeWay Christian Store serving you.

Moving Beyond Your Past is written with the assumption that you have received Jesus Christ as your Savior. If you have not yet made this decision, you will find in unit 4 guidance for doing so. You will benefit more from *Moving Beyond Your Past* if you have Jesus guiding you in the process.

Heart-to-Heart Support Group
COVENANT

- *I agree to make attendance at all 13 group meetings a top priority. If I must be absent, I will miss no more than three meetings. If I miss more than three meetings, the group may decide whether I can continue in the group.*

- *I agree to identify one or more compulsive behaviors and work on removing the behavior(s) from my life during the next 13 weeks.*

- *I agree to be on time for each meeting. I recognize that I hurt myself and other group members when I am late.*

- *I agree to stay until each meeting is adjourned. I recognize that I affect the dynamics of the group in a negative way if I leave early. My desire to leave early may be an expression of my unwillingness to face up to the feelings I am feeling in response to what is happening in the group. If I must leave the meeting early, I will explain my reasons to the group before I leave. I will be open to discussing my early departure at the next group meeting.*

- *I agree that what takes place in the group is CONFIDENTIAL. If I break my commitment to confidentiality, I understand that I will be asked to leave the group.*

- *I agree to do everything I can to help create an atmosphere of trust in the group.*

- *I agree to be supportive of other group members as they struggle with their emotions. When needed I will encourage other group members with the words, "I support you."*

- *I agree to engage in rigorous—not brutal—honesty toward myself and other group members.*

- *I agree to let other group members confront me in love so that I can grow.*

- *I agree to complete assigned homework so that I can grow and have meaningful interaction with group members during the group sharing times.*

- *I understand that some sessions of the group may be emotionally intense. I agree to let my group leader know about any physical problems which might affect my participation in the group.*

- *I agree to share with my group any developments in one-to-one relationships with other group members that occur outside the group meetings because relationships outside the group can hamper the group process.*

*Signed*_____ *Date:*_____

You are strongly encouraged to abstain from using any drug, including alcohol, that alters your feelings. Although this recommendation is not part of the covenant, you are asked to avoid substances that could interfere with your efforts to get in touch with your feelings.

If you are using a prescription drug that alters your feelings and cannot safely stop using it, please inform your facilitator. Do not violate your doctor's instructions. Some prescription drugs require gradually reducing the dosage. Follow your physician's advice.

You are challenged to abstain from any sexual involvement outside marriage. Compulsive sexual behavior can numb feelings.

Recovery

**In this Unit you'll work on—
Turning Point 1**
I admit my powerlessness in the face of my painful past and my current compulsions. I am ready to believe that God truly is more powerful than I am and that He can restore me to spiritual and emotional wholeness.

The Recovery Cycle
An attitude of BROKENNESS accompanied by the action of SURRENDER leads to RECOVERY.

CRAIG AND THE SUPERVISOR

Craig could feel his stomach churn every time the boss approached his desk. *It's curtains for me now*, Craig thought. *I just know he's coming over to tell me how badly I messed up on the contract.*

"Craig, about the dollar figure you reached on the Jones agreement . . .," Mr. Denton began, but Craig cut him short. "You just didn't explain it well enough to me," Craig fired back at his boss. "I just didn't understand what I was supposed to do."

Mr. Denton was puzzled. What had gotten into Craig? The boss had started to commend him on his work and hadn't expected such a defensive response. Earlier Mr. Denton had decided that Craig was showing promise and should be promoted to a higher spot in the corporation, but now he wasn't sure. If Craig couldn't control his responses, he certainly couldn't be put into a supervisory position.

This incident with Mr. Denton wasn't the first time Craig had experienced difficulty with authority figures. On his past two jobs his sharp remarks cost him promotions. Craig came from a dysfunctional family where blame was a big issue. When an authority figure asked him a question, he assumed the person was trying to trap him into a wrong answer so he could assign blame. This fear interfered with his job performance and held him back from reaching his potential. (On page 16 read more about what Craig needs in his life.)

Why you will find this unit useful

This unit will help you to define how you want your life to be different. You will develop an understanding of a three-stage process of growth (brokenness, surrender, recovery) which you will apply during the remainder of this study.

Breaking the Cycle of Pain	Receiving God's Cleansing	Discovering God's Power	Getting Close to Others	Continuing to Grow
DAY 1	**DAY 2**	**DAY 3**	**DAY 4**	**DAY 5**

This week's memory verse

Do not conform any longer to the pattern of this world, but be transformed by the renewing of your mind. Then you will be able to test and approve what God's will is— his good, pleasing and perfect will.
                                        –Romans 12:2

DAY 1

Today's Objective:
You will review the elements of emotional pain, denial, and control which characterize adult children from dysfunctional families and the cycle of brokenness, surrender, and recovery which leads to healing.

compulsive—adj. having power to compel (drive or urge forcefully)

Can you spot yourself?

Breaking the Cycle of Pain

Identifying the Cycle of Pain

In *Making Peace with Your Past* you learned the traits of an adult child from a dysfunctional family. Those of us who grew up in dysfunctional families have recognizable patterns in the way we deal with life. Does the cycle of pain and compulsion described below apply to you?

 Put a check in the margin beside any statement that you feel describes you.

1. As a child, you lived in a family that was out of control.
2. Because of being reared in that out-of-control family, you felt deep emotional pain.
2. To control the pain, you developed a survival system which utilizes some form of **compulsive behavior**.
   a. The feelings you want to avoid go away while you are engaged in the compulsive behavior.
   b. Time seems to stop while you act out the compulsive behavior.
   c. The behavior feels good and bad at the same time.
   d. The compulsion seems to have a life of its own.
   e. The compulsion is progressive.
   f. The compulsion is like a parasite. It does not care if it destroys you.
3. You deny the existence and/or the negative impact of your compulsive behavior.
   a. You seek an environment—such as being around others who practice the same behavior—which validates your compulsive behavior.
   b. To keep others from seeing how destructive your compulsions are, you alternate between compulsions.
   c. You occasionally stop your compulsive behavior until the emotional pain and the force of habit of your compulsion pull you back.
   d. You manage to hide your compulsive behavior.
4. You keep your denial system in place, or your denial system may break down. Your denial system can break when:
   a. You get tired.
   b. You get scared.
   c. You get caught.
   d. You lose the support of those who have been helping you keep the denial system in place.
5. When you experience more pain, you
   a. Choose to deny your pain and attempt to rebuild your denial system.
   b. Give up.
   c. Acknowledge your pain and choose to surrender to God.

 As you read the statements above, you identified where you are in the cycle of pain, denial, and control. Below, describe how long have you been where you are now in this process.

_____

_____

_____

As you work through the pages of *Moving Beyond Your Past*, we'll often ask you to identify where you are in the cycle of pain. The following illustration will help you visualize the cycle that this book describes.

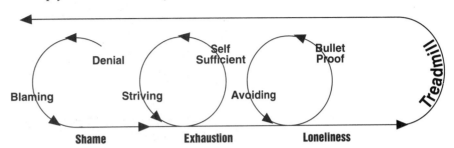

An attitude of brokenness, followed by surrender, begins and feeds the recovery process. Recovery means recycling brokenness and surrender. Often during this study we'll ask you to identify where you are in the recovery cycle. The chart below describes this cycle. On the inside back cover you can see how these two charts work together.

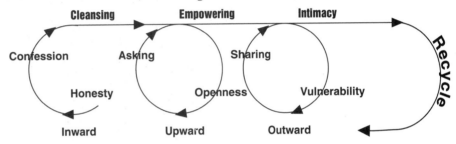

Connecting with the Recovery Cycle

The three-stage cycle of brokenness, surrender, and recovery is another way to view beginning a relationship with God through Christ. You begin a relationship with Jesus when you experience:

Brokenness

Surrender

Recovery

Brokenness—You arrive at the point where you can say, *I am a sinner, and I need forgiveness.*

Surrender—You then arrive at the point at which you can say, *Jesus, I give you my life. Take control and lead me.*

Recovery—You receive new life in Christ.

This same three-stage cycle continues as you experience growth in your Christian life. You do not need to re-experience beginning with Christ. When He enters your life, He enters to stay. However, part of the process of knowing Christ better is continuing the cycle of brokenness, surrender, and recovery.

You experience **brokenness** when you face an area of your life in which you must grow and change. For example, you admit to yourself, "I cannot stop eating compulsively."

Surrender occurs when you turn over that part of your life to God. You can say, "God, I am powerless over this compulsion. I give it to You."

Brokenness and surrender begin the process of **recovery**. At this point you learn to say, "God is giving me strength to overcome my compulsion and to love myself while I am fighting the battle." The cycle of brokenness, surrender, and recovery is a life-long cycle. It is a spiritual journey. If you desire to spend only a few weeks thinking about these things so you can move on and never think about them again, you have missed the point. Recovery is an ongoing process.

On the journey

"Are you saying that I must deal with the issues of brokenness, surrender, and recovery for the rest of my life?" you might ask. Exactly! None of us has arrived. We are on the journey.

Always Making Peace

Sometimes when I speak to a group, someone introduces me as a person who has made peace with his past because I wrote the book *Making Peace with Your Past*. In one sense I have made peace with my past, but in another sense making peace with my past is an ongoing process. Through my initial experiences with support groups, I experienced some major breakthroughs in overcoming my past. One example was shame. On a shame scale of one to 10, with 10 being high, I had been operating on a level nine or 10. I was living a shame-based life. Some immediate relief from shame occurred when I realized what shame was and how it was affecting me.

I had to admit that my addiction to work and ministry had left scars on my marriage and my parenting.

After I had been involved in the recovery process for a while, I discovered new areas of brokenness in my life. I had to face the fact that my inner emotional scars had affected the way I related to my wife. I had trouble being emotionally vulnerable with her. I had to admit that my addiction to work and ministry had left scars on my marriage and my parenting, and I felt some shame about this. Admitting to myself that I still had things to work on was painful. Often, the discovery of some new area of my life in which the need for growth was dramatic led to a deep feeling of brokenness. Brokenness feels a lot like failure.

 Below describe areas of brokenness in your life on which you feel you still need to work.

_____

_____

As you can learn by studying *Moving Beyond Your Past*, I have learned by experience that spiritual and emotional recovery is a process. When I encounter a new area in which growth is crucial, I have a decision to make. I can deny that a problem exists, or I can admit my brokenness. When I admit my brokenness, I can surrender it to God and begin to grow.

A way of life

Recovery is not just something that happened to me a number of years ago. It is a way of life. I still am growing. My marriage is growing. My relationship with my sons is growing. I never would choose brokenness, but I have found that God uses brokenness to help us grow.

Finding Victory in Brokenness

When the people of England first received news of the Battle of Waterloo, the news arrived on the south coast by ship. Signal flags on high places then sent it further. The message came through: "Wellington defeated," and then fog rolled in to conceal the signal flags. This news of defeat spread gloom through the land, but when the fog lifted the signals were completed: "Wellington defeated the enemy." The nation's joyful response was that much more intense because of the darkness that preceded it.[1]

When you face your own brokenness, the message seems to be D-E-F-E-A-T! The next step is surrender. Surrender also may feel like defeat. Surrender is painful because you want to be in control of your life. You do not want to admit what is broken in your life. You want to be in complete control of all that you do. In fact, you even may desire to control the lives of the people around you as well as any situation that affects you. In the margin box describe one reason why you don't want to admit what in your life is broken. Brokenness and surrender feel like defeat, but an attitude of brokenness accompanied by surrender leads to the victory of recovery. Out of the apparent defeat of brokenness can come the victory of recovery.

What God Had in Mind

Recovery is a return to what God originally had in mind for you. The Book of Genesis tells about Adam and Eve. They lived in the garden God made for them. The garden contained good food. It was a beautiful place. It had so much abundance that they did not need to work. God did not want Adam to be lonely. He made Eve as a companion for Adam.

God talked with Adam and Eve. They were not ashamed in the presence of God. God made them to be creative. God asked Adam to name the animals. The Evil One came in the form of a serpent. He said God was trying to keep something good from Adam and Eve. The serpent said the tree that God had forbidden to them really was something very special which God did not want them to enjoy. Enticed by the serpent, Adam and Eve chose to disobey God. After they had sinned against God, they were ashamed and hid from Him.

Recovery is a journey toward what God had in mind for humanity all along. God made the garden a place where people could be happy and fulfilled. The garden was not a place for loneliness. It was a place for meaningful companionship. The garden was not a place for shame. It was a place for openness with God. Adam and Eve had to leave the garden because of their sin. You and I lose the best God has for us when we choose to control our lives. Recovery is regaining the kind of life God meant for us in the first place.

✎ **After you read the above two paragraphs, check below the statements that are true.**

❑ Recovery has its origins only in modern times.
❑ Adam and Eve tried to control their own lives instead of letting God be in charge.
❑ We please God when we try to control our lives.
❑ Recovery is regaining what God had in mind for us all along.

God was not pleased with Adam and Eve when they—like us—tried to run their own lives. We recover when we let God back in the driver's seat, which was His original design. The second and fourth statements are the correct answers to the exercise.

Why I don't want to admit brokenness in my life:

_____

_____

_____

God made the garden as a place for companionship, but humanity foiled those plans.

DISCOVERING WHAT RECOVERY IS NOT

- Recovery is not compulsive living.
- Recovery is not living in fear.
- Recovery is not living in a rut.
- Recovery is not running from God.
- Recovery is not having to be in control all the time.
- Recovery is not living self-destructively.

RECOGNIZING WHAT RECOVERY IS

- Recovery is a lifestyle of spiritual and emotional health based on a growing understanding of who I am and who God is.
- Recovery begins with a spiritual and emotional transformation resulting from a change in the way you think. This change is powered by Jesus Christ. The verse appearing in the margin tells how this change occurs.
- Recovery means cleansing, empowering, and intimacy.

Do not conform any longer to the pattern of this world, but be transformed by the renewing of your mind.
—Romans 12:2

✎ **Are you willing to commit yourself to a life of recovery?**
❑ **Yes** ❑ **No** **What are your feelings as you think about making this commitment?**

_____

_____

God promises to help us through.

You may have written something like this: *I feel apprehensive about admitting that some areas of my life need major change, but I want God's best for my life, no matter what the cost.* Feeling apprehensive is normal, but God promises to help us through.

Work on Turning Points

Crucial decisions

Through this study and group experience you will encounter nine turning points. At each turning point you will be asked to make a decision which is crucial to your recovery process. You will begin to prepare for these turning points by answering questions like the ones below before you actually confront the turning point.

✎ **Are you ready to receive God's help in breaking the cycle of emotional pain and compulsion in your life?** ❑ **Yes** ❑ **No**

If you have reservations about breaking this cycle, what is holding you back?

_____

_____

What do you need to do to get ready to receive God's healing?

_____

What compulsive behaviors are you willing to work on during this study?

_____

➤ **Write twice this unit's memory verse, Romans 12:2. Begin to memorize it.**

_____

_____

_____

Today's Objective:
You will discover that recovery means cleansing from the guilt of past mistakes as you cultivate an attitude of honesty and engage in meaningful confession.

Receiving God's Cleansing

Connecting with the Recovery Cycle

Honesty, confession, and cleansing make up the Inward Cycle of recovery. An attitude of honesty accompanied by the action of confession lead to cleansing. Honesty is a form of brokenness. Confession is a form of surrender. Cleansing is a form of recovery.

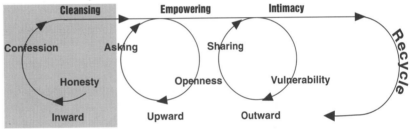

Identifying with the Cycle of Pain

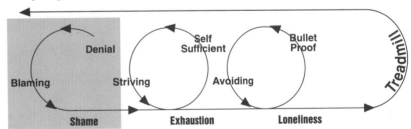

Denial
When your brokenness challenges you to admit you have a problem, you may choose to stay in denial. Below are some typical denial statements.

 Do any of these apply to you? Put a check in the left margin beside any of these statements that you've used to engage in denial.
- "I don't have a problem."
- "I may have a problem, but it's not that serious."
- "I have a problem, but I am bringing it under control in my own way."
- "I am not addicted. I can stop when I want to."

✎ **Do you have another denial statement which you frequently use? If so, write it below.**

_____

Denial may be occurring in your life when you think, "Someone else has this need. Not me."

Sometimes we deny our problems by focusing on others instead of ourselves. When you learned your church was offering a study like *Making Peace with Your Past*, you initially may have reacted by saying, "I certainly wish _____ (fill in the blank with someone else's name) would sign up for that; he has so many troubles." Instead of looking inside your own life and seeing healing that needs to occur, you may have focused on someone else.

Blaming

When your brokenness challenges you to admit you have a problem, you may choose to blame it on someone else. Blaming is a family sport in dysfunctional homes. The blaming may focus on the family member who filled the scapegoat role.

Blaming may be multi-directional—like arrows flying through the house in every direction. The family may be separated into the blamers and the blamees, with the blamers always firing shots and the blamees always running for cover.

If blame was a big issue in your family, you may have problems with questions from authority figures, as Craig did in the story on page 9. Like Craig, when an authority figure asks you a question you may be tempted to assume he or she is trying to trap you in the wrong answer so the authority figure can blame you. This interferes with your ability to give simple and direct answers to questions. You may answer imagined questions and avoid the actual questions.

The reason for probing the dynamics of your family of origin is to gain understanding.

"But isn't the whole area of recovery about looking at my family of origin and assigning blame?" you might ask. No! Assigning blame is different from understanding how your family of origin affected your personality and emotions. The reason for probing the dynamics of your family of origin is not so you can blame others and abandon responsibility for your own actions. The purpose is to gain understanding. You can get to know yourself so you can effectively change *your* attitudes and *your* behavior.

✎ **Was blaming others a major part of the dynamics of your family of origin?** ❏ Yes   ❏ No

If so, how has this affected you?

_____

_____

Have you followed the example of your family in developing the habit of blaming others? Below explain your answer.

_____

_____

You may have written, for example, that you have difficulty owning up to even the most simple mistake—forgetting to take out the garbage or snapping at your child unnecessarily when you have a headache—because saying "I'm sorry" wasn't something you heard your parents do.

Taking Responsibility for My Actions

Recovery means taking responsibility for your own behavior. You may have come from a severely dysfunctional family. Growing up in that family produced emotional scars. Some of the wounds still may be healing. What you experienced may have damaged your view of yourself and your view of life.

When you were a child, you could not control your family. You may have developed addictions or controlling behaviors to cope with the pain you felt. The addictions/compulsions may have developed before you understood what was happening.

You could not control your family, so you may have developed addictions or controlling behaviors.

Part of the Serenity Prayer states, *God grant me the serenity to accept the things I cannot change.* You cannot relive the past. You cannot reshape your family of origin. The Serenity Prayer is appropriate. *God grant me the serenity to accept the things I cannot change.*[2]

Being affected and even shaped by the past does not mean you should place responsibility for your behavior on someone else. You are responsible for your actions. The Serenity Prayer also leads us to *ask for the courage to change the things I can.* Today, you are responsible for making decisions that lead to recovery.

You are responsible for making decisions that lead to recovery.

✎ **Have you been willing to take responsibility for your behavior?**
❑ **Yes** ❑ **No**

What are some specific areas in which you habitually have blamed others?

I blamed my parents for . . . _____

_____

I blamed my brother for . . . _____

_____

I blamed my sister for . . . _____

_____

I blamed my spouse for . . . _____

_____

I blamed my children for . . . _____

_____

You may have written something like this: I blamed my parents for not sending me to a better school, when actually I myself chose not to switch school districts when I had the option. I blamed my brother for getting all my father's attention, when I didn't always take advantage of chances I had to spend time with my dad. I blamed my sister for being aloof and cold, when I am responsible for hurting her by teasing her when we were growing up. I blamed my spouse for nagging me, when I've not always been careful to correct my bad habits like sloppy table manners. I have blamed my children for talking back to me, even though I'm responsible for lax discipline when they have spoken abusively to me in the past.

Facing Shame

Taking responsibility for your behavior is not the same as wallowing in shame. A shame-based identity plays a continual message, "You are no good. You messed up." Shame condemns you to hopelessness. Blame and shame are deadly partners. Shame makes you feel miserable about yourself. Blame keeps you pointing a finger at others to make them feel miserable about themselves.

Separate your shame from that of others.

Choosing to wallow in shame and assigning blame is futile. The first step in dealing with shame is to separate your shame from that of others. People who are shame-based have learned to own the shame of others. My father was an alcoholic. I learned to feel shame for his alcoholism. Actually, it was his shame and not mine. I have learned mentally to give him back his shame.

I become honest about myself when I stop denying and blaming.

I must deal with my own shame and guilt. I have made choices which were wrong—choices which hurt others. Being honest about my attitudes and my behavior is the first step in this part of the recovery cycle. I become honest about myself when I stop denying and blaming. This too is a form of brokenness. It is the brokenness of acknowledging my own failures. Agreeing with God that I have done wrong and naming my sins is crucial. The result is cleansing. God always hears the sincere prayer of confession. He forgives and restores.

- Honesty is a form of brokenness.
- Confession is a form of surrender.
- Cleansing is a form of recovery.

Finding Someone Trustworthy

In this course we will ask you to complete a moral inventory, which begins on pages 205. The moral inventory is a thorough individual evaluation—a complete assessment of our good and bad traits, strengths and weaknesses, assets and liabilities, and how we use each. Begin to think about locating one person with whom you can share this moral inventory. This may be a person who is a member of your group, or it may be a person outside your group. It must be a person who has some understanding of the process of recovery. It could be someone who has participated in a 12-Step group or who understands the meaning of the Fifth Step, which is, "We admit to God, to ourselves, and to another person the exact nature of our wrongs."

A crucial choice

Choosing a person to hear your moral inventory is crucial. This should be someone who is the same gender as yourself. He or she must be someone who

Some names that come to mind are—

_____

_____

_____

is trustworthy and who will not break confidence. This must be a person who is willing to listen without being judgmental—someone who can give encouragement and support. During the seventh meeting you will report on your sharing experience. In the margin box write the initials of some people that come to mind as you begin to think about the person you'll choose.

➤ **Begin praying that God will lead you to the person with whom you will share your moral inventory before the seventh meeting.**

Work on Turning Points

✎ **Are you ready to move toward God's cleansing?** ❑ **Yes** ❑ **No**

How ready are you to begin the cycles of recovery?

_____

What obstacles stand in your way?

_____

Are you willing to accept God's help on His terms? ❑ **Yes** ❑ **No**

➤ **Repeat aloud three times this unit's memory verse. Check your memory on page 9.**

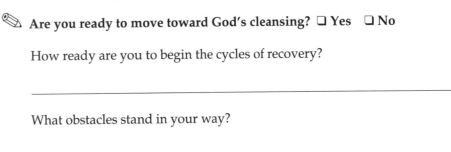

DAY 3

Today's Objective:
You will learn that recovery means getting in touch with God's power as you become more open to His involvement in your life and as you begin to ask Him for help.

Discovering God's Power

Connecting with the Recovery Cycle

An attitude of openness to God accompanied by specific requests for God's guidance helps you discover God's power in your life.

- Being open to God's work in my life and admitting that I am not self-sufficient is a form of brokenness.
- Asking for God's help is a form of surrender.
- Discovering the power of God in my life is a form of recovery.

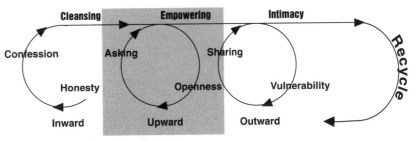

Identifying the Cycle of Pain

The alternative to the cycle of openness, asking, and empowering is self-sufficiency, striving, and exhaustion. Instead of being open to God, I may choose an attitude of self-sufficiency. I can do it myself. You may have such an attitude because of childhood experiences. You could not depend on key people in your life. You learned to fend for yourself. Now you continue to watch out for yourself. You carry the load. You may operate under a thin layer of trust in God, but the bottom line is that you are in control. Ultimately, this expression of the cycle of pain results in exhaustion. You will reach a point at which you must admit, "I cannot carry this load by myself anymore." See the pain cycle below.

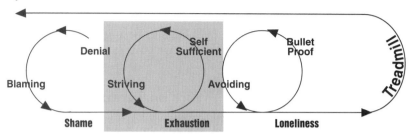

Expecting to See God at Work

Openness to God means expecting to see His work in your life. Even people who are deeply committed to God may lack a sense of expectancy about His work. I easily can get busy with religion while not really expecting God to be active in my life.

God and shaving cream

One day I was shaving my face with shaving cream and razor. I was listening to the radio. I looked into the mirror and realized that I had shaving cream on my forehead and on my nose as well as on the rest of my face. I was startled. Why had I put shaving cream on my forehead and nose? Why had I plastered my whole face with the white soap? Then I noticed that the radio was playing a commercial about facial cream. I had not realized that I was listening to the commercial. I subconsciously had picked up on the commercial's message and treated the shaving cream like facial cream. I was not totally present while I was shaving!

We can reach a point of not being present to God's daily activity in our lives. Those of us who travel on airlines sometimes watch the flight attendant give a routine speech about oxygen masks and seat belts. We say to ourselves, "I've heard this before. I know exactly what to expect." We begin to approach life with the attitude, *God isn't going to do anything special in my life today.* At the heart of a life of recovery is an expectancy that God is going to do something and that I will see some results of His presence in my life. God's love means growth.

Seeking God's Presence

When I expect to see God at work, I am more open to notice what He is doing. Living in the cycles of recovery means more than just being open. Recovery means actively seeking God's presence in my day-to-day activities.

✎ **What are you doing to seek God's presence in your life?**

_____

_____

_____

Sometimes those of us in recovery begin to see God through a whole new set of eyes. Instead of praying that God will change others, we begin to pray that

He will change our attitudes about ourselves. When we accept ourselves as people of worth, we stop trying to make others approve of us. We become comfortable with ourselves as God's treasured creations. That is one example of an ordinary, yet highly significant way, we can seek God's presence in the everydayness of our lives.

Experiencing God's Power

✎ **In the verses at left, underline the words and phrases that represent God's promises to us about how He will show His power in our lives.**

Do you not know? Have you not heard? The LORD is the everlasting God, the Creator of the ends of the earth. He will not grow tired or weary, and his understanding no one can fathom. He gives strength to the weary and increases the power of the weak. Even youths grow tired and weary, and young men stumble and fall; but those who hope in the LORD will renew their strength. They will soar on wings like eagles; they will run and not grow weary, they will walk and not be faint.

Isaiah 40:28-31

You may have underlined such phrases as *not grow tired or weary*, *understanding*, *strength to the weary*, *increases the power of the weak*, *renew their strength*, *soar on wings like eagles*, *run and not grow weary*, and *walk and not be faint*. What marvelous promises!

Recovery means strength and power. Isaiah 40:28-31 expresses the conviction that God will renew strength. Sometimes this strength is like flying. God is doing so much in my life, I feel as if I am soaring high in the sky.

At other times I may be involved in a challenging task, and God gives me a resurgence of strength like a second wind so I can keep on running. Sometimes, as the psalmist says, "I walk through the valley of the shadow of death" (Psalm 23:4). Even walking is a victory when you are in the valley of the shadow of death. You don't stop. You don't sit down. You don't quit. You don't give up. You walk, because you have His strength.

Sometimes God's power in your life will be obvious. At other times it may come from unexpected directions. In the book *The Fall of Fortresses*, Elmer Bendiner describes a bombing run over the German city of Kassel during World War II. While this particular B-17 crew was on a mission a 20 millimeter explosive shell landed in their fuel tank. The crew was amazed that the plane did not blow up.

Later the author of the book asked the pilot about the incident, and the pilot told him a remarkable story. He said not one, but 11 explosive shells were found in the fuel tank of the airplane. The shells were turned over to intelligence, so the crew did not learn until some time later the full story of what had occurred.

Intelligence found that these shells never had been loaded with an explosive. A rolled piece of paper containing a message written in Czech was found in one of the shells. They found somebody who could translate the message. It said, "This is all we can do for you now."[3] Captured patriots had been forced to load shells under the careful guard of the enemy, but they found a way to do one small thing that made a big difference for the bomber crew.

Sometimes God works as if through the back door. We are looking up and waiting for Him to light up the heavens for us, and then we find that He has been working from another direction more effectively than we would have ever hoped for Him to work.

How God works

God does not promise that all the battles will disappear. He does not say you never will be sick. He does not say that things always will go well in your work. He does not say that your relationships always will be trouble-free. He does promise always to be with you and to give you the strength you need to live life with a victorious attitude.

✎ **In what area of your life do you most need God's power at this time?**

_____

_____

_____

Sensing the Wonder of God

> And said, Verily I say unto you, Except ye be converted, and become as little children, ye shall not enter into the kingdom of heaven.
>
> Matthew 18:3, KJV

Along with this expectancy of seeing God at work comes a sense of wonder at what I see Him doing. In Matthew 18:3, appearing at left, Jesus told us that we need to become like little children to enter the Kingdom of Heaven. Children have great ability to experience wonder. When a little child sees a flower or an animal he never has seen before, he has the ability to say, "Wow!"

How sad when we get so "mature" and so "stable" as believers that we cannot see God do anything in our lives that makes us exclaim, "Wow! I never have seen anything like that before." How long has it been since you have seen something that caused you to say, "That's amazing!"? Recovery means being able to see God at work and being able to feel wonder at what you see.

✎ **What do you expect God to do in your life this week?**

_____

_____

The last time I experienced a sense of wonder—

_____

_____

_____

_____

_____

In the margin box describe the last time you saw or felt something that made you experience a sense of wonder.

Work on Turning Points

✎ **Are you ready to begin the cycles of recovery?** ❑ Yes ❑ No

Are you ready to receive God's power as you face your compulsions?
❑ Yes ❑ No

What obstacles stand in your way?

_____

_____

_____

Are you willing to accept God's help on His terms? ❑ Yes ❑ No

➤ **Pray for each member of your Heart-to-Heart group by name today.**

➤ Continue praying that God will lead you to the person with whom you will share your moral inventory.

✎ In the margin write this unit's memory verse. Check your work on page 9.

Check your work on page 9.

DAY
4

Today's Objective:
You will learn that recovery opens the door to close relationships with other people as you learn to become vulnerable and to share yourself with selected safe people.

passive-aggressive–a dishonest method of controlling or punishing others by refusing to make a decision or to perform an action. This behavior seems passive since it is a refusal to act or decide, but it actually is aggressive because: (1) it forces the other person to decide or act and (2) often it contains an element of hostility or punishment.

Getting Close to Others

Identifying the Cycle of Pain

Growing up in a dysfunctional family may have taught you to be bullet-proof. It hurt too much to hurt. You developed a suit of emotional armor. You learned not to feel. You gradually learned that getting close to people meant giving them more power to hurt you. Being frightened by the thought of giving anyone more ability to hurt you, you developed ways to avoid closeness to other people.

Maybe you learned to control people rather than relate to them. Perhaps you learned to manipulate through the web of **passive-aggressive** behavior. You never directly asked for anything, but you always got what you wanted. Maybe you isolated yourself from other people. Ultimately, the end result always is the same—loneliness.

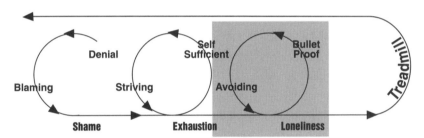

Connecting with the Cycle of Recovery

The alternative to loneliness is emotional intimacy. Emotional intimacy means being close to other people. It means learning to be honest about your feelings. Emotional intimacy requires vulnerability. This does not mean that you must be emotionally vulnerable with everyone you meet. It means that you must learn to identify selected safe people who are worthy of trust. You can learn to share yourself with others. You can take off the emotional masks you have worn.

Vulnerability is a form of brokenness. Sharing is a form of surrender. Intimacy is a form of recovery.

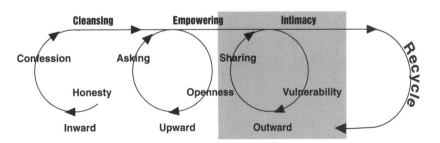

Healing Broken Relationships

Recovery means healing of broken relationships. When you surrender broken relationships to God and when you are able to say, "God, I cannot fix this relationship," you are in the right place to see healing begin.

Sometimes relationships are broken beyond repair. Things cannot be the way they used to be. Even in such cases, God can bring healing to the painful hurts the brokenness of those relationships causes. Even though the relationship may not be restored, God can remove your hostility. He can bring you to the place where the brokenness of the relationship does not control you.

✎ **List below the broken relationships in your life. What type of healing does the relationship need in each case?**

	Broken Relationship	Healing Needed
1.		
2.		
3.		
4.		
5.		

You may have listed a relationship broken by a quarrel with a friend or broken by the desertion of a parent or spouse. You may have listed a relationship in which no angry words occurred but where the relationship was damaged because you had unrealistic expectations of it. The healing needed may involve a conversation with the person, or it may need an amend—an action to indicate to that person your heartfelt desire to repair the breach.

The healing needed may involve merely a letting go on your part— you may need to forgive the person for not being able to give you the kind of relationship you need. You may need to look elsewhere for the type of relationship that person can't provide. Regardless, God can heal this relationship to the point that your grieving over it does not control you, but the love of God does control you.

Discovering Healthy Relationships

Divine intersections

Recovery means new relationships with people who understand spiritual and emotional health. God has a way of creating divine intersections in your life— a way of putting you in the place where you need to be to encounter the people you need in your life.

✎ **Make a list of some healthy relationships in your life. These do not necessarily have to be intense relationships.**

1. _____

2. _____

3. _____

4. _____

5. _____

Does the list include any authority figures? ❑ Yes   ❑ No

You may have listed people who seem to be interested in your welfare without an unhealthy dependency, who affirm you without manipulating you, and who are open enough to state what they need in the relationship without expecting you to read their minds.

Discovering Intimacy in Relationships

Trust is not a blind shot in the dark. It is a skill you can learn to exercise.

As you move through the process of recovery, you can learn to trust. You will learn that some people cannot be trusted, but others can. You will learn that no one is perfect. People who care about you sometimes may let you down through oversight and sometimes by intention, but trust is worth the risk. Trust is not a blind shot in the dark. It is a skill you can learn to exercise.

An essential element of trust is vulnerability. Trust always involves some degree of risk. You must be willing to be vulnerable to build relationships with other people. You must follow an attitude of vulnerability with a sharing of yourself. When you are willing to share who you really are with another person, you can move to a new kind of relationship.

Intimacy refers to emotional closeness. Honesty and genuine communication characterize an intimate relationship. An attitude of vulnerability accompanied by a sharing of your true self with another person opens the door to emotional closeness in relationships. Vulnerability is a form of brokenness. Sharing is a form of surrender, and intimacy is a form of recovery.

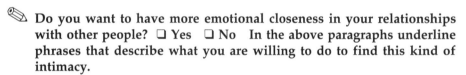 **Do you want to have more emotional closeness in your relationships with other people? ❑ Yes   ❑ No   In the above paragraphs underline phrases that describe what you are willing to do to find this kind of intimacy.**

You may have underlined phrases like *learn to trust, be willing to be vulnerable, sharing of yourself,* and *honesty and genuine communication.*

Paul's conversation

People who want emotional closeness may need to examine their communications with others. Paul wondered why he didn't feel emotionally close to people. One day he began to study what happened when he talked to a friend. He noticed that the conversation was not between two people but was a monologue. Paul talked about himself all the time.

Paul began to try to ask the friend questions about himself. He started to be a better listener and to follow up on comments his friend made. He noticed mementos in his friend's office and asked him questions about them. His friend seemed to appreciate Paul's efforts to become better acquainted. Soon Paul's relationships improved. Sometimes people are surprised to see how emotional closeness develops when each person feels that the other is genuinely interested in him or her.

Work on Turning Points

 Are you ready to receive God's healing in the relationships of your life?
❑ Yes   ❑ No

What obstacles stand in your way?

_____

 In the margin write this unit's memory verse. Check your work on page 9.

Today's Objective:
You will be challenged to an ongoing commitment to the cycles of recovery.

Recovery

Surrender

Brokenness

Continuing to Grow

Connecting with the Cycle of Recovery

God enables us to grow by permitting us over and over again to experience the cycle of brokenness, surrender, and recovery, as the illustration in the margin shows. The process begins when you bring the brokenness of your life to God. It continues when you surrender yourself to Christ. God continues to show us broken areas of life that need to be fixed. "Here is a broken area," God says. "Surrender it." Now the ball is in your court. You have to decide if you will surrender. When you surrender, you experience a recovery in your spirit.

I've been a Christian for more than 30 years, but still I am growing. God is working in my life. I have some brokenness—some areas where I am still hurting. But praise God, He is teaching me about growth and serenity. Brokenness is no picnic. Surrender is no picnic. But recovery makes the struggle worthwhile.

Recycling Recovery

After you have experienced an introductory walk through the three recovery cycles you can learn to recycle.
The recovery cycles are:
The Inward Cycle: Honesty, Confession, Cleansing
The Upward Cycle: Openness, Asking, Empowering
The Outward Cycle: Vulnerability, Sharing, and Intimacy

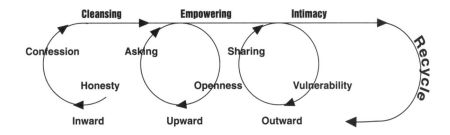

These three cycles are forms of brokenness, surrender, and recovery. Recycling recovery means walking back through these cycles as you see new areas for growth in your life.

introspection–n. the examination of one's own thought and feeling; self-examination (Webster's)

The Inward Cycle

Introspection calls you back to the cycle of honesty, confession, and cleansing. If you are living in the cycle of pain, you try to avoid introspection. You run from yourself. Looking inside is too painful. You feel that you cannot cope with what you will see. You may deny this fear, but it is present whether or not you deny it.

Introspection means that you continue taking a personal inventory. You learn to evaluate where you are spiritually and emotionally. When you find areas that need to change, you make appropriate confession to God and to other people. This introspection is not a pathway to shame but is a journey into cleansing. Introspection calls you away from blame and back to personal responsibility.

The Upward Cycle

Prayer takes you back to the cycle of openness, asking, and empowering. You may have made prayer a compulsion. You may be moving too fast to stop and pray. Healthy prayer is an expression of openness to God. It is a way of listening for God's voice. Prayer is the avenue of asking God for help. Prayer is a way of saying, "I am not self-sufficient." Prayer is a way of connecting with God's power.

The Outward Cycle

Service calls you back to the outward or relational cycle: vulnerability, sharing, and intimacy. When you live in the cycle of pain, you are pulled toward codependent relationships. Codependent relationships involve giving with strings attached. Serving others can be a form of controlling others. I will help you, but I expect a payback.

Service is a call to recycle vulnerability, sharing, and intimacy. Service is a call to help others out of the fullness of your experience with God. Service means learning to give with no strings attached.

You will not experience emotional closeness with everyone you help, but you will connect with some people. You will learn to be vulnerable as you share yourself. As you take measured risks, you will move out of loneliness into fellowship with others.

Experiencing Serenity

Recovery means receiving cleansing and starting over. Recovery means receiving the strength of God. It means new relationships.

Recovery means that I have decided to let God be in control. I have given God permission to be God in my life.

One important result of giving God control is *serenity*. Everything around me may be in turmoil, but I can know serenity because I know that God is in control. At the heart of the recovery process is the Serenity Prayer:

> *God grant me the serenity to accept the things I cannot change,*
> *the courage to change the things I can,*
> *and the wisdom to know the difference.*[4]

✎ **Write five statements describing what your life would be like in a state of spiritual and emotional health.**

Examples: I will take responsibility for my actions, but I will refuse to carry the shame of others. I will let God take charge of relationships instead of always trying to fix and rescue.

1. _____

_____

2. _____

_____

3. _____

_____

4. _____

_____

5. _____

_____

What do you need to surrender to gain these five things? What are you willing to surrender?

_____

For example, I might write that in order to take responsibility for my actions, I may have to turn over to God my compulsion to surround myself with certain people who are emotionally damaging to me. Now, read again Turning Point 1 that you first saw appearing on the unit page. In unit 2 you'll continue to work on this turning point.

Turning Point 1
I admit my powerlessness in the face of my painful past and my current compulsions. I am ready to believe that God truly is more powerful than I am and that He can restore me to spiritual and emotional wholeness.

Notes
[1]A. Philip Parham, *Letting God: Christian Meditations for Recovering Persons* (San Francisco: Harper and Row, Publishers, 1987), April 3rd reading.
[2]Reinhold Niebuhr, "The Serenity Prayer," (St. Meinrad, IN: Abbey Press)
[3]Elmer Bendiner, *The Fall of Fortresses* cited by Scott Wenig, "Quiet Influence," *Leadership*, Spring, 1983, Vol. IV, Num. 2, p. 93.
[4]Niebuhr.

Brokenness

**In this Unit you'll work on—
Turning Point 1**
I admit my powerlessness in the face of my painful past and my current compulsions. I am ready to believe that God is more powerful than I am and that He can restore me to spiritual and emotional wholeness.

The Recovery Cycle
An attitude of BROKENNESS accompanied by the action of SURRENDER leads to RENEWAL.

BOB DRAWS THE LINE

Bob's wife Sally ruined every couple friendship that they tried to form. When Bob arranged for the two of them to dine with friends, Sally always managed to have a business conflict.

Bob made flimsy excuses for Sally when such situations arose. Actually, Sally was a workaholic, and Bob covered for her.

Then one day the engagement Sally broke involved an outing with Bob's business partner and his wife. This time Sally had gone too far. Bob refused to endure the consequences and disrupted relationship that could occur with his business partner if he weaseled out yet another time. He told Sally he would cover for her no longer.

(Read more about Bob on page 39 and how drawing the line helped bring about an end to his brokenness.)

Why you will find this unit useful
This unit will challenge you to acknowledge your brokenness. Adult children of dysfunctional families experience brokenness as they cope with the pain of an emotionally deprived childhood. Shame teaches you to hide your brokenness and to pretend you are strong. Hiding your brokenness keeps you in emotional pain and stunts your spiritual growth. You will discover that acknowledging your brokenness connects you with God's healing power.

The Admission of Brokenness	The Anatomy of a Denial System	The Collapse of a Denial System	The Fork in the Road	The Victory of Brokenness
DAY 1	DAY 2	DAY 3	DAY 4	DAY 5

This week's memory verse
The LORD is close to the brokenhearted and saves those who are crushed in spirit.
–Psalm 34:18

The Admission of Brokenness

Connecting with the Recovery Cycle

Brokenness is the first step toward recovery. This does not mean that you must create brokenness in your life to experience recovery. Recovery occurs when you admit to brokenness that already is present. You and I have something inside us that is broken—something that we never can fix by ourselves.

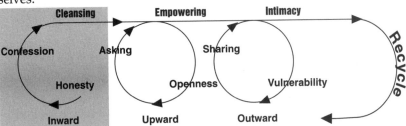

Keith Miller said it like this: "In human nature and experience there is a basic inner conflict. There is something 'broken' that cannot be 'fixed,' something wrong that cannot be made right by all the success, effort, money, pleasure, power, or ability in the world. There is a basic fear, an aching pain and frustration in life, that cannot be covered up forever by smiles and outward trappings of success."[1] Many of us have something broken inside us that we cannot fix by ourselves. This brokenness shows up in different ways in different people.

Kathy's story

For example, Kathy was a popular college student who seemed to have many friends. A drama major on her small campus, Kathy was in charge of casting for all the campus productions. Walking across campus with Kathy was like walking alongside a hurricane, because so many students swirled around her and wanted her attention. But Kathy had a brokenness inside that all the adoring crowds could not fix. Her relationship with her father, who died during her freshman year, had been a stormy one. His death left her full of unresolved conflicts. This brokenness caused her to feel alone, even when masses of students surrounded her.

Kathy's example illustrates one kind of brokenness. Here are some ways brokenness affects other people.

- For some it is a fear—a pinpointed fear—about a certain thing or place or situation. For others the fear is generalized. It hangs overhead like a cloudy sky.
- Still others feel brokenness as an inner pain—sometimes dull and distant, sometimes so close and so intense that they cannot ignore it.
- For some individuals, the brokenness shows up over and over as shame—a weight that will not go away.
- Often the brokenness makes people unable to feel feelings. They find it difficult to identify what is happening emotionally.

Identifying the Cycle of Pain

Many of us have this brokenness inside us, but something about it or about us makes us feel ashamed that we are broken. It is as if an inner voice says,

An inner voice says, "Keep your brokenness a secret."

"Above all else, never let anyone know that you have brokenness within you. You must keep it a secret at all costs, for if anybody—even for a moment—sees what is going on inside of you, they will turn in disgust. They never will look your way again. You will be alone." We choose to hide our brokenness. We deny it. We learn to wear masks.

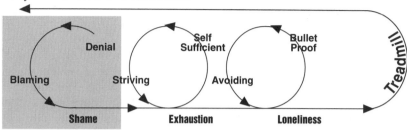

Sometimes the church can be a good place to hide this brokenness. To be broken before you make a commitment to Christ is OK, but after you become a Christian, people expect you to be whole. At least, that is how it seems. Kathy, the college student you just read about, was a committed Christian and was active in her campus church—and highly popular there, as well. Her smiles, however, covered the pain that controlled her life. Despite being a professing Christian, she felt anything but whole. Because many people wanted Kathy to give her testimony, church was the last place where she would admit her brokenness. Have you ever used church as a place to hide your brokenness? If so, in the margin box describe the things you did to hide.

Church was the last place Kathy would let on that she was in pain.

You may have written something like, "I taught Sunday School so that I could have a lot of people around me, but I never could form close relationships with any of the members of my class. Actually I'm afraid to let anyone get to know me."

You have learned to live under a denial system which says that everything is fine even if the opposite is true. If you work diligently, you may succeed in hiding your brokenness from other people. You even may be able to convince yourself that you have no brokenness.

You can reach a point of believing your own lies. You hurt inside. Someone asks, "How are you? I really want to know." You answer, "I'm fine," and you really believe it because you have learned to believe your own denial.

✎ What is broken inside you?

Specific Fears: _____

_____

General Fears: _____

_____

Loneliness: _____

_____

Inner Pain: _____

_____

How I hid behind my brokenness while at church—

_____

_____

_____

_____

Persistent Shame or Guilt: _____

_____

Blocked Feelings: _____

_____

You may be blocking feelings about how much you hurt.

You may have written that fears or even failure of success contribute to your feeling of brokenness. From studying *Making Peace with Your Past* you may recall my story about wanting to be successful, yet at the same time fearing my success. As I experienced success, I feared that something would burst the bubble. I felt that if things were going too well, a catastrophe would result. You may feel lonely because you have a relationship you would like to improve, but you fear letting someone get to know you well enough to see your pain. Your inner pain may spring from some unresolved event, like the death of a parent or the loss of a relationship. You may feel shame over and over because of a wrong decision you once made. You may be blocking feelings about how much you hurt when your mother raged at you or when your parents divorced.

The feeling of brokenness is a miserable, terrible feeling, but Christ's healing and unconditional love can repair it. This study will help you through the brokenness and into the healing power of God.

Work on Turning Points

✎ **Below, describe the progress you are making toward working Turning Point 1:** *I admit my powerlessness in the face of my painful past and my current compulsions. I am ready to believe that God is more powerful than I am and that He can restore me to spiritual and emotional wholeness.*

_____

_____

✎ **Respond to these questions.**

Are you ready to receive God's help in breaking the cycle of emotional pain and compulsion in your life? ❏ Yes ❏ No

If you have reservations, what is holding you back? _____

_____

What do you need to do to get ready to receive God's healing? _____

_____

What compulsive behaviors are you willing to work on during this study?

_____

➤ If the following prayer expresses the desire of your heart, today tell it to God in your own words. "God, help me to see through my own denial. Something in me is broken. I cannot fix it. Help me to face my brokenness. I am ready for You to go to work in my life."

➤ Mark Psalm 34:18, the unit memory verse, in your Bible. Spend five minutes beginning to memorize it.

The Anatomy of a Denial System

DAY 2

Today's Objective:
You will learn how we use compulsive behaviors to deny and to control emotional pain.

Even compiling a list of compulsions could become a compulsion!

Compulsive Behavior as a Survival Tool

As a child you experienced the emotional pain of living in a dysfunctional family. Your life had an "out of control" element about it. You were unable to express the depth of your pain and shame. You needed to find a way to survive emotionally.

You developed your own system for survival. The system probably included some form of compulsive behavior. You learned that acting out a compulsive ritual would make the pain go away, at least for a while.

Types of Compulsive Behavior

Here is a list of some compulsive behaviors.

1. Addiction to alcohol or other drugs
2. Work addiction
3. Addiction to gambling
4. Addiction to overspending or spending too little
5. Addiction to cigarettes or other tobacco products
6. Sex addictions (pornography, sex, romance)
7. Food addictions
8. Compulsion to control others
9. Compulsive need to please people
10. Compulsion to rescue others

The list is endless. You can turn just about anything into a compulsion. Even compiling a list of compulsions could become a compulsion! Notice that society frowns on some types of compulsive behavior such as drug addiction, but it rewards other compulsions such as work. The acceptable compulsions may be more difficult to confront because people generally view them as OK.

✎ Review the list of compulsive behaviors above. Which ones have you practiced or do you currently practice? Circle them in the list.

Characteristics of Compulsive Behavior

While the list of compulsive behaviors varies, the different forms of compulsive behavior have several things in common.
• Feelings that I want to avoid go away while I am engaged in the compulsive behavior.

- At least for a while the compulsive behavior makes the pain go away. For a while I feel, "Maybe I am not broken after all."
- Time seems to stop while I am busy with the compulsive behavior.
- The behavior feels good and bad at the same time.
- The compulsion seems to have a life and identity of its own.
- The compulsive behavior is progressive in nature. What was enough for me yesterday may not be enough today.
- The compulsion has no regard for my wholeness or my survival.

✎ **In the list you just read, mark the characteristics of your compulsive behavior. Can you list any other traits of your compulsions? Below write your response.**

_____

_____

Denial of Compulsive Behavior

Because I don't know any other way to deal with the pain, I may deny my compulsions. Perhaps I am afraid to try any other way. I know that my compulsions work. They feel like friends to me. I cannot face the negative side of my compulsiveness. I *need* to deny the destructive force of this important survival tool. I look for ways I can reinforce my compulsions.

I May Seek an Environment Which Validates My Compulsive Behavior

Reinforcing my denial

- If I am a work addict, I will enjoy a work environment that will reward or approve of my compulsive work habits.
- If I am a sex addict, I will gravitate toward friends who see my sexual behavior as a mark of a liberated person.
- If I am addicted to religion, I will seek others who choose a rigid moralism over a sensitive spirituality.
- I may marry someone who is codependent. My spouse outwardly may complain about my compulsions while at the same time helping me to continue in them.

Keeping it hidden

I May Alternate Between Two or More Compulsive Behaviors to Avoid Facing the Evidence that My Compulsions Are Destructive

- I may eat compulsively and then diet compulsively before my weight gets too far out of control.
- I may gamble my earnings away and then work compulsively to catch up financially.
- I may engage in sexual promiscuity and then attend church religiously to cover the guilt and shame I feel.

Living a lie

I May Keep My Compulsions in Place through Sheer Willpower
I may become a successful compulsive. I will live a compulsive lifestyle, but I also will work hard to cover any negative results of my compulsive behavior. Outwardly, I seem to be able to make the compulsion work for me. The extremism of my compulsive lifestyle may feel like a key to my success. For example, I fear that if I stop working compulsively, I will lose my job. I am doubly afraid of living any other way. Even though the compulsion hides my pain, I live in fear that someone will find me out or that I will lose what I have.

✎ **What features have you built into your life to reinforce your compulsive behaviors? Below describe these built-in features.**

_____

_____

You may have written something like this: "Because I am a compulsive speeder, I always try to do more than actually is possible in a day so I must go fast," or "Because I am a compulsive overeater, I find that I actually add stressful situations to my life so that I feel that I must overeat to help me cope with the stress."

Your compulsion is a mask designed to cover your brokenness.

Our compulsive denial systems become very important to us. If we feel somebody chipping away at our denial system, we likely will fight or flee. We become like a ducks swimming on a quiet pond. They glide across the water apparently without effort or without expending energy. Under the water, the ducks paddle furiously. From the outside, we may look as if everything is in order, but inside, we are frantic, hurting, struggling, seeking. The energy we devote to our compulsion expresses the turmoil inside us. Our compulsions help us cover our brokenness.

✎ **What kind of pain are you hiding under your compulsions?**

❑ Loneliness   ❑ Fear
❑ Sadness   ❑ Shame
❑ Guilt   ❑ Anger
❑ Other _____

You may have written something like: My compulsive busyness hides my fear that if I slow down, I'll have to address some areas in my marriage that are not working well. My compulsive work habits enable me to hide my sadness about a friendship that has gone awry. My compulsive disorganization allows me to cover my shame about a painful incident in my past.

Face Your Compulsions

Throughout the rest of *Moving Beyond Your Past* you will see the exercise below, or a modification of it, regularly. Becoming aware of your compulsive behaviors and developing a plan to manage them is crucial to your recovery. Please take time to complete this exercise.

✎ **The compulsive behaviors I am working on are:** _____

_____

Below describe how you managed these compulsive behaviors yesterday.

_____

_____

Work on Turning Points

 Below describe the progress you are making on working Turning Point 1: I *admit my powerlessness in the face of my painful past and my current compulsions. I am ready to believe that God is more powerful than I am and that He can restore me to spiritual and emotional wholeness.*

_____

_____

Are you willing to accept God's help on His terms? ❏ Yes ❏ No

➤ If the following prayer reflects the desire of your heart, express your version of the prayer to God. "God, help me to see through my own denial. Something in me is broken. I cannot fix it. Help me to face my brokenness. I am ready for you to go to work in my life."

➤ Say aloud five times this unit's memory verse.

DAY 3

Today's Objective:
You will learn some ways in which denial systems break down.

The Collapse of a Denial System

Your Denial System Can Break Unexpectedly

If you are fortunate, your denial system will break one day. When your denial system breaks, you will "hit bottom." You may hit

1. "A physical bottom"
2. "An emotional bottom"
3. "A spiritual bottom"[2]

Some people make it all the way through life with a denial system intact. The denial system is buried with them. They never come to grips with it. They never face it. We can pity them. They escape the pain of facing painful truth but miss the opportunity for growth that only brokenness can bring.

In today's lesson, you will learn about these five situations that can cause your denial system to break. It can break—
• when you get tired;
• when you get scared;
• when you get caught;
• when others stop helping you deny;
• when you decide to face the truth and to begin recovery.

When You Get Tired

Compulsive behavior requires large amounts of energy. Pretending that everything is OK when it is not OK is exhausting.

Jack's story

Jack was a compulsive perfectionist. He believed that every single thing had to be exactly right. He exerted tremendous energy organizing life. Jack began dating Susan, who had a relaxed, carefree attitude and was just the opposite of his perfectionistic ways. In one sense Jack knew that Susan had something that was missing in his life. As a perfectionist Jack found this attractive and was drawn to it. For a while after Jack and Susan married, this change of pace felt good. It was a breath of fresh air. After a while the traits that attracted Jack to Susan became the traits that drove him crazy. He protested, "You're not like me! Why can't you organize things the way I organize them? Why can't you do things the way I do them?"

Now Jack had to expend not only the energy necessary to make his own life perfect but also the energy necessary to make Susan's life perfect. Later, the children arrived, and did they ever resist perfection! Perfection is totally against children's nature. Now Jack tried to keep himself, Susan, and his children in line. "Do this. Straighten this up. Don't do it that way! Why did you do that?" One day Jack woke up and said, "I am exhausted. I cannot go on like this."

Perfectionism is not the only denial method that requires large amounts of energy. Regardless of the exact nature of your denial system, it can break when you get tired of maintaining it.

✎ **Has your compulsive behavior ever brought you to a point of exhaustion? ❏ Yes ❏ No If so, write a description of a time this happened.**

_____

_____

When You Get Scared

The more energy you spend to keep your denial system in place, the more anxious you become. A part of you asks, "How can I keep this up?" The anxiety overload eventually may emerge in the form of panic or panic attacks. You develop an overwhelming feeling inside that something terrible is about to happen. You are not sure what you fear, but you sense that everything will be exposed. You fight to control the panic. You try to hold on, but one day your fear gets the best of you. Your denial system snaps.

You are not sure what you fear, but you sense that everything will be exposed.

✎ **Have you ever felt feelings like the paragraph you just read describes? ❏ Yes ❏ No If so, write what you think these feelings mean.**

_____

_____

When You Get Caught

Removing the mask

A thief looking for a hiding place saw what looked like a perfect place to hide. He went inside. He saw a rope. He climbed the rope, but as he climbed, a church bell rang. He was climbing the rope that rang the church bell. He was caught as he sounded his own alarm.[3]

An alcoholic calls in sick one time too many. A sex addict gets caught with the other woman (or man). The compulsive spender goes bankrupt. The mask is off. The denial is over.

✎ Has your compulsive behavior ever caused you to be "caught" in a way that brought you out of denial? ❑ Yes ❑ No If so, describe the circumstance.

_____

_____

When Others Stop Helping You Deny

In recovery groups people often hear the comparison that living with a family member who is in denial is like having an elephant in your living room. The family rule is that life revolves around the elephant. Nobody crosses the elephant. Let him do what he wants to. Walk around him. Clean up after him. The elephant is king of this house. Family members fear that one day somebody will come into the house and see the elephant and ask, "Why in the world do you have an elephant in your living room?" The rule is, "Don't talk about the elephant," so the possibility of being asked a point-blank question about the elephant scares them. Everyone in the family works together to keep the elephant secret.

It takes a whole family system to maintain this kind of denial. The elephant may be alcoholism. The elephant may be rage. It may be abuse in the home.

Stewart's story

Sometimes family members decide to quit the denial team. In public the Stanton family looked successful, happy, and very upper class. Stewart and his wife led the parents' organization at their daughter's school. They looked like a model couple. The family was active in a large church. Their daughter Lisa was cheerleader. They lived in an expensive home. Friends described Stewart as gracious and kind. But Stewart had a drinking problem. He physically abused his wife, and she had filed for a divorce. Stewart's wife had said, in effect, "I am quitting the denial team. I am no longer going to make it possible for you to carry on the facade you have been hiding behind."

Alcoholics need someone to help them in their denial. Most alcoholics are not on skid row. The skid-row alcoholics have lost their helpers in the game of denial. Most alcoholics have some people around them who are willing to pretend that the drinking isn't really there, or that it is not really that bad.

Stewart had a drinking problem. When his wife said she was quitting the denial team, Stewart began to see that he would have to face the consequences of his brokenness. Other people saw the family as whole and healthy, but the trappings of success and happiness only hid their brokenness. Brokenness becomes obvious when your denial team resigns and your denial system collapses.

✎ List people who help you maintain your compulsive behavior. Write the name of each person and how that person helps you maintain the behavior.

_____

_____

When You Decide to Face the Truth and Begin Recovery

Along with the gloomy list of situations we just reviewed, one positive option exists. One other possibility is that you would decide to face reality—not just the past, but also the present. You can decide to confront your denial system. You will need help. You cannot do it alone. You can begin to grow. You do not have to wait for things to cave in on you.

Bob and Sally's story
Bob's wife Sally ruined every couple friendship that they tried to form. When Bob arranged for the two of them to dine with friends, Sally managed to have a business conflict. Bob made flimsy excuses to their friends about why Sally had to cancel. Sally actually was a workaholic and Bob covered for her. Then one day the engagement Sally broke involved an outing with Bob's business partner and his wife. This time Sally had gone too far. Bob refused to endure the consequences and disrupted relationship that could occur with his business partner if he weaseled out again. He told Sally he would cover for her no longer. Bob confronted his denial system and decided to face the truth about Sally. Then healing could begin in his life. Are you ready to face the real truth about yourself?

Face Your Compulsions

✎ **The compulsive behaviors I am working on are:** _____

_____

Below describe how you managed these compulsive behaviors yesterday.

_____

_____

Work on Turning Points

✎ **Below, describe the progress are you making toward working Turning Point 1:** *I admit my powerlessness in the face of my painful past and my current compulsions. I am ready to believe that God is more powerful than I am and that He can restore me to spiritual and emotional wholeness.*

_____

_____

➤ **If the following prayer reflects the desire of your heart, express your own version of the prayer to God. "God, help me to see through my own denial. Something in me is broken. I cannot fix it. Help me to face my brokenness. I am ready for you to go to work in my life."**

➤ **Write in the margin three times your Scripture memory passage for this week.**

The Fork in the Road

Give Up or Grow

When we recognize our brokenness, we have an opportunity to give up or to grow. In the illustration in day 3, Stewart's story had a happy ending. He decided to get help. He began a process of emotional and spiritual healing that eventually saved his marriage. He could have chosen to give up, but he decided to grow instead.

Today's Objective:
You will recognize that when your denial system breaks, you can choose to find healing or to give up.

Any difficult situation can be a reason to fail or a reason to succeed. Somerset Maugham, world-renowned author of more than 20 books, 30 plays, and many essays and short stories, had a speech handicap. When he was 86 years old, he commented that his speech handicap had affected him to the good more than any other factor in his life. He said, "Had I not stammered, I would probably have gone to Cambridge as my brothers did . . . and every now and then published a dreary book about French literature."[4] His handicap became a means for greatness.

 Write in your own words what the story of Somerset Maugham says to you. What handicap in your own life could this story inspire you to overcome?

_____

_____

Perhaps you wrote that your pain of being reared in an alcoholic home could become a springboard for understanding and improving relationships with your co-workers. Perhaps you could overcome your addiction to food, and you could channel that energy into improving your marriage. In Somerset Maugham's case, his handicap became a means for greatness. The brokenness that has held you back could become the very force that pushes you forward.

At a decision point

When you stop denying your brokenness—and when your brokenness stares you in the face—you may feel overwhelmed. Your denial system held back the horror of looking into the mirror of your soul. You probably do not like what you see. You always feared it would crush you. Now that you look at it, your fears seem justified. You are at a point of decision.

In the book _Putting Faith to Work_ Robert McCracken tells a story about Leo Durocher, the manager of the Giants baseball team. Durocher had a 20-year-old player who was going through a bad time in his baseball career. He had been up to bat 26 times but had only made one hit. Finally this young player approached Leo Durocher crying and begging to be benched. He knew he was doing poorly. Durocher put a fatherly arm around the 20-year-old player and said to him: "Don't worry, Son, you are my center fielder, even if you don't get another hit all season." Twenty-year-old Willie Mays strolled out of Leo Durocher's office with a buoyant step, and he started hitting the ball. He went on to become one of baseball's greats.[5]

Brokenness led to victory. Why? It was because the manager, Leo Durocher, did the right thing. He had enough understanding to say the right things at the right time, and the player made a decision to respond to the opportunity.

Your brokenness could be the death of you if you go on denying it, or it could be the beginning of life. It depends on what you do with it. In the margin box describe a time in which you faced a crisis and had to make a decision to grow or to give up.

 What crisis—large or small—are you facing today that presents the same option—grow or give up? Will you let your brokenness crush you, or will you choose to let your brokenness become the first step to wholeness? Below write your response.

_____

_____

Face Your Compulsions

 The compulsive behaviors I am working on are: _____

_____

Below describe how you managed these compulsive behaviors yesterday.

_____

_____

Work on Turning Points

 Below, describe the progress are you making toward working Turning Point One: _I admit my powerlessness in the face of my painful past and my current compulsions. I am ready to believe that God truly is more powerful than I am and that He can restore me to spiritual and emotional wholeness._

_____

_____

DAY 5

Today's Objective:
You will learn how brokenness can become wholeness when it is placed in the hands of God.

The Victory of Brokenness

Giving Your Brokenness to God

In the spring of 1988, I went to a treatment center to confront issues resulting from growing up with an alcoholic parent. The center offered help for family members of alcoholics as well as for alcoholics and drug addicts themselves. The five days at the treatment center changed my life. At one point in my week, the leader of my group asked me a question which irritated me. He said, "Who is your God?" I answered quickly, "Jesus Christ is my God." As soon as I completed my answer he asked me again, "Who is your God?" This time with some annoyance in my voice, I answered again, "Jesus Christ is my God." As soon as I answered, he asked again. I gave the same answer.

Our group dismissed. As we left the meeting place, I asked another member of the group about the question our group leader had asked me over and over. I said, "I don't understand what he meant." Frankly, I was angry that the leaders had questioned me, a Baptist minister, about the identity of my God.

My fellow group member said, "Let me put it another way for you. Who is in control of your life?" Then I understood the question and why my group leader asked it repeatedly. My group leader sensed what I did not want to admit. Stating your belief in God is one thing; giving Him control is another. I had to face the fact that much of the time, God was not in control of my life.

Turning Point 1 states:
I admit my powerlessness in the face of my painful past and my current compulsions. I am ready to believe that God is more powerful than I am and that He can restore me to spiritual and emotional wholeness.

At the end of your rope

Another way to state this turning point is, "I admit that something in me is broken." Still another way to say it is, "God, I am at the end of my rope." I imagine God might respond to us, "When you are at the end of your rope, that's where I step in to be sufficient for you. Take hold of my rope."

 Below describe how you feel knowing that God offers to step in to be sufficient for you when you are at the end of your rope.

The sacrifices of God are a broken spirit; a broken and contrite heart, O God, you will not despise.

Psalm 51:17

Admitting brokenness sets the stage for repentance, because when we honestly see our brokenness, we become ready to turn to God. We come before God saying, "Yes, God, my life is broken, and I cannot patch it up by myself." As you stand before God in your brokenness, be honest with Him, as the verse at left describes. Your prayer could be, "Here I am. My life is broken. Here it is. Take it." He always will receive you with open arms.

In the cross we see the greatest example of God's ability to turn brokenness into wholeness. God turned the cross—formerly a horrible symbol of execution of the worst kind of criminal—into a symbol of hope, life, and forgiveness because He can turn brokenness into wholeness. In Galatians 2:20 Paul wrote, "I have been crucified with Christ, and I no longer live, but Christ lives in me." He might have said, "I laid my life, broken, at the foot of the cross, and gave it to Christ."

 After you read the above two paragraphs, check below the statements that are true.

❑ God will accept you sometimes if you are honest with Him.
❑ God expects us to be on our own when we're trying to patch up the brokenness of our lives.
❑ The cross demonstrates God's power to turn brokenness into hope, life, and forgiveness.
❑ God can turn brokenness to wholeness.
❑ Honesty about our brokenness leads us to God.

The last three statements in the above exercise are true and the first two are incorrect. God always accepts us when we are honest, and He wants us to turn to Him in our brokenness instead of trying to patch things up on our own.

What God Does with Brokenness

When you give your brokenness to God, He will—
• increase your spiritual stamina;
• help you change your life;
• remold you.

Let's look at how this occurs.

Increasing Your Spiritual Stamina
The central mystery of the Christian faith appears as God transforms our weakness into strength. We cannot be sure how this works, but Paul wrote: about God, "My power is made perfect in weakness" (2 Corinthians 12:9). When we honestly admit we cannot govern our lives, God provides the wisdom and strength we need.

Helping You Change Your Life

Trying to grow

One evening as I led a recovery group in my church, I told the members, "I want you to pray for me, because I have more to do this week than I possibly can do." Making such a request was not easy. I do not like to admit that anything is too difficult for me. Normally my attitude is, "Tackle it head on and work until it's done," but I was trying to grow. I wanted to be honest about my brokenness. I trusted the people in this group. The next day when I woke up, I gave the day to Jesus. During the next two days, some things changed that removed about eight hours from my work load for the week. I said, "Thank you, God. Forgive me for not having more faith than I did."

Sometimes God changes circumstances. He does not always work that way. Sometimes He seems to say, "You need to work through this and find out that I am going to give you more strength than you knew you had." Sometimes it seems that God wants you to have the experience of not getting everything done and letting people love you and accept you anyway.

Remolding You
God turns brokenness into wholeness by reshaping us in the broken areas of our lives. See what the Scripture appearing at left says about this kind of remolding. God takes our brokenness and molds us into what we need to be.

 After reading the above paragraph and the verse at left, describe below what you think that you would be like if God remolded you into a person who was whole and not broken.

_____

_____

So I went down to the potter's house, and I saw him working at the wheel, but the pot he was shaping from the clay was marred in his hands. So the potter formed it into another pot, shaping it as it seemed best to him. Then the word of the Lord came to me, 'O house of Israel, can I not do with you as this potter does? Like clay in the hands of the potter, so are you in my hand, O house of Israel.'"
Jeremiah 18:3-6

The passage in Jeremiah 18:3-6 says that the potter shaped the clay "as it seemed best to Him." For us, wholeness would mean attaining God's best for us. In the above exercise, you might have answered that wholeness would mean that you could endure your mother's criticism without feeling demeaned or hurt. It might mean that you could forgive a former boss who dismissed you from a job and not allow that incident to paralyze you with bitterness for the rest of your life. It might mean that you accept people with their limitations and not allow your disappointment about less-than-ideal relationships to control your life.

Telling Safe People About Your Brokenness

Finding those who care

When I tell selected safe people about my brokenness, they can choose to help me. My denial system will lead me through life wearing a mask and acting like everything is OK when it is not. Inside I am crying out, "Why doesn't anybody know I am lonely? Why don't people know that I need them?" They do not know because I will not let them see it. I act as if I don't need anyone. When I become honest about my brokenness, I can discover people who will reach out and love me.

Taking the First Step Toward Wholeness

Brokenness can be a state of disrepair in your heart, but it also can be an attitude that says, "God, I am ready for you to go to work in my life." This is how you start the Christian life, and this is how you live it.

When you give your life to Christ, you immediately experience wholeness and healing. Down the road somewhere, He makes you aware of more areas where you need healing. He seems to say, "Here is an area of brokenness I have not shown you before. I didn't want to mention it earlier, because I knew it could overwhelm you. Now you are ready to see it. This part of your life is broken." Maybe it is a habit. Maybe it is your temper. Maybe it is your attitude about money. Maybe it is your attitude about other Christians. Maybe your attitude about your work is broken. God seems to say, "This part of you is broken. I want you to be willing to say the same thing about it that I say about it. I want you to acknowledge this brokenness. Give me your brokenness. Let me work on it."

Let God show you who you are. Let Him reveal what He needs to reveal.

Perhaps you now are in a state of wholeness. Maybe you are not broken. It is OK to be OK. Maybe you simply are reading this to increase your understanding of how these issues affect other people. It is OK to be on the other side of brokenness. Whatever your spiritual and emotional state is, do not try to be broken. Attempt to be open. Let God show you who you are. Let Him reveal what He needs to reveal.

Don't be surprised if the thought of admitting brokenness frightens you. Brokenness may be more difficult for men to admit than for women, because our culture says that men always must be in control. Though we as men may say we are free from such outdated ideas, we may have a tough time looking at brokenness because it implies that we are weak and out of control.

✎ **Does the thought of admitting brokenness frighten you?** ❏ Yes ❏ No
If so, check below what frightens you the most.
    ❏ I'm afraid I might cry or express other strong emotion.
    ❏ I'm afraid of what others would think.
    ❏ I'm afraid I'd realize that I need to fix too many areas in my life.
    ❏ I'm afraid it would cause other relationships in my life to change.
    Other _____

Admitting brokenness does result in changed relationships and an openness to expressing feelings. It does result in discovering other areas that need repair. Yes, those close to you are bound to notice that something is different in your life. However, in the honesty of the brokenness is wholeness. God does not intend for your brokenness to be permanent. God sees brokenness as a path to lead you to wholeness.

Do not try to break somebody else. You will fail. That is not your job. When you try, the results may be opposite of what you intend. You may break the person, but not in a way that brings healing.

We all need honest and affirming people in our lives. I have committed for the rest of my life to always have people around me who will be honest with me about what they see. I do not want somebody mean. I do not want a gossip. I do not want somebody who is out to get me. I do want somebody I can trust and who will look at me and say, "This is what I see," and then leave me with the freedom to decide what I will do with it. I also want to be that kind of person for others.

> Brokenness is an opportunity to give up or to grow.

Brokenness becomes wholeness when we place it in the hands of God. Not only that, with God brokenness can become beauty.

During World War II a beautiful stained glass window in the Reims Cathedral in France was shattered. After the disaster, members of the community gathered in the place where the fragments of the window had fallen. One by one they picked up the tiny pieces of glass and lead. When the war was over, they hired skilled artists to build a new window out of the tiny broken pieces of the original. When the artists finished, the window was more magnificent than it was before.[6]

Letting God go to work

That is how God works. Give Him your brokenness. You can say to Him something like this:
- "God, here is my life. It is in a state of disrepair."
- "Here is this part of my life, God. It is broken."
- "God, I'm tired of taking this matter in my own hands."

✎ **Below write a statement of what you'll say when you give your brokenness to God. (In the next unit we'll carry this further when we actually give Him our brokenness.)**

_____

_____

_____

_____

What you just wrote represents the attitude of brokenness. This is the first step to spiritual wholeness.

Face Your Compulsions

✎ The compulsive behaviors I am working on are: _____

_____

Below describe how you managed these compulsive behaviors yesterday.

_____

_____

Work on Finding a Listener/Sponsor

Sharing your inventory

As we mentioned earlier, you will need to find someone to listen to you as you share the contents of your moral inventory. Choosing a person for this role is highly important. We'll review the following characteristics of a good sponsor/listener. This person needs to be someone who is—
• the same gender as yourself;
• trustworthy and will not break confidence;
• willing to listen without judging you;
• an encourager and supporter;
• has some understanding of the process of recovery;

Your sponsor could be someone who has participated in a 12-Step group and who understands the meaning of the Fifth Step. During the seventh meeting of the group you will report on the experience you've had in sharing your inventory with this sponsor. You will not share your inventory with the group. You will report on what it was like to share your inventory with a sponsor. In the box at left write the initials of some people that are now on your mind as you think about the person you'll choose. If you've already decided on who what person will be, write his or her name on the lines.

Potential sponsors

_____

_____

_____

_____

> **Turning Point 1**
> I admit my powerlessness in the face of my painful past and my current compulsions. I am ready to believe that God is more powerful than I am and that He can restore me to spiritual and emotional wholeness.

Notes

[1]J. Keith Miller, *Sin: Overcoming the Ultimate Deadly Addiction* (San Francisco: Harper & Row Publishers, 1987), 24.

[2]Robert Hemfelt and Richard Fowler, *Serenity: A Companion for Twelve-Step Recovery* (Nashville: Thomas Nelson Publishers, 1990), 25.

[3]*Dynamic Preaching*, March, 1989, p. 10, citing J. David Long, ed. Devotion: December (Cincinnati: Standard Publishing Co., 1981).

[4]Jack Gulledge, *Proclaim*, April, May, June, (Nashville: The Sunday School Board of the Southern Baptist Convention, 1989), 32.

[5]Robert McCracken, *Putting Faith to Work* cited by G. Curtis Jones, *One Thousand Illustrations for Preaching and Teaching* (Nashville: Broadman Press, 1986), 327.

[6]Philip Parham, *Letting God: Christian Meditations for Recovering Persons* (San Francisco: Harper and Row, Publishers, 1987), March 27th reading.

In this Unit you'll work on—
Turning Point 2
I surrender control of my
life to God.

Surrender

The Recovery Cycle
An attitude of BROKENNESS accompanied by the action of SURRENDER leads to RECOVERY.

BECKY AND HER MOTHER

Becky's mother lived 40 miles away from Becky and her family, but she kept Becky on a string constantly. She repeatedly telephoned Becky to ask her to run errands. When Becky did not respond immediately, her mother laid on a guilt trip! She told Becky, "My friend Gladys' daughter always drives her to the doctor. It's too bad you're so selfish and won't do that for me!" Even when Becky dropped everything to visit her mother, her mother was highly critical. She criticized the way Becky reared her children, cleaned her carpet, and wore her hair. On their wedding anniversary Becky's husband Joe planned a special weekend away. He obtained a hotel room and arranged for someone to care for their children, but Becky's mother called just as the couple was about to drive away for a romantic weekend. Joe was furious when he had to delay the trip for several hours so Becky could go to pick up a prescription for her mother.

Becky dreamed of an ideal mother-daughter relationship—one in which her mother appreciated her and did not make demands on her. Becky thought if she only did enough tasks for her mother, she could "fix" whatever was wrong with things between her and her mother. What did Becky need in her life? (Read more about Becky on page 62.)

Why you will find this unit useful
The call to surrender confronts you with the issue of control. Surrendering your life to God and retaining the right to control every aspect of your life do not go together. Adult children of dysfunctional families need to control people and situations. Giving someone else control feels frightening. The call to surrender raises the issue of trust. We have learned that trusting can be dangerous. In this unit you will find help in dealing with the issues of being in control and learning to trust. The unit will challenge you to make a decision to let go and to surrender to God.

Isn't Surrender for Cowards?	I Am in Control and in Pain	Authority Figures Bother Me!	Surrender Requires Trust	I Must Give My Brokenness to God
DAY 1	DAY 2	DAY 3	DAY 4	DAY 5

This week's memory verses
Come to me, all you who are weary and burdened, and I will give you rest. Take my yoke upon you and learn from me, for I am gentle and humble in heart, and you will find rest for your souls.
                                                                    –Matthew 11:28-29

47

Isn't Surrender for Cowards?

Today's Objective:
You will learn about a kind of surrender that is a mark of courage rather than cowardice.

Recovery

Surrender

Brokenness

EMOTIONAL PAIN

Denial

Control

Pain

Ron's story

Connecting with the Recovery Cycle

We live in a throwaway world. If something breaks, we toss it out and buy a new one. When a relationship or even a life is broken, we too quickly may assume that it is beyond repair or that fixing it would be too costly.

Broken lives can be fixed! Broken relationships can be healed! The power for these repairs must come from God. He will give you the strength you need to experience healing. Your role is surrendering your will and your life to Him. Surrender is what you do with brokenness. (See illustration in margin.)

The word "surrender" presents an immediate problem. When we hear this word, we often think the following things:

- Surrender is for cowards.
- Surrender is for quitters.
- Surrender is for losers.
- Surrender means giving up.
- Surrender involves saying to another person, "You are stronger than I am," or "You are right and I am wrong."

 Below describe what feelings come to you rmind when you think about the word *surrender*.

_____

_____

You may have written that you believe surrender is a form of weakness. You may have said that it represents giving up the control you think you have when you are in a situation. You may have written that surrendering allows someone else to dominate you. You may have said that surrendering gives someone else the right to abuse you.

Ron struggled with pain in his past because his father was absent during his growing-up years. Ron's father always was dashing off on a business trip. In his *Making Peace with Your Past* group, Ron told group members, "He always brought me little souvenirs from places he went. I didn't want his souvenirs. I wanted him there to listen to my frustrations when I broke up with my girlfriend. I wanted him there to see me get a trophy in basketball."

Ron felt that past pain still had control on his life. He felt that because he had a poor role model of husband and father, he never could have a satisfactory dating relationship. Thoughts about his father held him in a stranglehold. When Ron thought about the concept of surrender, he thought that would mean admitting that his father always would overpower him in his thoughts.

Admitting that someone else is stronger than him was exactly what Ron needed to do. Ron needed to say, "Something in my life is broken, and I do not have the ability to fix it. I need someone else who is stronger than me to help, and that someone is God."

Only God has such superior strength. Only He can give you the help you need in your brokenness. Surrendering in the middle of a battle may mean you are a coward, but surrendering to God takes courage. Surrendering in the face of life's challenges may mean you are a quitter, but surrendering to God is the path to victory.

How Ron could surrender

Ron could turn over to God his feelings of resentment about his father. He could admit to God that he cannot heal himself. He could ask God to step into the middle of the battle and take over the feelings that were raging inside him. This type of surrender to God would be the path to victory in Ron's life.

On the previous page we read some concepts—all wrong ones—that the word *surrender* often brings to mind. Here's a true picture of surrender:

- Surrender is giving God permission to be God in your life.
- Surrender is giving God control of the things that control you.
- Surrender is letting go.
- Surrender is giving back to God what He has given you.
- Surrender is experiencing "the honor of defeat at God's hands." [1]

Below are some comments others have made about surrender:
When asked to describe the reason for her success, Florence Nightingale said, "I have only one explanation. As far as I was able or aware, I have kept nothing back from God." [2]

I hereby resign my self-appointed position as directing superintendent of my own life and of the world. I cannot level all the mountains of injustice, or fill in all the valleys of selfishness. There is too much of it in me. I hereby turn over to you for your disposition and use my life, my money, my time and talents to be at your disposal. [3]

Jesus said, "If anyone would come after me, he must deny himself and take up his cross daily and follow me. For whoever wants to save his life will lose it, but whoever loses his life for me will save it" (Luke 9:23-24).

Needing more of God

"Recovery does not depend on finding yourself; it depends on losing (yourself). Real self-discovery is in losing ourselves by discovering God. We don't need more of us, we need more of God." [4]

✎ **Take a few minutes to write a letter to God that expresses how you feel about surrendering your life to Him.**

_____

_____

_____

_____

_____

_____

Face Your Compulsions

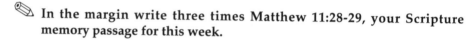 The compulsive behaviors I am working on are: _____

_____

Below describe how you managed these compulsive behaviors yesterday.

_____

_____

Work on Turning Points

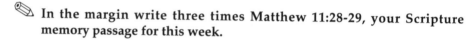 Below, describe the progress you are making toward working Turning Point 2: *I surrender control of my life to God.*

_____

_____

_____

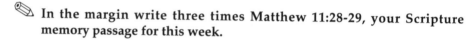 In the margin write three times Matthew 11:28-29, your Scripture memory passage for this week.

DAY 2

Today's Objective:
You will learn some ways people running from surrender try to stay in control rather than giving in to God.

I Am in Control and in Pain

Identifying the Cycle of Pain

The alternative to surrender is control. The cycle of pain works like this. You experience emotional pain. You fear this pain. You learn to deny the pain. You begin to live in denial of what you feel. The drawing in the margin on page 48 illustrates this.

To maintain your denial you need control. First, you need to control yourself, especially your own feelings. Eventually, other people will threaten your denial system. They also need to be controlled. When you were a child, your life felt out of control. As you grew older you decided you were better off to be in control than to let others control you. Now you are in control. Your tendency toward control is a barrier in your relationship with God and with other people. While brokenness and surrender lead to recovery, denial and control lead to more pain.

Staying in Control

Dysfunctional families feel out of control. Children of dysfunctional families develop a feeling of helplessness. They realize, "This is happening to me. It hurts. I cannot do anything about it." An internal dream develops: "One day, I will get out of this situation, and I will gain control of my life." The adult child then may live by this motto, "Whatever I do, wherever I go, I will do my best to be in control."

Amanda's story

Amanda's motto could have been described as, "Just the facts, ma'am." Her whole approach to life was just that—extremely factual. For example, when she returned from her grandfather's funeral, she described to her support group every detail of every flower arrangement. But when group members asked her, "But how did you *feel*, Amanda, about losing your grandfather?" Amanda looked at them like they were speaking a foreign language. Words to describe her feelings weren't part of Amanda's vocabulary. Her inability to express feelings was affecting every relationship—her friendships, her work associations, and especially her marriage.

Amanda learned that her inability to express her feelings originated from her need to stay in control. Her childhood as the daughter of a drug-addicted father was chaotic. When she returned home from school, she never knew whether her father would be raging, sick, sullen, or physically absent. She learned that the expression of her emotions was one thing she could control, so she kept a tight lid on them.

✎ **Think about Amanda's story. Can you identify with her in any way? Why is it important for you to be in control? Below write your answer.**

_____

_____

One person wrote: *It is important for me to be in control because my father often got drunk when I was a child. When he was drunk, my whole family felt out of control. Sometimes he would lose control of his car. Sometimes he would lose control of his money. Being out of control feels very frightening to me. When I am not in control I feel I will get hurt.*

✎ **What are some ways you control people?**

_____

_____

Some of us respond: *I control people by being right as much as possible. I control people by being more prepared than they are. I control people by reminding them of their failures. I control people by locking them out emotionally when they disappoint me. I control people by changing my plans constantly so that I can keep their plans off balance and therefore stay in control myself.*

✎ **What are some ways you control situations?**

_____

_____

Example: *If I am in a new situation, the first thing I do is move into the background to "scope it out." I try to get a good sense of what is happening and what the rules are. I am very careful not to make a mistake. I don't say anything unless I am sure it is right. The problem is that when I live like this, the situations really are controlling me.*

✎ **What are some ways you control your feelings?**

_____

_____

You may have written: *I do not allow myself to feel anything intensely. I control my feelings by working long hours at things I enjoy. I control my feelings by eating. When I am not eating or working, I often feel empty.*

Running from Surrender

A feeling of panic

When your brokenness and the need to surrender confront you, you may feel panic. You depend on being in control. Life without control is frightening. The paradox of the matter is that the more you try to control, the more things get out of control. Compulsive habits control you. People eventually rebel at being controlled. The need to control is so great, you want to hold on to it even when you know in your head that it can harm you. As the call of surrender comes closer to you, you may want to run and hide.

Below are some ways you can run from surrender. You'll read more about them in this lesson.
• You may deny the need to surrender.
• You may fight the call to surrender.
• You may engage in self-destructive behavior rather than surrender.

You May Deny the Need to Surrender

You may use denial to stay in control. You may be like the breathless mountain climber who climbs halfway up a mountain and says, "I think this is the best spot from which to see the view."[5] The truth is that the hiker cannot go any farther. He is exhausted. Rather than say, "I am weak. I am tired. This is as far as I can go," the hiker says, "I don't want to go any higher." When the challenge to face your brokenness and surrender confronts you, you may reply, "I'm OK. I don't have any problems. I'm fine." This digging in of your heels can occur even after you have done initial work in recovery. You may say, "I had some problems in the past, but I have dealt with them." It hurts to say, "I cannot let go. I am hurting. I do need help."

✎ **Do you have areas in your life that you need to surrender?**
❏ Yes ❏ No

Are you "in denial" about certain areas of control in your life?
❏ Yes ❏ No

If yes, in what areas?
❏ Self-esteem
❏ Use of alcohol
❏ Compulsive eating
❏ Compulsive sexual behavior
❏ Compulsive religious activities
❏ Work addiction
❏ **Emotional enmeshment** with another person
❏ Other: _____

emotional enmeshment—Our emotional life is tied to that of other people. If they are happy, we can be happy. If they are not happy, we cannot be happy.

You May Fight the Call to Surrender

A mother punished her five-year-old son in an abusive way. She locked him in her closet. At first the mother heard noises coming from the closet. Then all became very quiet. Out of curiosity the mother opened the door of the closet. Her son was sitting on top of all her clothes. He looked at her with a scowl and said, "I pulled all your clothes down; I spit all over them, I spit all over your shoes, and now I'm just sitting here waiting for more spit."[6]

The little boy chose to fight rather than surrender. When someone is abusing your basic rights as a person, you act in a healthy way when you resist and fight. However, as one man said, "When I wrestle with God, I hope to lose." Some people wrestle with God and hope to win. They assume that God cannot be trusted—that He is like a parent who locks you in a closet. They may wrestle with God openly, or they may do it in more subtle ways. They learn to run, to hide, to inwardly resist God, and to keep Him at arm's length.

People may wrestle with God openly, or they may do it in more subtle ways.

✎ **Are you fighting with God?** ❑ **Yes** ❑ **No** **What makes you think you are fighting with God? What do you hope to win from Him in your struggle?**

_____

_____

You May Engage in Self-Destructive Behavior Rather Than Surrender

A last resort

Some people view surrender as so frightening and so much of a last resort they would rather destroy themselves than let go and give everything to God. Some destroy themselves with a slow, self-destructive pattern—inhaled through every drag on a cigarette. Others use the downward spiral of drug addiction. Some follow a socially acceptable practice like working themselves to death or a compulsion to eat or an obsession with sexual activities.

In Berlin in 1908, a 21-year-old Polish pianist named Arthur Rubenstein was in despair. He was lonely, hungry, and in debt. His career was at a standstill. He decided nothing was left to do but take his own life. He did not have a gun. He did not have poison. The idea of jumping out a window and possibly surviving as a cripple repulsed him.

He placed a chair under his feet. He took a belt from his robe and hooked it onto a hook overhead. He wrapped the belt around his neck. He kicked the chair out from under himself. The worn out belt broke immediately. Rubenstein fell to the floor with a crash.

For a while he just lay on the floor. Later he went to the piano and cried himself out in music. He went back out onto the street. Later he said that he saw the world as if he had been reborn. He learned that day to "love life, for better or for worse, without conditions."[7]

By refusing to surrender, some people pull themselves down slowly but surely into an early grave.

Not every self-destructive individual is so fortunate as young Arthur Rubenstein. Rubenstein went on to become a famous pianist, but many self-destructive individuals succeed in their attempts at self-destruction. Some people pull themselves down slowly but surely into an early grave. That grave may be a physical one, or it may be an emotional or spiritual grave. People can die many different ways.

> Some people are willing to do anything but surrender.

We so value staying in control that we deny we are in control. We deny we need to let go and give things to God, or we insist that we already have done so. We will do anything but surrender.

✎ **Are you engaging in self-destructive behavior? ❑ Yes ❑ No If so, what is it and how much control does it have over your life?**

_____

_____

What aspect of surrender scares you? _____

_____

God understands our fears

You may have written that you fear surrender because it might cause you to make changes in a harmful relationship that has been like a crutch for you. You may fear surrender because you're afraid it will make you too spiritual. After all, if you're depending on God, you might have to pray more often than you do now in order to stay in touch with Him as the source of power in your life. You may fear surrender because if you surrender, God might show you that you need to begin having some intimate conversations with your spouse rather than the surface ones you have now. Whatever your fears about surrender, God understands them and does not condemn us for them. He wants us to be honest so that healing can begin.

Face Your Compulsions

✎ **The compulsive behaviors I am working on are:** _____

_____

Below describe how you managed these compulsive behaviors yesterday.

_____

_____

Work on Turning Points

✎ **Below describe the progress you are making toward working Turning Point 2:** _I surrender control of my life to God._

_____

_____

➢ **Say aloud five times your Scripture memory passage for this week.**

Authority Figures Bother Me!

Responding to Authority Figures

Mixed Feelings Toward Authority Figures

As adult children from dysfunctional families we may have mixed feelings about authority figures. We may engage in silent mental conversations with the authority figures in our lives. These conversations may sound like this:

- "I want you to like me, but I am afraid of you."
- "You probably don't like me, so I'll keep my distance."
- "Why don't you notice me? You probably don't care."

Fear of Authority Figures

The adult child from a dysfunctional family may fear authority figures and think thoughts like:

- "If I fail and you find out, you will hurt me."
- "You may accuse me when it was not my fault."
- "When you ask me a question, I must quickly figure out what the catch is. I probably will answer wrong, but maybe I can anticipate what you want me to say."
- "When you tell me what needs to be done, the things you say become garbled in my mind. I am afraid to say, 'I didn't understand what you meant.'"

From Where Do These Feelings Come?

Parents Teach Us About Authority

What is the source of such feelings toward authority figures? The first authority figures you encounter are your parents. How your parents deal with their authority over you strongly affects your view of authority figures. If they are reasonably consistent and worthy of trust, you learn to trust authority figures. If one or both of your parents were addicted to a substance or a behavior, your view of authority figures was harmed. If you experienced deep anger toward your parents because of the way they related to you, and if you are unable to process that anger, you still may be transferring some of that anger to other authority figures.

Childhood Leaders Teach Us About Authority

Lasting impressions

Significant adults in your childhood years also shaped your view of authority figures. Teachers, church leaders, doctors, nurses, and others likely made lasting impressions on your view of authority figures. If you experienced abuse by an adult authority figure, you may find it difficult to trust authority figures even now that you are an adult.

✎ **Read the following statements and pretend you are saying them to an adult authority figure from your childhood years. Do any of these statements represent ones you would say in this conversation? Why?**

- ❑ "I want you to like me, but I am afraid of you."
- ❑ "You probably don't like me, so I'll keep my distance."
- ❑ "Why don't you notice me? You probably don't care."
- ❑ "If I fail and you find out, you will hurt me."

❑ "You may accuse me when it was not my fault."
❑ "When you ask me a question, I must quickly figure out what the catch is. I probably will answer wrong, but maybe I can anticipate what you want me to say."
❑ "When you tell me what needs to be done, the things you say become garbled in my mind. I am afraid to say, 'I didn't understand what you said.'"

✎ **What did your parents teach you about authority figures? How did they communicate these ideas to you?**

_____

_____

_____

Besides your parents, what other authority figures made a big impact on you during childhood? How did they shape your view of authority figures?

_____

_____

A big impact

You may have answered that your parents made fun of each other's discipline of you. You may have said that they communicated to you that you do not need to take seriously rules authority figures make. Or, you may have written that your parents were highly critical of any task that you performed. Their constant stream of criticism without affirmation may have shaped the way you feel today about a supervisor, a law enforcement officer, a minister, or a committee chairperson.

Perhaps you listed a favorite aunt or a coach as another authority figure that made a big impact on you. Perhaps you said that this person influenced you positively because he or she called attention to your strengths instead of your weaknesses.

Authority Figures Exercise Control

If you feel compelled to stay in control, you will struggle with authority figures. You will resent and resist anyone who exercises control over you, even if that control is necessary and fair. In the margin box write the initials of people who represent the authority figures in your life today.

✎ **Mark the descriptions that apply to people who exert authority in your life today.**

❑ Supervisors
❑ Teachers
❑ Physicians
❑ Ministers
❑ Other church leaders

❑ Police
❑ Parents
❑ Leaders in community organizations
❑ Other: _____

Authority figures in my life today—

_____

_____

_____

_____

Do your relationships with people in these roles reflect problems with authority figures? In what ways?

_____

_____

_____

Where Does God Fit In?

God is the ultimate authority figure. Unfortunately we sometimes transfer our feelings toward human authority figures to God Himself. Even people who are deeply sincere believers may make this transfer.

Judd and Helen's story

Judd studied to be a minister. When he and his wife Helen married, Helen automatically believed that the couple would have a prayer time together each day. Imagine her surprise when Judd told her he thought praying to God was a waste of time because God never heard his prayers anyway!

Helen couldn't believe that a preacher-to-be would have such thoughts. Their lack of a family devotion time became a big issue in their marriage. Judd had developed a view of God as a non-provider because his own father had neglected his family and left them with big debts. The Heavenly Father seemed distant in Judd's mind because of his experience with his earthly father. When Judd understood the source of his feelings, he began to make some major adjustments in the way that he and his wife related to God.

✎ **To test yourself, ask yourself whether the statements below describe how you often think of God.**

❑ "I want you to like me, but I am afraid of you."
❑ "You probably don't like me, so I'll keep my distance."
❑ "Why don't you notice me? You probably don't care."
❑ "If I fail and you find out, you will hurt me."
❑ "You may accuse me when it was not my fault."
❑ "When you tell me what needs to be done, the things you say become garbled in my mind. I am afraid to say, 'I didn't understand what you said.'"

But the fruit of the Spirit is love, joy, peace, patience, kindness, goodness, faithfulness, gentleness and self-control.
Galatians 5:22-23

You may need to re-evaluate your view of God. Here is a good test. Begin by reading the Bible passage at left. These verses list the fruit of the Holy Spirit. God exists as Father, Son (Jesus), and Holy Spirit. The fruit of the Spirit are attributes of God.

✎ **Look at the list of the fruit of the Spirit below. Check which of these traits describe your heartfelt view of God? Notice the term "heartfelt," as opposed to what you may have been taught about God or what you feel you're "supposed to believe."**

❑ Love   ❑ Joy
❑ Peace   ❑ Patience
❑ Kindness   ❑ Goodness
❑ Gentleness   ❑ Self-control

If your heartfelt view of God does not connect with these attributes, could your heartfelt view of God be inaccurate? Could your concept of God be an idol, obstructing your path to a relationship with God? I urge you to dismiss this false god. Invite the true God in. Let your heartfelt view of God come into line with what the Bible says about Him.

➤ **Take a few minutes to remind yourself about the true nature of God. Say each of these attributes aloud three times.**

God's true nature

- God is loving.
- God is joyful.
- God is peaceful.
- God is patient.

- God is kind.
- God is good.
- God is gentle.
- God is in control.

➤ **Stop and pray, asking God to help you to see Him as He really is.**

Face Your Compulsions

✎ **The compulsive behaviors I am working on are:** _____

_____

Below describe how you managed these compulsive behaviors yesterday.

_____

_____

Work on Turning Points

✎ **Below describe the progress you are making toward working Turning Point 2: *I surrender control of my life to God*. Write your thoughts below.**

_____

_____

Work on Relating to Authority Figures

✎ **For the next 24 hours be sensitive to how you relate to authority figures. By this time tomorrow attempt to accomplish at least two of the items below.**

❑ Give a sincere compliment to an authority figure.
❑ Look an authority figure in the eye when you speak to him/her.
❑ Say no to an impulse to talk behind an authority figure's back.
❑ Exercise the courage to politely disagree with an authority figure when appropriate. (Don't overdo it!)
❑ Greet an authority figure in a friendly manner.
❑ Instead of presuming that you know an authority figure's view on something, ask the person what his or her opinion is.

➤ Pray for each member of your Heart to Heart group by name today.

➤ Say aloud this unit's memory passage. Identify the phrases in the memory passage that bring you the most assurance and comfort. Repeat those phrases several times.

➤ If the following prayer expresses how you feel, pray your own version of it now. "God, show me the areas of my life which need to be surrendered to you. Show me any compulsive behaviors which rule over me. Give me the strength I need to surrender these to you."

Today's Objective:
You will examine the issue of trust as it relates to surrender.

Surrender Requires Trust

Surrender Can Be Frightening

Here are some things you might fear about surrender.

Fear #1: The Last Time I Trusted . . .
Surrender frightens some people because it requires trust. Perhaps you fear surrender because you tried trusting, and you got hurt. You put your faith in a parent, a friend, a teacher, or a spouse, and this person let you down HARD! You tried trusting again, and you got hurt again. You experienced the same results over and over again. You learned that trusting can be very dangerous. You can get hurt! When somebody starts talking about letting go and trusting God, you feel fear. You have learned to be afraid of surrender and trust.

Fear #2: The People Who Do Not Surrender Will Pass Me By
Do you fear that if you surrender to God, the people who do not surrender will pass you by and have a better time in life? Do you worry that they will have more joy while you're stuck serving God?

What God did for us

This fear grows from a misunderstanding of the nature of God. Think about who God is. Think about how He made the world. He made birds and flowers and blue skies and beautiful mountains and all the good things. God made those things for you.

Danger originates from our human self-centeredness. We want the things God did not intend for us to have. We take the good things God has given us and use them improperly or to excess. The fact that something is unavailable makes it more desirable to us.

The people who have not surrendered to God may appear to drink deeper from the springs of life, but theirs is a frantic quest for more because they have not learned to be satisfied with what they taste. An abundance of experiences means nothing without the serenity to appreciate the present.

Fear #3: God May Hurt Me
A church member once told me, "My friend prayed that my son who was away at college would come home for a visit. She received word he was coming home. On the way home, he was killed in an accident." This church member said to me, "That just goes to show you, you better be careful what you pray for."

What a twisted view of God! Such a view imagines God saying, "If you say the wrong thing in your prayer, I am going to get you." God is not like that. A God like that wouldn't send His Son to die on the cross for you.

You may fear surrender because a significant person in your life who let you down shaped your heartfelt view of God more than the biblical picture of God has. Or, you may have a very accurate intellectual knowledge of God with a very inaccurate heartfelt view of God. The thought of surrender to God frightens you because in your heart you see Him as mean or as a trickster who is out to get you.

God puts His arms around your neck and hugs you!

A Sunday School teacher talked about the biblical passage in which Jesus said, "My yoke is easy" (Matthew 11:30). She told the girls in her class that a yoke is something you put on the neck of an animal. Then she asked them, "What is the meaning of God's yoke?" One wise child answered, "God puts His arms around your neck." When God puts His arms around your neck He does not reach out and strangle you. He hugs you. He holds you, and He loves you.

 Go back to the paragraphs you just read about fear. Circle the fear that you feel most often stands in your way of trusting God.

Surrender Means Trusting God

You must make the decision to trust God. The decision to trust God and surrender yourself to Him may feel like a big step in the dark. Trusting God requires faith. You decide to express and to exercise faith.

Faith is your decision

Write one thing you plan to do in the next 24 hours that will be an outward expression of your willingness to develop your trust in God.

_____

_____

_____

You may have written that you will begin keeping a prayer journal to write your prayers and keep a record of God's responses. Or you may demonstrate your willingness to trust Him by surrendering one area of your brokenness. For example, if your brokenness involves your relationship with your mother, you may tell God that you surrender this relationship to Him. You would tell Him you trust Him to give you strength to resist running to her aid the next time she calls you to manipulate you with guilt.

Face Your Compulsions

The compulsive behaviors I am working on are: _____

_____

_____

_____

Below describe how you managed these compulsive behaviors yesterday.

_____

_____

Work on Turning Points

✎ **Describe the progress you are making toward working Turning Point 2:** *I surrender control of my life to God.* **Write your thoughts below.**

_____

_____

Follow Up on Relating to Authority Figures

✎ **How well did you do on yesterday's assignment to be sensitive to how you relate to authority figures? Which of the following items did you complete?**
❑ Give a sincere compliment to an authority figure.
❑ Look an authority figure in the eye when you speak to him/her.
❑ Say no to an impulse to talk behind an authority figure's back.
❑ Exercise the courage to disagree politely with an authority figure when appropriate. (Don't overdo it!)
❑ Greet an authority figure in a friendly manner.
❑ Instead of presuming that you know an authority figure's view on something, ask them what their opinion is.

✎ **In the margin write from memory this unit's memory passage.**

DAY 5

Today's Objective:
This book will challenge you to a conscious act of surrender to God.

I Must Give My Brokenness to God

Facing Surrender

Many of us who have grown up in church or who have spent significant time as church members may say, "I've trusted Jesus as my Savior. Why do I need to surrender any more?"

I answer that many of us know how to talk "church-y" language. We know what to do and what not to do. We know what to say when someone asks us a question in Sunday School, but we may not have a day-by-day relationship with the living God.

Even those of us who are life-long Christians can be constantly surrendering. I accepted Christ when I was a child. To the best of my ability and understanding I gave myself to Jesus Christ. I believe it was a genuine decision. I have not experienced serious doubts about that decision. Later, when I was a teenager, I discovered that being a Christian meant adopting

Therefore, I urge you, brothers, in view of God's mercy, to offer your bodies as living sacrifices, holy and pleasing to God—this is your spiritual act of worship. Do not conform any longer to the pattern of this world, but be transformed by the renewal of your mind. Then you will be able to test and approve what God's will is—His good, pleasing and perfect will.

Romans 12:1-2

some values that I did not even know existed when I was a child. The issue of surrendering new areas of my life to Jesus faced me. As I have grown older, I have learned more about what it means to live the Christian life. Year by year, month by month, I reach new levels of realizing, "I've not given some area of my life to God, and I need to give it to Him." Read in the margin what Paul wrote about surrender.

Surrender hurts because I want to be in control. Surrender frightens me because it involves faith and trust. However, we must surrender if we want to live in the will of God. We begin the Christian life by surrender. We live the Christian life through surrender. Surrender is what you do after you have turned to God and said, "God, help me to face my brokenness. Show me myself as I really am." Surrender is what you do with your brokenness.

✎ **Check the following that are true statements.**

❑ We do not need to surrender any more after we become Christians.
❑ Surrender means that I must give control of my life to Christ.
❑ I can live within God's will without surrender.
❑ Surrender allows God to show us ourselves as we really are.

A mirror of our lives

The second and fourth statements are true; the others are false. When we surrender, God takes control of our lives and holds a mirror up to show us how He sees us. From that point on, healing can begin.

Giving Broken Things to God

Do not throw your life away because it is broken. Do not throw a relationship away because it is damaged. Choose surrender!

Don't throw a relationship away because it is damaged. Choose surrender!

After the anniversary weekend incident, Becky, whose story appeared on page 47, was at the point of withdrawing totally from her mother. The relationship was so damaged that she thought she had no choice but to avoid her mother. In her support group, however, she learned about the concept of surrender. "I wonder what things would be like if I surrendered this relationship to God instead of trying to fix things myself," Becky pondered with her group.

In a prayer, Becky offered this broken relationship to God. She said, "I can't fix this. I want more than anything to have a perfect relationship with my mother, but that may not be possible. Lord, I give this relationship to you." Soon God began moving in Becky's heart. When her mother called again to make her demands, Becky tried a new approach. She said, "Mother, I can't visit you this weekend. I was there last weekend, and I've promised Joe that we'll take the children to the beach. I'll call to check on you when I get back."

Becky feared that her mother couldn't exist without her care, but when Becky and her family returned from the beach, she found that her mother had recruited a friend to help her. Becky's mother, of course, yelled at her and called her irresponsible, but this time Becky did not react. In another week Becky called her mother to set up a schedule for visiting her. She also helped her mother locate neighbors and fellow church members that could assist with her mother's needs. Each time her mother yelled at her, Becky continued matter-of-factly with her schedule planning. Becky learned to set boundaries with her mother and not bite when her mother baited her. Becky began to realize that she never would have the dream relationship with her mother that she desired, but she also felt better that she no longer allowed the brokenness of the relationship to defeat her.

Letting God be God

Surrender means giving the broken things of your life to God. When you surrender, you give God permission to be God in your life.

✎ **Look over the story of Becky again. Describe here how Becky gave God permission to be God in her life in the relationship with her mother.**

_____

_____

You may have written something like this: When Becky gave up her need to be needed and her ideal of a perfect mother-daughter relationship, God took this defeat and helped Becky become strong.

Carrying Us on His Shoulders

An early painting of Jesus portrayed Him as a shepherd carrying a lamb on His shoulders. Is it difficult for you to think of yourself as the lamb and Jesus as the shepherd? Some of us find this concept quite difficult. In the margin box describe how you feel when you think about Jesus carrying you. You may have written that thoughts came to your mind like, "I'm too important to be helped like this," "I'd feel humiliated," or "I can take care of myself."

However, life has a way of getting us to a point where we figure out that we can't carry the load alone. We call that process *brokenness*. It involves saying, "I cannot fix my life by myself. I am broken. If I am honest, I will admit that I cannot take care of myself." Sheep are not self-sufficient. They may be wayward, unruly, stubborn, or even stupid, but they are not independent or self-sufficient. Isn't it interesting that Jesus chose to portray Himself as the shepherd and us as the sheep? The sheep is not the animal you and I would choose as a symbol of who we are. We would like to be smart as a fox, strong as an ox, wise as an owl, but who wants to be a sheep needing a shepherd?[8]

Surrender threatens us because we want to be in control. Surrender frightens us because we must trust God to surrender. But, surrender is essential if we want to live in God's will. Don't play games with surrender. Don't fight with God. Don't destroy yourself. Surrender and let Him have your life. Surrender is a vital issue for every Christian. Give Him whatever you are holding back. You are the sheep. Let Him be the shepherd.

✎ **Which of the items in the list below hold you back from surrendering to God?**

❑ Selfishness
❑ Love of sin
❑ Fear of what people think
❑ Hiding behind work in the church
❑ Feeling that surrender is not something that an "intellectual" does
❑ Other: _____

How I feel about Jesus carrying me—

_____

_____

_____

_____

You are the sheep. Let Him be the shepherd.

Face Your Compulsions

✎ The compulsive behaviors I am working on are: _____

_____

Below describe how you managed these compulsive behaviors yesterday.

_____

_____

Now, read again the second turning point that you've been working on during this unit. Be prepared to share with your Heart-to-Heart group where you are in regard to Turning Point 2.

> **Turning Point 2**
> I surrender control of my life to God.

A Reminder: Find a Listener/Sponsor

Continue to work on finding someone to listen as you share the contents of your moral inventory. During the seventh meeting you will report on your sharing experience. As a reminder to you, your sponsor must be a person who has some understanding of the process of recovery. This person could be someone who has participated in a 12-Step group and who understands the meaning of the Fifth Step. Your listener should be someone who is the same gender as yourself. He or she must be a person who is trustworthy and will not break confidence. This must be a person who is willing to listen without being judgmental and someone who can give encouragement and support.

➤ **Pray for each member of your group by name today.**

➤ **If the following prayer expresses how you feel, pray your own version of it now.**
"God, today I surrender myself to you. I give special emphasis to the fact that I am surrendering my compulsion to _____ to you. I am a broken person, and I am asking you to help me to overcome this compulsion. I am willing to be accountable to the members of my group about how I deal with my compulsion for the next 10 weeks. AMEN."

Notes
[1]Philip Parham, *Letting God: Christian Meditations for Recovering Persons* (San Francisco: Harper and Row, Publishers, 1987), July 3rd reading.
[2]Parham, August 3rd reading.
[3]Ibid., October 3rd reading.
[4]Ibid., September 17th reading.
[5]Leslie Weatherhead, *Discipleship* (New York: Abingdon Press, 1934), 20.
[6]Parham, November 3rd reading.
[7]King Duncan, ed., *Lively Illustrations for Effective Preaching* (Knoxville: Seven Worlds Publishing, date), 137.
[8]Ibid., March 19th reading.

Cleansing

In this Unit you'll work on—
Turning Point 2
I surrender control of my life to God.

The Recovery Cycle: An attitude of HONESTY accompanied by the action of CONFESSION leads to CLEANSING.

JEFF AND THE CHURCH COMMITTEE

Jeff was chairman of the missions committee at his church. Although he really wanted to serve the Lord, he began bungling things badly. He refused to make any specific plans for projects. Whenever he did make plans and announced them to the group, he later changed everything totally.

Phillip, Jeff's best friend in the church, was on Jeff's committee. Phillip rearranged his weekend so he could help Jeff with a food collection drive, but just as Phillip was about to leave his house for the project, Jeff called him and canceled the drive. Jeff thought the committee members were being too rigid when they complained about his erratic behavior. "Why can't they just roll with the punches?" Jeff asked himself. Jeff's erratic behavior actually stemmed from his childhood with a father who had an addiction. Read on page 68 about what Jeff needed in his life.

Why you will find this unit useful

Shame and guilt are powerful forces. The more you run from them, the more powerful they become. When you stop to face the shame and guilt of your past, you begin to remove their power. This week you will begin work on a moral inventory. When a store takes an inventory, the employees count everything in the store. Your moral inventory is an examination of the strengths and weaknesses, the victories and failures of your life. For the next several days you will work on the moral inventory. You do not need to do this perfectly. Work on your assignments each day. Don't put this off! At the end of this period, we will ask you to share your moral inventory with another person.

Cleansing of Childhood Shame	Cleansing in Your Relation- ships	Cleansing of Resent- ments	Cleansing and the Power to Say No	Cleansing in the Context of Grace
DAY 1	DAY 2	DAY 3	DAY 4	DAY 5

This week's memory verses

Have mercy on me, O God, according to your unfailing love; according to your great compassion blot out my transgressions. Wash away all my iniquity and cleanse me from my sin. For I know my transgressions, and my sin is always before me. Surely you desire truth in the inner parts; you teach me wisdom in the inmost place.

–Psalm 51:1-3,6

Cleansing of Childhood Shame

Today's Objective:
You will list ways in which childhood shame affected the development of your identity.

Connecting with the Recovery Cycle

You are seeking spiritual and emotional wholeness. You have learned about a three-stage process of healing: brokenness, surrender, and recovery. You have discovered that an attitude of brokenness accompanied by the action of surrender leads to recovery.

During this study we will examine three cycles of recovery: the inward cycle, the upward cycle, and the outward cycle. This week we begin looking at the inward cycle. An attitude of HONESTY (brokenness) followed by the action of CONFESSION (surrender) leads to CLEANSING (recovery).

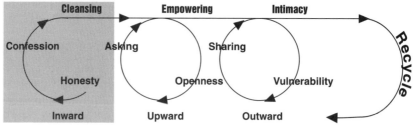

Emotional and spiritual growth often involves pain. Such growth involves the difficulty of making painful discoveries about myself. I may see my own self-centeredness. I may see my own weaknesses. When we grow spiritually and emotionally, we often endure the pain of confronting our failures as well as the struggle of letting go and giving God control. We must remember that beyond the pain we experience cleansing.

Identifying the Cycle of Pain

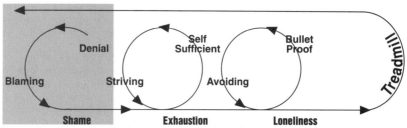

Children in severely dysfunctional families learn to feel the shame of others. Maybe you felt shame for a parent's alcoholism. You were not the alcoholic, but you felt shame. Perhaps you felt shame for a parent who lived an immoral life. You lived a moral life, but you felt shame for your parent's immoral behavior. Perhaps one of your parents abandoned you. You began to believe that somehow it was your fault. You decided that if you could have done things better, your parent would not have left. In the margin box describe a source of shame from your childhood.

This shame builds a nest somewhere deep inside you and begins to deliver the message, "You are inadequate. You are not like other people. You are different. You are strange and other people know it. You should be ASHAMED!" This shame is so powerful that you eventually can't distinguish it from yourself. It becomes a part of you, part of your identity, part of how you see yourself.

> **Describe a source of shame from your childhood.**
>
> _____
>
> _____
>
> _____
>
> _____
>
> _____

You win a major victory when you identify this shame and call it by name. Learning to say inwardly to someone else, "I give you back your shame," begins the release from the vice-like grip of shame.

A major victory

Hopefully, in *Making Peace with Your Past* you learned to release the shame that is not your own. By the time you reach Turning Point 4, *I will share my moral inventory with another trusted person*, we would like you to claim an official, historic victory over your shame about your childhood.

> A painful childhood causes wounds. Wounds can heal. Scars need not give pain.

As part of your moral inventory, you will list some key facts about your childhood in a dysfunctional family and how it has affected your adult life. Later in your life you may have responded to your family of origin in some ways that were morally wrong. You must claim responsibility for such behavior, but today's work does not focus on that.

You had no vote on determining the dynamics that existed in your childhood family of origin.

We are looking at the shame that occurs simply as a result of being a member of a dysfunctional family. You had no vote on determining the dynamics that existed in your childhood family of origin. You were just there, and you had nothing to say about it.

Cleansing for this aspect of your life does not require you to confess wrongdoing. It requires honestly admitting what life was like and how it felt to you. It requires the courage to give the shame of others back to them.

✎ **After reading the section on shame, check the statements below that are true.**
   ❑ 1. We never can recover from the feelings of shame in our childhood.
   ❑ 2. Honestly admitting what life was like for us in a shame-bound family is the first step toward cleansing from shame.
   ❑ 3. We must confess wrongdoing to gain release from shame.
   ❑ 4. The shame of our childhoods can affect many decisions we make in our adult lives.

Everything we do as adults—how we relate to our children, the decisions we make while on the job, the way we respond when someone asks us to serve as a Scout leader or fund-raising volunteer, even the way we react when a friend asks us out to dinner—can spring from our reactions to childhood shame. The good news is that we can recover from these feelings, and we start that by honestly admitting what things were like for us. The correct answers to the above exercise are statements 2 and 4.

Face Your Compulsions

✎ **The compulsive behaviors I am working on are:** _____

_____

Below describe how you managed these compulsive behaviors yesterday.

_____

_____

Work on Turning Points

Go to the Moral Inventory section of this book beginning on pages 205. Today, begin working on the section of the inventory titled, "How My Childhood Shaped Me." Your moral inventory is a picture of who you are and how you became who you are. Under the heading "Shame I Felt for the Behavior of Others," list five things about the behavior of significant persons in your life that made you feel shame. Be honest with yourself. Describe how these things have affected your thoughts and your behavior in the past and in the present.

Work on Finding a Listener/Sponsor

By now you likely have found someone to listen as you share the contents of your moral inventory. If you have not found this person yet, you may want to look back at page 18 to review the characteristics of this person. During the seventh meeting you will report on your sharing experience.

➤ **Read and begin to memorize this unit's memory verses, Psalm 51:1-3,6.. Underline words or phrases that you feel offer you the most hope and comfort.**

Cleansing in Your Relationships

DAY 2

Today's Objective:
You will learn that cleansing offers a release from the painful prison of sin.

Release from Your Shame

As a child you learned to feel shame for the actions of other family members. Dealing with that shame means letting go and acknowledging that it was not and is not your shame.

At some point you made moral and spiritual decisions about how to react to your family of origin. You made choices that hurt other people as well as yourself. You may have followed a parent's example by copying his or her compulsive/addictive behavior. You may have chosen new compulsive behaviors to deal with your inner pain.

Jeff's story

Jeff was in charge of the missions committee at his church. He recruited some qualified, dedicated people to serve as committee members. But the committee could not progress because Jeff refused to plan activities for the year. When members urged Jeff to commit to some definite dates and goals, he gave them a rough outline, only to change his mind about his plans by the next meeting. His best friend Phillip, a committee member, arranged his weekend schedule around a committee food drive, but Jeff cancelled the project at the last minute. Several of the committee members resigned in frustration. Phillip was one of those who resigned. All of them were hurt and puzzled about Jeff's conduct in chairing the group. Jeff scoffed, "These people are just too rigid. They need to learn to be flexible, like me." But the committee members believed Jeff had asked them to be flexible too many times. They felt Jeff's behavior was immature and insensitive.

Based on his childhood shame, Jeff made some decisions about how he conducted the committee. As the son of a drug-addicted father, Jeff lived from crisis to crisis, without much room for careful planning for the future. The goal was to get through today and to make it through this crisis, then worry about the future. Even when he was an adult and outside his family of origin, Jeff had a difficult time planning for the future. This explained why he resisted making plans and resisted the committee members' efforts to pin him down on precise dates for projects.

In adulthood, we have choices about how our childhood shame causes us to act today.

Jeff had no choice about being reared in a dysfunctional family, but he did have a choice about how he acted now as a result of this shame. Jeff's actions hurt his fellow committee members—and they also hurt his service to the Lord. The committee did not accomplish much in the missions areas that year because Jeff would not come to terms with how his past was affecting his present.

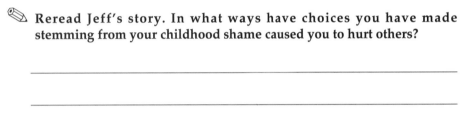 **Reread Jeff's story. In what ways have choices you have made stemming from your childhood shame caused you to hurt others?**

_____

_____

_____

Responsible for our choices

You are responsible for your choices. The Bible uses the term "sin" to describe behavior that violates God's plan for living. Cleansing, as you will experience it, deals not only with cleansing from the shame of others, it also deals with cleansing from the shame of your own sinful behavior.

Release from the Prison of Sin

Cleansing marks the beginning of release from the prison of sin. Imagine that you enter a large room. The room is beautifully decorated and contains every possible luxury. You begin to walk around in the room and enjoy its decor. You sit in a comfortable chair. You turn on some relaxing music. The room seems like a wonderful place. You decide to stay in the room. Day after day you spend hours in the room. You like the way you feel when you are in it.

After you have been in the room for a while, something starts to bother you. You don't know exactly what it is, but you know something is wrong with this room. You go on enjoying all the room has to offer you, but day after day you cannot escape the sensation that something is wrong with the room.

One day you finally realize what is happening. This large, beautiful room gradually is getting smaller. Being in the room is so pleasant that you go on with your daily activities. Week after week you stay there, but you have more and more difficulty ignoring the fact that the room is getting smaller and smaller. Even though it is getting smaller, you don't want to leave. You are not sure you know how to leave. You are not even sure you could leave if you decided to leave.

One day you realize that not only is the room getting smaller but some of the beautiful things in the room are starting to disappear. Finally, you wake up and find that the room has become a small, gray cell. The room is cold and damp. You hardly can move without touching walls or the ceiling. You realize that you are in a prison. It was a prison even before it looked like a prison.

Sin is the attempt to exercise God-like control over everything around you.

The room illustrates what sin is like. Sin involves the refusal to let God be God. Sin is the attempt to exercise God-like control over everything around you—your life, your feelings, the people around you, everything you possibly can control.

Sin is an attitude of self-centeredness that says, "I will play the role of God in my life. I will be in charge. I will be in control." Sin denies the promise that God loves you and wants the best for you. It is a challenge to God. It says, "No, God, you don't want the best for me! I will take control of my life because I know better what I need."

Compulsive/addictive behavior is like the room. The feelings you want to avoid go away while you engage in your compulsive behavior. Time seems to stop. Your compulsive behavior feels good. You like it.

Somewhere along the way you begin to realize that while the behavior feels good, it also hurts. You may begin to see that your compulsion has a life of its own. It is progressive.

If you leave the compulsion alone, it eventually will destroy you, and it does not care. It will use you up and throw you away.

Buried deep inside are feelings you do not want to face. Maybe it is pain. Maybe it is shame. Maybe it is guilt. Maybe it is fear. Your compulsive behavior helps you keep these feelings at arm's length.

The attitude at the very bottom of it all says, "I cannot trust God to take my life and control it. I cannot trust God to be in charge, so I am going to be in charge." That is the essence of sin. Sin is a prison. Sin is a form of spiritual and emotional death.

You walk through the motions of life, but you seldom make contact with another human being's spirit.

Some people are dead before they die. Living only for self and living under the compulsion to control brings a form of spiritual death. You have a deadness of spirit. You walk through the motions of life, but you seldom make contact with another human being's spirit. You keep your distance from the God who loves you and wants to fill your life with His love.

 In the section you just read about sin as a prison, go back and underline statements that you feel describe you and your struggle with sin.

You may have underlined such statements as, "The feelings you want to avoid go away while you engage in your compulsive behavior," "Buried deep inside you is a feeling you do not want to face," or "You keep your distance from the God who loves you and wants to fill your life with His love." Regardless of what you underlined, your honesty took courage.

Release from the Path of Sin

Cleansing also means that you begin to experience healing from the pain of sin. Sin feels good at first, but then it becomes like the shrinking room. Eventually, the walls start to move in on you. Then sin starts to feel bad. When it starts to feel bad, you already may be hooked. You cannot stop. At least you don't think you can. The pain of sin builds and builds. Your response to the pain may be well hidden, or it may be etched in the lines of your face.

You don't have to live the rest of your tomorrows the way you have lived life until today.

Cleansing means hope. If you can be cleansed of the pain and the mistakes of your past, you can have hope that tomorrow does not have to be like yesterday. You don't have to live the rest of your tomorrows the way you have lived life until today. Many factors push toward making tomorrow like yesterday. Your childhood, your habits, and your personality all try to push your tomorrows into the mold of yesterday. Remember Jeff's story from the previous page? Shame from his childhood pressed him into some harmful habits that affected his relationships as an adult. Jeff truly wanted to serve the Lord and to be a good friend, but he needed consciously and deliberately to break this harmful cycle so that he could be whole.

Cleansing from God is a reminder that you have hope. Without cleansing, the only alternative is despair. Jesus Christ died on the cross so that you could be forgiven. He died so that you could receive healing from the pain that sin causes. He felt that pain and paid the price for all our sin. He stretches His arms out to you today and says, "Come to me, all you who are weary and burdened, and I will give you rest" (Matthew 11:28).

My yoke is easy and my burden is light.
Matthew 11:30

Jesus is not a stern taskmaster with a whip in His hands. In the Scripture appearing at left, He spoke against the religious leaders of His day who turned the power of the living God into a cold, ritualistic religion. He brought a message of hope, healing, and cleansing.

✎ **Describe below how you feel when you realize that Jesus wants to heal you from the pain sin has caused.**

_____

_____

_____

An invitation to you

You can trust Christ's death and resurrection to pay for your sin. In Acts 16:31, Luke wrote, "Believe in the Lord Jesus, and you shall be saved." If you have not done so already, you can receive Jesus Christ right now by invitation. If you desire to trust Christ and accept His payment for your sins, tell that to God in prayer right now. You may use this sample prayer to express your faith.

Lord Jesus, I need You. I want You to be my Savior and my Lord. I accept Your death on the cross as payment for my sins, and I now entrust my life to Your care. Thank You for forgiving me and for giving me a new life. Please help me grow in my understanding of Your love and power so that my life will bring glory and honor to You. Amen.

_____ (signature) _____ (date)

Trusting in Christ does not guarantee that you will be delivered instantly from problems in life. It does not mean that instantly you will be free from patterns your childhood shame has caused. It means that you are forgiven, that you are restored to a relationship with Him that will last throughout eternity, and that you will receive His unconditional love and acceptance, as well as His strength, power, and wisdom, as you continue to grow in recovery.

Face Your Compulsions

✎ **The compulsive behaviors I am working on are:** _____

_____

Below describe how you managed these compulsive behaviors yesterday.

_____

_____

Work on Turning Points

Work on the section of your moral inventory titled "My Relationship with God" (see page 206). Write some of the ways you have disobeyed God repeatedly through your life. I don't mean for this to be a list of specific sins you have committed. Rather, it is a description of patterns in your life. For example, you might write, "Consistently I have placed climbing the career ladder in a more important place than my family." You might write, "I have made a habit of lying when the truth made me uncomfortable." You might write, "I have hurt friends by snubbing them when they started to get close to me," or "When someone has tried to confront me in love, I have refused to talk with that person because of my compulsion to control."

A reminder: Don't be compulsive in working on your moral inventory. Don't get hung up on attempting to write everything that applies to each question. Write what comes to mind. If nothing comes to mind, go to the next question. A compulsion to do this perfectly may be a way of refusing to face the task.

Areas of faithfulness

Then list some positive things about your relationship with God. Hopefully, as you look back over your life, you not only will see failures but also areas of moral and spiritual strength. In this section, list some areas of your spiritual life in which you have been faithful to God. What are some spiritual convictions you have kept? For example, you might write, "I never have stopped believing in God." Or, "I have refused to take God's name in vain." You might write, "I always have tried to pray in both the good times and the bad times," or "I have tried to tell others about Jesus."

✎ **Below write this unit's Scripture memory verses. Try to do it without looking back at the unit page.**

_____

_____

DAY 3

Today's Objective:
You will list your resentments toward others.

Great partners—denial and blame

More of Jeff's story

If therefore you are presenting your offering at the altar, and there remember that your brother has something against you, leave your offering there before the altar, and go your way; first be reconciled to your brother, and then come and present your offering.

Matthew 5:23-24,NASB

Cleansing of Resentments

Moving Beyond Blame and Resentment

Rick, a friend who is a pastor, shared an incident that graphically illustrated the pain of his early years. As a senior in high school, he was preparing to go to bed one evening when he heard a loud splash in the family's swimming pool. He ran outside and found his mother at the bottom of the pool. Trying to commit suicide, she had tied some of Rick's barbells around her neck and jumped into the pool. Rick pulled her out of the pool and called for help. His action saved her life.

The next day Rick's father said to him, "If you had put your barbells away like you were supposed to, this would not have happened."

Dysfunctional families are big on BLAME. When something goes wrong, families must assign BLAME as soon as possible. Apparently Rick's dad could not face the fact that his wife needed help. Denial and blame are great partners. The dysfunctional family does not consider the fact that some things just happen or that many things can combine to cause mishaps.

Members of dysfunctional families learn to prepare themselves for accusations. They always have a good defense ready. Family members may decide that blaming someone else first is the best defense. Because of the confusion that blaming and defending create, over time the family loses the ability to understand clearly why a particular event occurred. The saddest part of all this is that the family also loses the ability to learn how to avoid the same unpleasant events in the future.

This pattern of blaming also makes healthy communication unlikely. People reared in dysfunctional families are so ready with their defenses that they immediately shut out people who try to confront them in love. When Jeff, the church committee leader described on page 68, through his bungling offended his friend Phillip, Phillip tried to approach him in love about the matter. Phillip told Jeff that he felt hurt when Jeff constantly altered plans without explanation.

Instead of listening thoughtfully to Phillip's concerns and trying to work things out as the Bible encourages Christians to do (see verse appearing at left), Jeff had his defense ready. He immediately fired back to Phillip, "It's all your fault. If you just wouldn't be so sensitive and so rigid, things would be just fine." He greatly resented Phillip for approaching him in this manner.

Resentment is one of the by-products of a blame-oriented family. Like a low-grade infection, resentment drains something from you. Resentment always is at work behind the scenes. It saps spiritual and emotional strength.

> Recovery means moving beyond blame and coming to grips with your resentments.

✎ Below describe a time in which you, like Jeff, have been quick to place blame instead of responding to a situation objectively.

_____

_____

Face Your Compulsions

✎ The compulsive behaviors I am working on are: _____

_____

Below describe how you managed these compulsive behaviors yesterday.

_____

_____

Work on Turning Points

Continue working on your moral inventory. Move to the section entitled "My Relationships With People." Focus on the topic, "Identifying Your Resentments." Make a list of your resentments. Name the people toward whom you have felt resentment.

➤ Pray for each member of your Heart-to-Heart group by name today. Ask God to give you strength as you continue to look within.

➤ Say aloud three times this unit's Scripture memory verses.

DAY 4

Today's Objective:
You will learn that cleansing offers a release from the guilt of self-destructive habits.

Cleansing and the Power to Say No

Forgetting What Is Behind

Can you receive the promise that this passage makes?

No temptation has seized you except what is common to man. And God is faithful; he will not let you be tempted beyond what you can bear. But when you are tempted, he will also provide a way out so that you can stand up under it.

–1 Corinthians 10:13

This promise states that you will not face a temptation that somebody else has not faced. You will not face a unique temptation.

When you are tempted, a part of you says, "No one in the world ever has faced a temptation like this. Nobody else has ever felt such a powerful pull to commit this wrong like I have." This is not true. Someone *has* faced a temptation like yours.

God is faithful. He does not push you aside and say, "This is nothing new." With the temptation He will see that a way out exists. If you choose, you always can walk through that door of escape.

Cleansing helps you to claim the promise of 1 Corinthians 10:13, which appears at left. You can best deal with the present after you have let God deal with your past. The cleansing work of Christ brings healing from the pain and prison of sin. His cleansing work also gives you the strength to say no to wrong and to live a changed life.

In one sense the victory occurs when you invite Christ into your life, as you may have done some time ago or just did during day 2 of this lesson. In another sense, the victory is gained day by day. It is a day-by-day walk—one day at a time, one step at a time.

Read the passage appearing at left that tells what Paul wrote the Philippian church on this matter. Are you forgetting what is behind? Have you let go of the things God already has forgiven, or do they still weight you down?

When you are honest with God about who you are, about your weaknesses, and your powerlessness, you can lay your life before Him in an act of confession. You can say, "God, this is who I really am. It is all I can give you."

Then God begins to do His work of cleansing that brings your release from the prison of sin. You begin to lose the feeling that the walls are closing in. Life begins to open up. You begin to see a broad horizon and a beautiful world!

His work of cleansing means that you begin to experience healing from the pain of sin. It also means that you have new power to say no to sin.

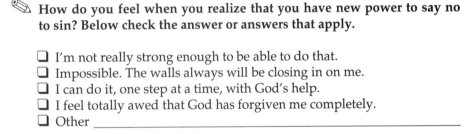 **How do you feel when you realize that you have new power to say no to sin? Below check the answer or answers that apply.**

- ❑ I'm not really strong enough to be able to do that.
- ❑ Impossible. The walls always will be closing in on me.
- ❑ I can do it, one step at a time, with God's help.
- ❑ I feel totally awed that God has forgiven me completely.
- ❑ Other _____

No doubt, we still will have moments when we feel weak and imprisoned, but one step at a time God can deliver us from that closed-in feeling and can help us claim that power to reject the practice of sin. We hope you were able to say that the last two sentences apply to your life.

Fortunately, the story of Jeff has a happy ending. When his church formed a support group for people who had painful pasts, Jeff joined. The work that he did in this group helped him begin to understand some of his adult patterns that stemmed from the shame of his childhood. He began to experience healing in many areas of his life.

One day at work one of Jeff's employees approached him. The employee told Jeff he was disappointed that Jeff had changed his work schedule without letting him know in advance. He told Jeff he would miss his daughter's birthday party because Jeff rescheduled him. At first Jeff felt irritated. He believed that the employee was being far too sensitive. He started to yell at the

---

No temptation has seized you except what is common to man. And God is faithful; he will not let you be tempted beyond what you can bear. But when you are tempted, he will also provide a way out so that you can stand up under it.

1 Corinthians 10:13

Not that I have already obtained all this, or have already been made perfect, but I press on to take hold of that for which Christ Jesus took hold of me. Brothers, I do not consider myself yet to have taken hold of it. But one thing I do: Forgetting what is behind and straining toward what is ahead, I press on toward the goal to win the prize for which God has called me heavenward in Christ Jesus.

Philippians 3:12-14

Healing in Jeff's life

worker. Then he caught himself. "It's my old shame and blame pattern again," he thought. He prayed, "God, help me say no to sin. Help me to keep from responding in a way that would hurt this person." With God's help, Jeff responded in a healthy way. He apologized to the employee, and the two of them sat down to arrange a new work schedule.

Face Your Compulsions

 The compulsive behaviors I am working on are: _____

_____

_____

Below describe how you managed these compulsive behaviors yesterday.

_____

_____

Work on Turning Points

Continue working on your moral inventory. Go to the "Affirmations" section of the Moral Inventory. List some positive habits in your life. Think of things you do consistently which you want to continue doing.

 In the margin write what the Scripture memory verses mean to you.

Today's Objective:
You will think about the presence of God's grace in your life as you continue to work on your moral inventory.

Cleansing in the Context of Grace

Examining Myself in the Context of Grace

In his book *The Screwtape Letters*, C.S. Lewis wrote about a senior servant of Satan who trains some underlings to work with individual humans to lead them away from God. In discussing one of the humans, the senior servant of the devil says, "You must bring him to a condition in which he can practise [sic] self-examination for an hour without discovering any of those facts about himself which are perfectly clear to anyone who has ever lived with him or worked in the same office."[1]

Do you understand the strategy of this evil advisor? "Don't try to scare him away from self-examination. If he thinks he is avoiding self-examination, he will feel like he needs to grow. Let him learn how to examine himself, but teach him how to look at himself without ever seeing those things that really need to change, the things that are obvious to everybody else but him." You may need help in seeing yourself as you are. Read what the following Scriptures say about how God sees us as we are:

O LORD, you have searched me and you know me. You know when I sit and when I rise; you perceive my thoughts from afar. You discern my going out and my lying down; You are familiar with all my ways. Before a word is on my tongue you know it completely, O LORD. Search me, O God, and know my heart; test me and know my anxious thoughts. See if there is any offensive way in me, and lead me in the way everlasting.

–Psalm 139:1-4,23-24

When I kept silent, my bones wasted away through my groaning all day long. For day and night your hand was heavy upon me; my strength was sapped as in the heat of summer. Then I acknowledged my sin to you and did not cover up my iniquity. I said, "I will confess my transgressions to the Lord"—and you forgave the guilt of my sin.

–Psalm 32:3-5

✎ **Describe below what you think God sees when He looks at you. I have filled in the first line for you as an example.**

He sees someone too afraid to depend on Him totally.

_____

_____

_____

_____

Around the time of World War I a girl who had a wonderful voice did not have money for vocal training. Her music so touched some friends in her church in Philadelphia that they started a collection. They called it "The Fund for Marian Anderson's Future." They raised $126 and used it to buy singing lessons for her.

Marian took the lessons. When she was 18, her high-school teachers set up an audition with a world-famous singing instructor. Again people in the church raised money for more lessons. Her future looked so bright.

A mother's wise words

Things moved too quickly. A group who believed in her sponsored her in concert at New York City's famous Town Hall. She wasn't quite ready for it, and the critics destroyed her. For more than a year she wallowed in pity. She would not go to see her teachers. She had given up. Then one day her mother talked to her. She said, "Marian, grace must come before greatness. Why don't you think about this failure and pray about it a lot?"

Years later Marian Anderson, having helped many young singers survive the kind of defeat she had overcome, made this statement: "Whatever is in my voice, faith has put it there. Faith and my mother's words: grace must come before greatness."2

Grace must come before greatness, and confession is the friend of grace. We want greatness now—no pain, no brokenness, just greatness. But grace must come before greatness. Grace comes when I have been honest about my weakness and my failures. Grace comes when I have confessed these things to God. Grace comes when I have laid my life before Him, just as I am. At this point I can begin to understand that God's grace means He loves me even when I cannot understand why.

A man once told a famous minister, "You are a good man." The minister replied, "I'm not a good man. I am sinful, selfish and sick; Jesus Christ has laid His hands on me, that's all."[3]

Face Your Compulsions

✎ The compulsive behaviors I am working on are: _____

_____

Below describe how you managed these compulsive behaviors yesterday.

_____

_____

Work on Turning Points

Continue working on the Moral Inventory. Go to the "Affirmations" section of the Moral Inventory and write about the following areas:
- **Positive Character Traits**—Turn to the appropriate page of the Moral Inventory and make a list of positive character traits. Give yourself a pat on the back.
- **Positive Gifts from My Family of Origin**—List some good things that you gained from your family of origin.
- **Positive Talents, Abilities, and Gifts**—Brag on yourself!
- **Positive Permissions**—List some positive things that you have given yourself permission to do (for example, permission to be happy.)
- **Positive Recovery Processes**—What recovery principles are you implementing in your life? An example would be, "I am committed to identifying shame that is not my own and letting it go when I recognize it," or "I am committed to stop trying to control everything and everyone and let God take over."

➤ **Pray for each member of your Heart-to-Heart group by name today. In three more weeks you will be ready to share your moral inventory with another person. If you have not already selected this person, ask for God's leadership in finding the right person. Look back at page 18 if you need a reminder about the type of person you are seeking.**

Notes

[1]C.S. Lewis, *The Screwtape Letters* (New York: Macmillan Pub. Co. Inc., 1961), 16.

[2]King Duncan, "The Secret of His Success," *Dynamic Preaching*, June, 1989, (Knoxville: Seven Worlds Publishing), 12.

[3]A. Philip Parham, *Letting God: Christian Meditations for Recovering Persons* (New York: Harper & Row, 1987), March 11th reading.

Honesty

In this Unit you'll work on—
Turning Point 3
I will take an honest moral inventory of my life.

The Recovery Cycle: An attitude of HONESTY accompanied by the action of CONFESSION leads to CLEANSING.

DONNA'S GOOD-NEIGHBOR POLICY

When a new family moved into her neighborhood, Donna was the first person to greet them. She introduced them to other neighbors and helped them locate piano teachers and baby-sitters for their children. She and her husband took the new couple out to dinner and gave them many helpful insights into the community. The people who Donna befriended were immensely grateful. Others who admired her from a distance wished they had her gift of hospitality.

A puzzling thing happened, however, after the new couple had been in place for several weeks. Donna seemed to drop them. The scene repeated itself with every new family that moved in. On the surface, Donna looked like she had many friends, but she ran when someone tried to develop a close friendship. On page 88 read about how Donna developed this unhealthy pattern and how it affected all parts of her life.

Why you will find this unit useful

This unit will challenge you to continue work on your moral inventory as you prepare to share it with another person. Last week the task of beginning your moral inventory may have overwhelmed you. You may have skipped some of the questions until you could go back and complete them with greater exactness. Do not aim for perfection. When you read a particular question, simply respond with the things that come to mind. This unit will challenge you to go a step further in being honest with yourself. Although working on current compulsive behaviors in your life requires some looking back, the focus is on present issues. Moving ahead with present issues requires a tougher honesty than you exercise when you review childhood experiences. Besides looking back, you will look honestly at your relationship with God and with other people. We will challenge you to face honestly any destructive habits in your life.

Honestly Facing My Past	Honestly Evaluating My Relationship with God	Honestly Examining How I Relate to Others	Honestly Confronting Self-Destructive Behavior	Honestly Assessing Myself
DAY 1	DAY 2	DAY 3	DAY 4	DAY 5

This week's memory verses

Search me, O God, and know my heart; test me and know my anxious thoughts. See if there is any offensive way in me, and lead me in the way everlasting.

–Psalm 139:23-24

Honestly Facing My Past

Today's Objective:
You will evaluate the extent
to which you have been honest
about the past and how the past
has affected you.

Connecting with the Recovery Cycle

As we think about honesty, we consider more than issues like robbing banks or cheating on tax returns. We focus on an honest attitude about ourselves.

One of the traits of adult children of dysfunctional families is: "Adult children . . . lie when it would be just as easy to tell the truth."[1] The greatest lies I tell may be lies I tell myself. An attitude of honesty starts with a decision to stop denying the very reality that surrounds me. It means looking in the mirror and seeing what really is there and admitting who I am and how I am living. The experience of cleansing starts with honesty.

Identifying the Cycle of Pain

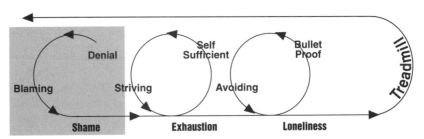

Denial perpetuates the cycle of pain. You still may be hoping that "yesterday will get better." Of course, that is impossible, but do you choose to hope for it anyway? Do you choose not to see the past as it actually was?

During the last few years I have listened to many people talk about their childhood years. I have heard the voice of denial many times.

It Did Not Hurt, Or , It Did Not Hurt that Much
Sometimes the voice of denial says, "It didn't hurt." Sometimes it says, "It didn't hurt that much." As one woman began honestly to face her past, she began to talk to her mother about family issues. Her mother said, "It wasn't really that bad." The adult daughter responded, "What about the time dad shot you?" The mother's reply was, "He didn't mean anything by it." Wouldn't you say that's a pretty good example of saying, "It didn't hurt that much," when it really hurt a lot?

I Have Dealt with It
At other times the voice of denial says, "It was painful, but I have dealt with it." This may be a true statement. However, if you say, "I have dealt with it," and then insist, "I am not willing to talk about it," have you actually dealt with it? "I have dealt with it" may mean that you simply swept the issue under the table.

You may have swept some issues under the table.

Others Were Hurt More
Sometimes the voice of denial says, "Yes, I was hurt, but others have been hurt more." The truth is that you still hurt even if others seemed to suffer more than you did. Your hurt does not go away because someone else hurt more than you did.

Suppose two people permitted me to hit their fingers with a hammer. Before I hit either person's fingers, I explain that I am going to hit the second person's fingers twice as hard as I am going to hit the first person's fingers. After I hit them, I ask the first person whose fingers I hit only half as hard as the fingers of the second person, "Do your fingers hurt?" Do you think he will say, "No, because you hit the other person's fingers harder"? It does not matter how hard the other person was hit. The first person's pain results from what the hammer did to his fingers.

You hurt without regard to how much someone else may be hurting. Emotional pain does not have to reach some magic threshold to be valid. Your pain is your pain, and you have a right to feel it.

Recognizing the Importance of Yesterday

You may ask, "If I am looking for wholeness in my day-to-day life now, why do I need to get caught up in the past?" Dealing with present emotional issues is difficult if you have not been honest about yesterday.

Author David Seamands writes that four types of pain from the past—hurts, humiliations, hates, horrors[2]—need to be addressed. In the exercise below we'll focus on those four types of pain.

✎ **You already may have done a lot of work on being honest about your past. Perhaps you have faced your past with a high degree of courage and honesty. Regardless of how boldly you have looked into your past before, take a few minutes to look for denied pain in the areas listed below.**

A hurt: List one childhood experience that still causes pain when you think about it.

_____

_____

_____

A humiliation: List one humiliating experience that happened when you were a child. How do you feel when you think about it?

_____

_____

_____

A hate: Does a nickname you had in your childhood evoke hatred when you think of it? What is the name? Why does this name make you feel as you do?

_____

_____

Denial
is a powerful poison.

Honesty
is the antidote.

A horror: Can you remember two things that deeply frightened you as a child? Have you discussed them with anyone? Do these events still exert control over you? How?

_____

_____

_____

_____

Here are examples of the kinds of responses you may have written: When you wrote about a hurt, you may have thought about the time when someone pushed you down on the pavement and you ran home to the comforting arms of your mother, only to hear her say, "You're too big to cry." The fact that you couldn't get the comfort you needed hurt you then and still does. When you wrote about a humiliation, you may have mentioned the time when your father showed up drunk at the PTA box supper and everyone could smell the alcohol on his breath.

When you wrote about a hate, you may have mentioned something like this: "My family always insisted on calling me Pudge; they did it to tease me because I was fat, and I hated it." A horror you experienced may have been the time your father beat your mother while you hid crouched in the closet for fear he would strike you, too.

Facing the present with wholeness

Writing about these incidents may be painful, but taking an honest look at the things that caused you pain is the first step toward facing the present with wholeness.

Face Your Compulsions

✎ The compulsive behaviors I am working on are: _____

_____

Below describe how you managed these compulsive behaviors yesterday.

_____

_____

_____

Work on Turning Points

Go to the "How My Childhood Shaped Me" section of the Moral Inventory on page 205. Complete the "Hurts, Humiliations, Hates, Horrors" section.

➤ **Repeat aloud three times this unit's memory verses, Psalm 139:23-24. Look on page 79 to check your memory.**

Honestly Evaluating My Relationship with God

Today's Objective:
You will learn some ways in which you may be pretending to honor God.

Playing Games with God

Today I want you to think about your relationship with God. If you have gone through the outer motions of saying yes to God when you continually say no to Him on the inside, being honest about your relationship with Him will be challenging and complex. Let's examine four ways we play games with God.

Assuming God's Role

Children play like they are police officers, soldiers, parents, and nurses. Adults sometimes play like they are God. The key to playing God is to look as though you are not playing like you are God.

Playing God does not mean you go around speaking in a booming voice. Playing God means attempting to control other people. It means attempting to control situations. You may exercise control directly, or you may exercise control in a passive way. You may be so good at controlling behind the scenes that other people do not even realize that you are manipulating them.

Greg's story

As an adult, Greg, who grew up in an out-of-control home situation, was determined to control any area of his life he could. When co-workers appeared at his office door to ask him a question, Greg kept his eyes riveted on his computer screen and left his visitors to wait for him to acknowledge them. Sometimes Greg kept them waiting several minutes at a time before he turned around to address their inquiries. Yet Greg was his office's worst offender about barging in on co-workers and monopolizing their time for long periods. Greg constantly irritated his fellow employees—and thus controlled them— with this type of manipulation.

✎ **Do you need to be in control? If so, list those things or people you attempt to control.**

_____

_____

_____

_____

You may have written something like this, "I control by withdrawing. When I withdraw from people, I like to watch them hover around me and beg for my attention." Or, you may control through complaining or whining. When you complain constantly, you enjoy watching people scramble to make you happy and to try to get you back into a good mood. Whether you control in these ways or others, you play like you are God.

Choosing Compliance Over Obedience

More sophisticated ways

You may not be bold enough to shake your fist at God and say, "God, I am going to be in charge. Leave me alone." You may find more sophisticated ways of resisting Him.

Compliance is not the same thing as obedience. Think of a nine-year-old boy whose mother tells him to take out the garbage. He could do the job in about 60 seconds. When the boy hears the assignment, "Take out the garbage," a look of deadness and sluggishness comes over him. Somehow he manages to stretch the task into a 15-minute job. When the mother looks outside, she finds he has left a trail of garbage from the house to the garbage bin. He is acting out of compliance—merely going through the motions.

When compliance motivates me, I will go to church and sit in the pew when I am supposed to. I will act the way I am supposed to act. I do these things because I am supposed to. I act not from a deep internal obedience but out of compliance.

Brokenness and surrender—active obedience—lead to renewal, but brokenness followed by compliance leads to a form of spiritual decay.

You may forget how it feels to do something for God because you want to.

On compliance, you can go a long way in your religious life. You can be a leader in the church—a teacher, even a preacher. You may do it for so long that you forget how it feels to do something for God because you want to.

A Personal Experience
For many years compliance filled my spiritual life. From childhood I wanted so badly to be a "good boy." I wanted to do the right thing. I was afraid to do the wrong thing. My attitude was, "Tell me the right thing to do, and I will do it." Somehow compliance became my lifestyle. Compliance meant that I did not always think through the issues involved in my spiritual life. I did not always know how I felt about an issue. I frequently lied to myself about my inner motives and drives.

Acting from the heart

When I began the process of personal recovery, I began to think more carefully about my behavior. I became more aware when I was tempted to do the wrong thing. Actually, the temptation had been there all along, but I had largely denied it. Though often tempted more severely, I also began to feel more joy in my decisions to do the right thing. I was discovering a new aspect of my life. I was making my own willful decisions about right because it was what I had decided to do. I had begun to act from the heart.

> Compliance is going through the motions.
> Obedience is acting from the heart.
>
> Compliance is playing a game.
> Obedience is living out what you feel inside.
>
> Compliance is a puppet-like existence.
> Obedience is a self-actuating lifestyle.

✎ **Write your own definition of compliance.**

_____

_____

_____

In what ways are you compliant in your relationship with God?

_____

In what ways are you obedient in your relationship with God?

_____

Choosing Ritual Over Worship

In a ritual, you act but don't experience.

We play another game with God. We walk through the motions of worship without making contact with God. God is alive. Worship has meaning when you touch the living God. Your spirit can make contact with His Spirit. In a ritual, you act but don't experience. You mouth songs of praise. You stand and sit when someone tells you to do so. Inside yourself, you resolve, "I will not open my heart to God. I will hold back. I will stay in control. I will not yield my full devotion to Him." You may love the rituals you adopt more than you love the God toward whom they point.

 Are you caught in ritualistic behaviors that replace a genuine openness to the presence of God? What are your rituals? Why do you pursue these rituals?

_____

_____

You may have answered something like this: "I never miss a church activity, and I frown on people who do. I believe that if I go to church without fail, it will make up for the shame in my life. Yet I sleep through most sermons and go through the motions of singing and praying. I'm afraid that if I ever truly opened myself to God's leading, He would make me look at some areas in my life where I need to be more honest."

Choosing Moralism Over Morality

Doing moral acts without being a moral person

Moralists took Jesus to the cross. These men obeyed the religious rules. They observed the Sabbath. They gave money to support God's work. Jesus offended them because He sometimes healed sick people on the Sabbath. These people performed moral acts, but they were not moral people. Love and compassion were not priorities for them. The things that meant everything to Jesus meant nothing to them.

Jesus told a story about a prodigal son who prematurely took his inheritance and left home. The young man soon realized that he had made a big mistake. He went back home and hoped to become a servant in his father's house. His father saw him returning and ran to meet him. His father welcomed him back and gave him a ring and a robe. He held a party in his honor.

The young man's older brother was not happy about his brother's recovery. He was offended. If I may paraphrase, he said, "I always have done what is right. I never left home. I have been good, and no one has ever given me a party." The older brother is an example of moralism.

Moralism is one of the main reasons why many people from dysfunctional families believe that churches have not provided them with significant emotional help. A church consumed by moralism will not have much room for compassion. A church that sees its main mission as telling people what they have done wrong without introducing them to a dynamic relationship with the loving God actually prolongs the pain of wounded emotions.

I am in favor of values that grow out of a living relationship with God. I am against living by a cold set of rules that turn you into a harsh, judgmental, and uncaring person.

 Go back to the above paragraphs. Underline with one line words and terms that are characteristics of a moralistic person. Underline with two lines words and terms that are traits of a moral person.

For the "moralistic" category, you may have underlined terms like *telling people what they have done wrong; harsh, judgmental, uncaring; obeying religious rules;* for the "moral" category, you may have underlined words and terms like *love and compassion; values that grow out of a living relationship with God.*

Playing games with God does not lead to a strong spiritual life.

The central question is, "Will you let God be God?" Will you surrender your life to Him? Will you give your life to Him daily? Will you attempt to walk in His guidance and love? Playing games with God does not lead to a strong spiritual life. Living in an open relationship with Him results in spiritual power.

> Choose obedience rather than compliance.
> Choose worship instead of ritual.
> Choose morality rather than moralism.
> Most of all, choose to walk with God.

Where are you in your relationship with God? What needs to change?

_____

_____

_____

List some things you now are experiencing in your relationship with God that you want to continue experiencing.

_____

_____

_____

You may have written that you are playing games with God by having all the markings of a religious person while refusing to let Him show you the areas of your life in which you need to surrender your brokenness. You may have written that you've only recently been able to pray openly to Him and you want to see that prayer life continue as it grows more honest and more intimate.

Face Your Compulsions

✎ **The compulsive behaviors I am working on are:** _____

_____

Below describe how you managed these compulsive behaviors yesterday.

_____

_____

Work on Turning Points

Continue working on your moral inventory.

Playing God
Complete the section entitled, "Ways I Have Tried to Play God" (page 206)

Compliance
Complete the section of the moral inventory form labeled "Ways I Have Substituted Compliance for Obedience in My Relationship with God" (page 207).

Ritual and Moralism
Complete the section of the Moral Inventory entitled "Ways I Have Substituted Ritual and Moralism for Worship and Morality" (page 207). Write your thoughts on how these issues apply to your relationship with God.

➤ In the margin write what this unit's memory verses mean to you.

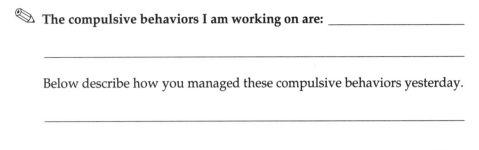

DAY 3

Honestly Examining How I Relate to Others

Today's Objective:
You will list some consistent patterns in your relationships with other people.

but if we walk in the light as He Himself is in the light, we have fellowship with one another, and the blood of Jesus His Son cleanses us from all sin.
1 John 1:7, NASB

Today I want you to honestly look at how you relate to people. Many of us want to relate in a more positive way to others in our lives. We need relationships with others. God intended for us to enjoy fellowship with others, as the Scripture appearing in the margin below illustrates. Yet issues from our past and how we respond to these issues in the present can keep our relationships with others from being healthy and productive.

We can study how we relate to people by looking for patterns in those relationships. Ask yourself honestly: If I examined my relationships with others, can I see some patterns of behavior on my part? Why might I have some of the same difficulties relating to my mother that I do to my neighbor and my boss and my best friend? Can I see some common reasons why my relationships fail? Can I, by being honest with myself, make some mid-course corrections that would strengthen all of my relationships?

Donna's story

When a new family moved into her neighborhood, Donna always was the first person to greet them. Toting a warm loaf of banana nut bread as she arrived at the family's door, Donna had a special way of helping new neighbors feel welcome in unfamiliar surroundings. She introduced them to other neighbors and often even tossed backyard barbecues to help them get better acquainted with others. She helped them locate piano teachers, pediatricians, and baby-sitters for their children.

Donna and her husband took each new couple out to dinner, related the history of the community, and provided many insights to help the newcomers adjust more easily. People who Donna befriended appreciated her. They credited her with keeping the move from being traumatic for their family. Others who from a distance saw Donna in action admired her and wanted to be like her. They wished that they had her gift of hospitality.

After a new neighbor family was in place for several weeks, however, a puzzling thing always happened. The people who Donna befriended in her frenzy of hospitality noticed that her attentions dropped off. When a couple that Donna and her husband had taken out for a get-acquainted dinner tried to return the favor or invited Donna and her husband to go to the movies or on some other type of outing, Donna always declined. When a new woman in the neighborhood offered to pick Donna up on the way to a church gathering, Donna always had some excuse. "We're just *so* busy," she always replied. This type of scenario seemed to repeat itself with every new family who moved in.

Only surface friendships

Although Donna was great at "rushing" newcomers and at first gave off many signals that she wanted to build an enduring friendship with them, her relationships actually all were on the surface level. Although from a distance Donna appeared to be a person with many, many friends, she had no close ones.

 Can you identify with anything you read about in Donna's story? Have you ever surrounded yourself with many people and yet actually been close to none of them? Below describe your situation.

_____

_____

Let's look at what formed the background of Donna's puzzling behavior. Donna grew up with an alcoholic father and a hypercritical mother. When her parents began having difficulties in their marriage because of her father's drinking, they took their stress out on Donna. "You're so dumb," Donna's mother told her. Donna made some failing grades in school—not because she wasn't intelligent but because she had such a poor concept of her abilities.

Learning to please

Donna learned she could do one thing confidently. She could please people. When people visited her family's home, Donna was a sparkling hostess. She believed that if she acted sociable and friendly, guests might not see her family's troubles or notice evidences of her father's drinking habits.

Even as a child, however, Donna never let anyone get close to her. She feared that if they knew what life really was like for her, they would run from her. So she ran from them first. When she became an adult, she kept up this same pattern. She could "rush" new neighbors like a pro, but when a new couple looked like they might want to develop a close relationship, she made excuses. If someone got close to her, they might learn about the shame that she carried around from her past.

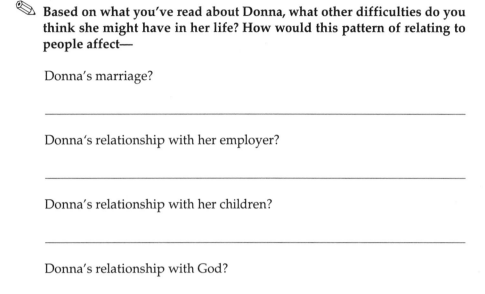 **Based on what you've read about Donna, what other difficulties do you think she might have in her life? How would this pattern of relating to people affect—**

Donna's marriage?

_____

Donna's relationship with her employer?

_____

Donna's relationship with her children?

_____

Donna's relationship with God?

_____

Regarding Donna's marriage, you may have written that pain from her past might keep Donna's conversations with her husband on a surface level so they would experience little intimacy in their marriage. Rather than dealing with the real issues in their marriage, Donna might take her frustrations out on her children in the same way her mother had—by being hypercritical. Or, her compulsive busyness in spending so much time orienting new neighbors might give her misplaced priorities that would keep her from spending quality time with her own family.

You may have written that on the job, Donna's history with a critical mother might cause her to overreact to a boss' instruction, or her sense of inadequacy from childhood might hold her back from trying to achieve. Donna might perceive God as critical like her mother or untrustworthy like her father. She might believe that she could only earn God's favor by her good works—by frantically wooing new neighbors or by other activities.

Letting the Light Shine In

Some tough honesty

For Donna to make a mid-course correction in these relationships required some tough honesty on her part. She found the courage to exercise that honesty. Donna learned to admit the pain that she felt because of her lack of friendships. She saw her own marriage faltering because of her misplaced priorities and her inability to talk with her husband about anything except food, movies, and kids. She felt pain in the other areas of her life as well.

Search me, O God, and know my heart; test me and know my anxious thoughts. See if there is any offensive way in me, and lead me in the way everlasting.
–Psalm 139:23-24

As she participated in a support group at church, she began taking seriously the words of Psalm 139:23-24—this week's memory verses, which appear in the margin. The passage challenged her to ask God to show her "any offensive way" in her and point her to the "way everlasting"——the way God would have her relate to people in her life.

✎ **How does it make you feel to know that God is available to help you see "any offensive way" in you and to show you the way He wants you to relate to others?**

_____

_____

As we mentioned at the start of this unit, taking an honest look at how you relate to others will cause you to grow emotionally and spiritually. God's Word promises His presence to help you and to show you the way. He can give you courage to face honestly these destructive habits in your life. You don't have to go through it alone! God will help you, and the members of your support group will help you in your struggles.

Face Your Compulsions

✎ **The compulsive behaviors I am working on are:** _____

_____

Below describe how you managed these compulsive behaviors yesterday.

_____

_____

Work on Turning Points

Go to the "My Relationships with People" section of your moral inventory on pages 208-215. Complete the following sections: Identifying How I Deal with Conflict; Parents; Authority Figures; Marriage; Children; Friends; Evaluating My Relationships with People

➤ **Pray for each member of your Heart-to-Heart group by name today. Ask God to give you strength as you continue to look within.**

DAY
4

Today's Objective:
You will learn to identify self-destructive behavior in your life.

Honestly Confronting Self-Destructive Behavior

Self-Destructive Behavior

Today we will think about three kinds of self-destructive behavior:
• behavior that damages my spiritual life,
• behavior that damages my relationships with people, and
• behavior that damages me physically or emotionally.

Self-destructive behavior is not logical. It generally is compulsive or addictive and has a life of its own. It does not care if it destroys you. Self-destructive behavior often feels good and feels bad at the same time. Such behavior may feel good because they keep you from feeling unresolved emotional pain. They feel bad because they hurt you and keep you stuck in emotional pain.

Behavior that Damages My Spiritual Life

Self-destructive behavior damages our spiritual lives because it causes us to put other gods before God. The Scripture at left reminds us of where God expects us to put Him in our priorities. This verse, one of God's Ten Commandments, instructs us to put God first. In the story of Donna that we read in the previous day's work, we saw that she put first pleasing others through her good deeds. She was guilty of idolatry—she allowed something to take the place of God in her life. Self-destructive behavior also damages our spiritual lives because it keeps us from worshiping God. If some addiction such as alcohol or drugs or even a more acceptable addiction like work controls my mind, my mind has difficulty receiving God's leading.

You shall have no other gods before Me.
Exodus 20:3

For the love of Christ controls us, having concluded this, that one died for all, therefore all died; Therefore if any man is in Christ, he is a new creature; the old things passed away; behold, new things have come.
2 Corinthians 5:14, 17, NASB

 Read 2 Corinthians 5:14, 17, the verses at left, and ask yourself, "What controls me to the point that it damages my spiritual life?" In the exercise below, fill in the blank with the word that represents the substance or behavior that sometimes takes the place of God in your life. Then say this exercise aloud to reject that control.

I say no to _____'s control of me. The love of Christ controls me, having concluded this, that one died for all, therefore all died; Therefore if any man is in Christ, he is a new creature; the old things passed away; behold, new things have come.

Behavior that Damages My Relationships with People

Self-destructive behavior damages our relationships with people because it causes us to hurt them. In day 3 you suggested some ways that self-destructive behavior in Donna's life might have affected her marriage, her relationships with her children, and her relationships in her workplace. Her compulsive people pleasing—the very behavior that on the surface looked like it was good for her—had its dark side. It attracted people to her that she then hurt when she rejected them. People who were new in town and could benefit from establishing an enduring friendship instead felt rejected when they saw that Donna had shown only a surface interest in them. This behavior felt good because it kept Donna from facing unresolved emotional pain—the hurts of her childhood. It felt bad because it kept her stuck in emotional pain—the lack of close friendships. Some other examples: Workaholism may make us feel good because it helps us achieve. It keeps us stuck in emotional pain because it hurts our families and it deprives them of our physical and emotional presence. Perfectionism keeps us stuck in emotional pain because it causes us to criticize ourselves. We believe nothing we do is ever good enough.

Which of the following statements reflect the way you feel after reading about how your self-destructive behavior affects others?

_____ 1. My self-destructive behavior feels good when I'm involved in it, so it must be good for me. Why should I want to give it up?

_____ 2. I depend on my compulsions too much; if it causes someone pain, that's too bad.

_____ 3. I'm the way I am, and I can't change. I had a painful childhood, and I'll never be able to cope in any other way than the way I do now.

_____ 4. Looking honestly at my self-destructive behavior will be tough, but I pledge to face it with God's help.

With us on the journey

Facing your self-destructive behavior takes courage. Giving up something that has helped you mask your emotional pain is one of the toughest actions you'll ever take, but God promises to be with you on the journey. Remember this week's memory passage? The psalmist took that brave step and asked God to show him harmful thoughts and to lead him in the right way. Hopefully you rejected the first three statements in the above exercise and listed statement 4 as the one that represented the way you feel about your self-destructive behavior.

Behavior that Damages Me Physically or Emotionally
Our self-destructive behavior not only harms our relationship with God and with other people, it harms our bodies and our emotions. We readily can see that physical addictions such as food, alcohol and other drugs, or sexual addictions can harm our bodies. But how about compulsions which are more socially acceptable—like workaholism, or even people-pleasing?

✎ **Thinking back to Donna's story on page 88, how could Donna's compulsion to please others harm her physically? emotionally?**

_____

_____

Or do you not know that your body is a temple of the Holy Spirit who is in you, whom you have from God, and that you are not your own?

1 Corinthians 6:19, NASB

Sometimes we're so determined to participate in our compulsion that we deprive ourselves of the rest we need. We fail to eat properly or to exercise, and we neglect to see physicians when we're sick. We harm ourselves emotionally because we use the compulsion to mask our emotional pain. We keep buried the real issues that we need to bring to the surface. This can show up in ways that harm us physically–such as heart trouble, intestinal trouble, or obesity. God created our whole beings, as the verse at left indicates. He intends for us to take care of His temple. Any self-destructive behavior that harms our physical bodies violates His temple.

Face Your Compulsions

✎ **The compulsive behaviors I am working on are:** _____

_____

Below describe how you managed these compulsive behaviors yesterday.

_____

_____

Work on Turning Points

Complete the section of your moral inventory labeled "Self-Destructive Traits" on page 216.

➢ **In the margin write three times this unit's memory verses. Check your memory on page 79.**

➢ **Stop and pray. Ask God to help you overcome your self-destructive acts.**

Honestly Assessing Myself

A Challenge to Be Honest

Pretend you have just died. A person who knew you well is writing your obituary. What would it say?

✎ **Fill in these blanks with the words you believe would apply to you.**

_____ died today. _____
was noted for his/her commitment to _____.
A friend said, "The thing we will remember most about
him/her was _____."
_____ spent most of his/her time
_____. Acquaintances
frequently said, "When you looked into
_____'s face you saw
_____. _____, who
had been ill for a few days prior to his/her death, said,
"I regret that I _____,
but I am glad that I _____."

The good news is that you can rewrite your "obituary" as you make changes in your life. Start with being honest about the past and present, relations with God and with people, self-destructive habits, and positive character traits. Different kinds of honesty exist. False honesty doesn't help anybody. Destructive honesty uses a brutal version of the truth to cause pain. Some honesty is neurotic and compulsive, but never cleansing.

False honesty doesn't help anybody.

A Personal Experience

When I was a seminary student, I became troubled about something I did in college. In a class, the professor assigned us to read five books and to write a brief report on each book. He said he wanted us to read every page of each book. Reading the first four books was agonizing because I was scrupulously honest. I agonized over reading every word. On the fifth book I ran out of energy. I just skimmed the book and wrote a report.

Later I became troubled by the feeling that I had cheated on this college assignment. I confessed to a Christian leader what I had done. My confidant helped me to find some relief about this incident, but he missed my most pressing problem—a compulsive need to feel I had done something wrong. I had erred, and I needed to confess it. However, I had a greater problem. I had a compulsive need to feel that I never did enough. I was experiencing neurotic honesty. Neurotic honesty is destructive. Rigorous honesty is what we need. Rigorous honesty goes beyond what is comfortable and confronts us enough to help us understand who we are. Rigorous honesty is part of the healing process.

As I start to be honest, I may be afraid that what I see in myself will be unmanageable. If I start to see my life as it really is, it may overwhelm me. I

Rigorous vs. neurotic honesty

may discover a problem with no known solution. I may have to say, "I don't know how to deal with this except to give it to God."

Rigorous honesty is painful but not deadly. If I want to see myself as I really am, I may not be able to do it alone. I am too much a part of the picture to stand back and look at it objectively. I need to let other trusted individuals help me. To experience the healing of cleansing, begin with an attitude of honesty. Make this a time of honesty with yourself and with God. Open yourself to Him and say, "God, show me what I need to see and begin the process of cleansing, growth, and healing." See the cycle of recovery below.

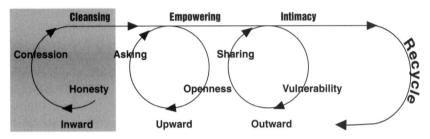

Face Your Compulsions

 The compulsive behaviors I am working on are: _____

_____

Below describe how you managed these compulsive behaviors yesterday.

_____

Work on Turning Points

Read again the third turning point you've been working on during this unit.

Turning Point 3
I will take an honest moral inventory of my life.

 Review the work you have done on your moral inventory. How honest have you been? Do you need to add anything?

If you have not already done so, choose the person with whom you will share your moral inventory. Ideally, this person should be someone who has done some work in recovery. Explain to the person what you need: absolute confidentiality; someone who will listen with a non-judgmental attitude; and someone who will affirm you for sharing yourself. Must you share your moral inventory with someone else? You don't have to do anything. However, sharing your inventory with another person is a pivotal turning point in your recovery process. Only you can decide what you will do.

Notes
[1]Janet Geringer Woititz, *Adult Children of Alcoholics* (Pompano Beach, Florida: Health Communications, Inc., 1983), 4.
[2]David A. Seamands, *Healing of Memories* (Wheaton, IL: Victor Books, 1985), 80, 84, 87, 90.

Confession

The Recovery Cycle: An attitude of HONESTY accompanied by the action of CONFESSION leads to CLEANSING.

Turning Point Three
I will take an honest moral inventory of my life.

"I MUST FIND SOMETHING WRONG"

Shawn was friendly, dependable, and talented in math. Her boss bragged on her accounting abilities. But Shawn could not see her abilities because she had much shame in her past. Her father had sexually abused her, and she was unable to see herself in a positive light because of the shame that her childhood produced. When her boss complimented her, she immediately told him about some mistake she had made on the job. She apologized for things that needed no apology.

When in her support group Shawn began writing her moral inventory, she approached the task in this same compulsive way. Shawn began to look for things to confess that she hadn't even done. She was determined to find flaws in her performance. What did Shawn need in her life? (Read more about her story on page 100.)

Why you will find this unit useful
This week you will work on finishing your moral inventory and sharing it with another person. You may be experiencing fear. You may even feel overwhelmed. This unit will offer you encouragement as you move toward completing this important task.

Barriers to Finishing the Moral Inventory	Reasons for Confession	Break-through to Reality	The Pain of Confession	Review of Basic Moral Values
DAY 1	DAY 2	DAY 3	DAY 4	DAY 5

This week's memory verse
He who conceals his sins does not prosper, but whoever confesses and renounces them finds mercy.

–Proverbs 28:13

DAY 1

Today's Objective:
You will become sensitive to some obstacles that you may face as you attempt to complete your moral inventory.

Barriers to Finishing the Moral Inventory

Connecting with the Cycle of Recovery

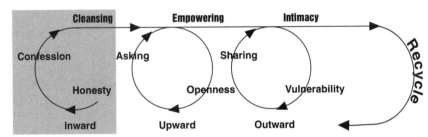

How is your work on finishing your moral inventory? Do you feel overwhelmed? Taking a personal moral inventory is a challenging task. Today, we will work on addressing some matters that may make completing your moral inventory and honestly dealing with issues difficult. These matters are:

• Denial
• Perfectionism
• Fear of Loss of Confidentiality
• The Size of the Task
• Present Painful Relationships
• Present Self-Destructive Patterns

Denial

The moral inventory brings you face to face with denial. Denial and confession cannot coexist.

We move out of denial in stages. Sometimes we take giant leaps out of denial. Sometimes we take a few steps backward into denial. Occasionally, we stumble across undiscovered pockets of denial. As you work on your moral inventory, remember that you are battling denial.

You may have as much difficulty listing your strengths as you do your weaknesses.

Denial works on you not only as you attempt to be honest about the wrongs you have done but also as you attempt to list your character strengths. Dysfunctional families often create situations that make us unable to feel good about ourselves. You may have as much difficulty listing your strengths as you do listing your weaknesses.

Denial does not like to call itself denial. It wears many disguises. It may speak to you with words like, "I don't have time for this." "This is too difficult." "Wait until you can do a better job on this moral inventory." Learn to call denial by its name and face it head on.

Perfectionism

Perfectionism is a form of compulsive behavior. You may believe that a moral inventory is a wonderful idea. You may believe that the moral inventory is so

**A time when
perfectionism has
kept me from a task—**

_____

_____

_____

_____

important that it has a once-in-a-lifetime quality about it and that you must do it perfectly. This attitude, which likely has held you back from completing some things in the past, also can keep you from finishing your moral inventory. In the margin box describe a time that your desire for perfection has kept you from doing something worthwhile.

Remember this: You do not have to give perfect answers on your moral inventory. You probably will leave some things out that you could have included. You still may be in denial about some things. Don't worry about it. Write down the things that come to mind. Push yourself enough to think about things even when they are painful to remember, but do not expect yourself to prepare an inventory that has no flaws in it.

Fear of Loss of Confidentiality

You may fear writing some things down because you are afraid someone will see what you have written. Perhaps you could make up your own code for some of the things you list on the inventory. You might use symbols to signify the things you list. However, writing out each item has great value. Find a safe place for your moral inventory. Lock it away if necessary. Don't let a fear that someone else will read it consume you.

You may hesitate to write some things down because you know we are asking you to share your moral inventory with another person. You may fear that if you write something, you will have to share it.

Not forced to share

Remember, no one will force you to do anything. You can decide how much of your moral inventory to share.

The decision to trust another person with the facts of your moral inventory is a big decision. Ask yourself whether you want to trust another person this much. You can decide. You may have a generalized problem with trusting others. The challenge to share the contents of your moral inventory brings you face to face with this basic issue of trust.

People who never take the risk to trust find a form of safety that includes loneliness.

 Go back to these first three barriers to completing your moral inventory. Below, state which of the three–denial, perfectionism, or fear of loss of confidentiality–blocks your progress the most and describe why.

_____

_____

The Size of the Task

A moral inventory is a big order. By its very nature, it is overwhelming. Work on the inventory a day at a time. Let it grow gradually. It is a big task, but do not let it overpower you.

Present Painful Relationships

Stop running!

The moral inventory may confront you with unpleasant realities about current relationships. Recognizing these realities hurts. A part of you may want to avoid the inventory rather than face the truth about present relationships. Stop running. Face reality. Now is the time!

✎ **What relationships in your life may the contents of your moral inventory threaten?**

_____

_____

You may have stated something like this: My relationship with my spouse will be threatened because I would have to change the surface way I relate to her if I am really honest in the inventory about how I interact. You may have stated: I would have to relate differently to my brother if I am truly honest in my inventory about how often I've snubbed him because I am competitive. Allowing yourself to be absolutely honest in your inventory will affect all your relationships.

Present Self-Destructive Patterns

Being unwilling to acknowledge and to stop self-destructive patterns can hinder your work on the moral inventory. The moral inventory brings you face to face with how you treat yourself. Looking into this mirror can hurt. It may be easier to say no to the inventory. Don't give up. Have courage! Look into the mirror of recovery and growth. You can do it! In the margin box describe what self-destructive habits your moral inventory will challenge.

You may have answered something like this: If I'm totally honest, I'll admit that I give in to my children too much because I want to be a "nice" mother to make up for neglect in my childhood. When I give in to them, I deprive myself. Or, I often don't have enough money to buy my family groceries because I let George sponge off me—I just can't learn to say no to him.

> **My moral inventory will challenge these habits—**
>
> _____
>
> _____
>
> _____
>
> _____

✎ **Go back to these last three barriers to completing your moral inventory. Below, state which of the three—the size of the task, present painful relationships, or present self-destructive patterns—blocks your progress the most. Describe why.**

_____

_____

_____

Face Your Compulsions

✎ **The compulsive behaviors I am working on are:** _____

_____

Below describe how you managed these compulsive behaviors yesterday.

_____

_____

Work on Turning Points

Your assignment is to finish sharing your moral inventory within two weeks. Your goal is to finish sharing the inventory with another person before the seventh Heart-to-Heart group meeting.

Review the work you have done thus far on the moral inventory. Have you been honest with yourself? Do you need to add some comments? Complete the section labeled "Addictions." The question is, "What statements would you add to your moral inventory?"

➤ **Pray for each member of your Heart-to-Heart group by name today. Ask God to give you strength as you complete your moral inventory and as you share it with another person.**

Today's Objective:
You will learn why confession is important and healthy.

Therefore confess your sins to each other and pray for each other so that you may be healed.

James 5:16

A state of brokenness causes you to look at things you do not want to see.

Reasons for Confession

Confession Is a Normal Aspect of a Healthy Christian Life

When you think about confession, you may think of a group of trench-coat-clad detectives trying to force a confession from someone sitting under a glaring light. The Bible has a different view of confession. The biblical view of confession is not a statement forced from an accused criminal. The Bible presents confession as a normal practice for anyone who seeks to live a life of obedience toward God. See what the Scripture appearing in the margin below says about confession.

An attitude of honesty followed by the action of confession results in spiritual and emotional cleansing. Cleansing is a form of recovery.

This week we are preparing for Turning Point 4: *I will share my moral inventory with another trusted person.* This turning point is not about confessing all the things you have done to all the people you have hurt. This step is about telling God and one trusted person the contents of your moral inventory.

This confession may occur as a part of the beginning of your walk with God. It may come later in your spiritual life during a time of brokenness. You may have had a spiritual walk for many years, but now you are experiencing brokenness. A state of brokenness causes you to look at things you do not want to see. You see brokenness. You see pain. You have to look at what you see and say, "God, I cannot fix what I see. I am inadequate."

The choice of the person to hear your confession is crucial. This should be someone who is the same gender as yourself. He or she must be someone who is trustworthy—somebody who can take what he or she hears and mentally lock it up as if he or she were locking something in a safe—a person who never will reveal the contents to anyone. This must be a person who is willing to listen without being judgmental—someone who can encourage and support.

You probably do not have a problem with the idea that you need to confess these things to God and to yourself. You may be struggling with the idea that somebody else needs to hear your confession.

Many evangelical Christians are turned off by the concept of confession because it produces an image of a weekly visit to a confessional booth. We can counter this by making confessional occasional, spontaneous, and voluntary instead of forced. We should not overlook the value of confession because of some negative images it may bring to mind.

James 5:16 says: "Confess your sins to each other and pray for each other so that you may be healed." A prayer for healing is not just about physical healing; it can refer to spiritual and emotional healing as well.

✎ **Based on what you've just read, check the statement(s) that is true about the biblical concept of confession.**

❏ Confession will not help us because so many negative images are associated with it.
❏ Confession must be required in order to be effective.
❏ Confession is useful only if someone who has been a Christian for many years does it.
❏ Confession is a normal practice for anyone who wants to live a life of obedience to God.

The last answer is the correct answer. The first three statements are incorrect concepts of confession.

Confession Is Not Automatically Healthy

Confession can be unhealthy. Confession can be neurotic and compulsive. It can be self-destructive. It can flow out of an attitude that says, "I must find something wrong with myself."

Sick confession will do more harm than good. It may inflict more spiritual damage than the actions being confessed caused.

Shawn was friendly, dependable, and talented in math. Her boss bragged on her accounting abilities.

Shawn's story   But Shawn could not see her abilities because she had much shame in her past. Her father had sexually abused her, and she was unable to see herself in a positive light because of the shame that her childhood produced. When her boss complimented her, she immediately told him about some mistake she had made on the job. She apologized for things that needed no apology.

When in her support group Shawn began completing her moral inventory, she approached this task in the same compulsive way. Shawn began to look for things to confess that she hadn't even done. She was determined to find flaws in her performance and refused to look at her strengths. Her confession became sick confession. It damaged her spiritually because it underscored her feeling that God was sitting in judgment of her, waiting for her to mess up.

Healthy confession grows out of a desire to be honest with one's self, with God, and with others. The focus of this honesty is being open with myself about the pain in my past, about the reality of who I am today, and about where I am headed if I don't change. Confession is a step beyond honesty. Honesty is looking at what's really there, but confession is admitting and naming what's really there.

Confession is admitting and naming what's really there.

> Healthy confession grows out of honesty. It is not driven by fear, compulsion, ritual, or habit.

Healthy confession grows out of a humility that comes from brokenness. You look into God's mirror and see a brokenness in your life. When you see that brokenness, you do not stand tall and say, "I'm great! I'm wonderful!" This brokenness causes you to admit, "God, I need you. I cannot deal with life by myself."

 In these paragraphs you just read under the heading, "Confession Is Not Automatically Healthy," underline words or phrases that you believe describe your attitude toward confession.

We hope you underlined phrases like *desire to be honest with one's self, with God, and with others; be open with myself about the pain in my past; about the reality of who I am today; about where I am headed if I don't change; admitting and naming what's really there.* We hope you were able to steer clear of words and phrases that described unhealthy confession.

Face Your Compulsions

 The compulsive behaviors I am working on are: _____

_____

Below describe how you managed these compulsive behaviors yesterday.

_____

_____

_____

Work on Turning Points

Take some time to continue working on your moral inventory. Have you selected the person with whom you will share your inventory? If you need help, contact your Heart-to-Heart group facilitator.

Breakthrough to Reality

Today's Objective:
You will discover how confession opens the door to living in the real world.

Facing Reality

Healthy confession grows out of a desire to live in the real world. When you behave in a way that violates God's value system, you begin to rationalize and deny the wrongness of that behavior. You may observe similar behavior in others and recognize it as wrong. When you engage in the same behavior, you act as if some device in your head enables you to see the behavior differently or excuse or deny it.

Harry's story

Harry criticized Tony for staying at the office too much and not spending enough time with his wife and children. Harry believed that he was the model family man because of the time he spent at home. He turned down numerous outside engagements because, as he put it, "My wife and children come first." When Harry was home, however, he had no more intimacy with his wife and children than did Tony when he was stuck at the office. Harry often invited people in spontaneously for dinner, so that Harry's home was a whirlwind of outside guests. Rarely did he and his wife and children eat by themselves as a family. When he spent time with his wife, Harry usually rented a video or took her to a movie or to some activity where many people were present. If his wife suggested that they take a walk or go somewhere alone to talk, Harry quickly excused himself by saying he had a headache. Harry was as guilty as Tony of neglect, but he was unable to recognize his own behavior as wrong.

 Have you ever been like Harry and condemned someone for a behavior that you were unable to spot in yourself? Explain.

_____

_____

Confession names inappropriate behavior and lets somebody else hear its name spoken. When you name the inappropriate behavior to another person, you have much more difficulty denying the true nature of the behavior. You are forced to bring your thoughts into reality by saying, "This is what really is happening. This is who I really am."

Taking Off Your Masks

Masks are essential if you are living in denial about compulsive/addictive behaviors.

You may be wearing several layers of masks. You may have different masks for different occasions. Masks are essential if you are living in denial about compulsive/addictive behaviors. You hide behind a mask. Confession means taking off the mask and saying, "This is who I really am." Confession marks a sincere desire to stop pretending.

What masks are you wearing? Below check them or add others.

❑ The "I'm a Christian and everything's OK" mask.
❑ The "I don't need anyone's help" mask.
❑ The "I'm a rebel" mask.
❑ The "party animal" mask.
Other _____

Seeing Others in a New Light

Confession may bring change in how you see other people. When you are honest about your own inappropriate behaviors, you may find yourself becoming more honest about others' behavior. You may have minimized inappropriate behavior on the part of someone close to you. You may have unfairly condemned the behavior of other people as a substitute for facing your own inadequacies.

More about Shawn

When Shawn, the accountant you met in day 2, entered recovery, she not only learned how harmful her compulsive fault-finding was, she also began to realize how often she allowed people to be rude and insensitive to her. For example, she learned to set better boundaries when her two teenagers spoke to her rudely. Previously she excused their behavior, but she began to leave the room when they belittled her. She imposed appropriate consequences on them if the behavior continued. As Shawn began to correct her own inadequacies, she gained courage to set limits for others as well.

✎ **How will honest confession affect the way you see other people?**

_____

_____

You may have answered something like this: I blamed my husband for being too controlling instead of facing the fact that I have been insensitive to how much of my time he needs. When I face the fact that I feel I must rescue and control my mother, I can see more objectively how I need to set boundaries when she tries to manipulate me through guilt trips.

Face Your Compulsions

✎ **The compulsive behaviors I am working on are:** _____

_____

Below describe how you managed these compulsive behaviors yesterday.

_____

_____

Work on Turning Points

Continue working on your moral inventory.

Remember, the goal is to share your moral inventory with another person before the seventh session of your group.

✎ **Memorize this unit's memory verse, Proverbs 28:13. Write it in the margin three times.**

DAY 4

The Pain of Confession

Today's Objective:
You will explore the painful side of confession.

Reality Sometimes Hurts

If you have been hiding behind a mask—if you have played denial games about the true nature of your behavior—the bright light of reality may be uncomfortable. When you take an honest look at yourself, and when you share with God and with another trusted person what you see, things may feel worse before they feel better.

Admitting your failures is painful. Confronting your failures may give you a temporary feeling of hopelessness. Your failures may seem powerful and overwhelming. When you stop denying, you can start dealing with the consequences of your behavior.

 What kind of pain do you feel when you think about sharing your moral inventory with another person?

_____

_____

Things Get Better After They Get Worse

Jesus told a powerful story about a man and his two sons. This story illustrates how things can get better after they get worse. One of the boys decided that he wanted to receive his inheritance early and to set out on his own. His father gave him his inheritance. He left home and began to violate God's moral laws and the values of his father. He did harmful things. Soon he found himself in the vocation of pig feeder.

How many of my father's hired men have food to spare, and here I am starving to death.

Luke 15:17

According to Jesus, at this point the young man "came to his senses" (Luke 15:17). He made an honest appraisal of his condition (see the Scripture appearing in the margin). The young man started to face reality.

So he got up and went to his father. But while he was still a long way off, his father saw him and was filled with compassion for him; he ran to his son, threw his arms around him and kissed him.

Luke 15:20

He decided he would return to his father and confess his wrong. At this point he was broken. He acknowledged his failure. If we could have interviewed the young man at this point, he probably would not have said that his problems were solved. He must have felt that sense of relief that comes from acknowledging reality, but he still was broken. Outwardly things had not started getting better, but this was not the end of the story. See the Scripture at left to see what happened next.

The son said to him, 'Father, I have sinned against heaven and against you. I am no longer worthy to be called your son.'

Luke 15:21

Even though the father welcomed the young man, the son still was broken, and he still saw the need for confession. (See the bottom Scripture at left.) The father accepted his son's confession and welcomed him back not as a servant but as a son. To celebrate the son's return, the father threw a big party (Luke 15:22-24).

God is full of mercy. Things may get worse before they get better, but at the end of the journey is a loving Heavenly Father with open arms. That Heavenly Father is ready to put those arms around you and to say, "Welcome back. I have been waiting for you. Welcome home!"

✎ **How do you feel when you read the last sentence, indicating that God will be waiting for you with open arms to welcome you at the end of your journey of confession? Below check the descriptions that apply.**

❏ Afraid
❏ Doubtful
❏ Encouraged
❏ Relieved
❏ Joyful
Other _____

You may be able to isolate one or two feelings, or you may feel a combination of all of those on the list. Believing that things will improve is difficult, but when that belief becomes a part of you, it can lead to feelings of joy.

➤ **Stop and pray, asking God to help you believe that things will get better even if they get worse.**

Face Your Compulsions

✎ **The compulsive behaviors I am working on are:** _____

_____

Below describe how you managed these compulsive behaviors yesterday.

_____

_____

Work on Turning Points

Troubleshooting
• I cannot find anyone with whom to share my moral inventory. What should I do?

If you are participating in a Heart-to-Heart group, contact your group facilitator for help. If you are working through this book on your own, look for a church that offers support-group ministries. Ask for help in finding someone who could listen to you share your moral inventory.

Moral inventory questions

• I simply am not ready to share my moral inventory with anyone at this time. What should I do?

If you are participating in a Heart-to-Heart group, talk at the next group meeting about your feelings. If you are working through this book on your own, pray about your struggle. Ask God to lead you to someone to whom you could talk. Perhaps a minister from a local church or a Christian counselor in your area could help.

✎ **In the margin write in your own words what this unit's Scripture memory verse means to you.**

<table><tbody><tr><td rowspan="2">DAY
5</td></tr></tbody></table>

Review of Basic Moral Values

DAY

5

Today's Objective:
You will review a simple checklist for evaluating the wrongs you have committed.

Basics

As you complete your moral inventory, take some time to review the basics. The Ten Commandments are a good place to start.

Here are the Ten Commandments in paraphrased form:
1. Have no other gods before the Lord God.
2. Don't make idols out of anything.
3. Don't misuse the name of God.
4. Set aside one day every week that is devoted to honoring God.
5. Find a way to honor your father and mother.
6. Do not murder.
7. Do not commit adultery.
8. Do not steal.
9. Do not lie.
10. Do not actively wish for things that should belong only to other people.[1]

Let's look at the Ten Commandments stated in a slightly different way.

1. Put God first.
2. Put God in a place all by Himself and don't let anybody or anything else stand in the place of God.
3. Honor the name of God. It is sacred.
4. Set aside a special day to honor God each week.
5. Honor your parents.
6. Treat all human life as sacred.
7. Honor marriage vows—your own and those of others.
8. Respect other people's property.
9. Tell the truth.
10. Find and appreciate the good in what is yours rather than looking for the good only in what is somebody else's.

'Love the Lord your God with all your heart and with all your soul and with all your mind.' This is the first and greatest commandment. And the second is like it: 'Love your neighbor as yourself.' All the Law and the Prophets hang on these two commandments.

Matthew 22:37-39

In the verse at left Jesus summarized the whole law. Think about the Ten Commandments. Think about how Jesus summarized the law. Measure yourself against them.

 Go back to the second list of the Ten Commandments. Writing in the left margin and using a scale of 1 to 10, with 1 indicating that you don't keep the commandment at all and 10 indicating that you keep the commandment faithfully, rate yourself on how well you keep God's laws. If you are concerned about confidentiality, then you may want to develop a code that would be meaningful to only you but that clearly would indicate how you feel you stack up on this list.

Moralism

If your review of the Ten Commandments leaves you feeling you have kept them all, go a little deeper. Check for moralism.

Moralism occurs when we outwardly obey God's laws but rebel against them inwardly. The religious leaders of Jesus' day engaged in moralism when they charged Christ with violating the rules of the Sabbath by healing the sick. The scribes and Pharisees practiced moralism when they held stones in their hands ready to throw at an adulterous woman while they also were guilty of sin (John 8:1-11).

We find moralism in the actions of the older son who was angry and confused when his father threw his arms around the prodigal son and celebrated with a party. (Luke 15:25-30). Moralism does not see how it deludes itself into believing that it knows everything and does everything right. Believing that it both knew God and God's will, moralism wanted Christ crucified.

Moralism wanted Christ crucified.

✎ **Now return to the Ten Commandments and check for moralism. Do you feel that you keep any of the commandments in a moralistic sense? Below describe how you do this.**

_____

_____

_____

You may have written something like this: I take pride in what I don't do to break the Ten Commandments, yet I shame others by reminding them when they break God's law.

Resentments

Check for resentments toward people. Keith Miller writes, "The first step I found valuable in making this inventory was to get out a pencil and paper and begin to list on paper everyone whom I resented or with whom I have been angry. After each name I put what it was that I felt led to my being angry. But the issue here is not what other people have done to me but my *own* behavior and reactions. So I wrote down my resentments, anger, fear, and jealousy about what happened."[2]

Feeling a positive impact

Remember that an attitude of honesty followed by the action of confession leads to spiritual and emotional cleansing. You may not feel the cleansing right away. Sometimes it takes a while to feel the positive impact of what you have done.

Take some time to meditate on the following passages.

O LORD, you have searched me and you know me. You know when I sit and when I rise; you perceive my thoughts from afar. You discern my going out and my lying down; you are familiar with all my ways. Before a word is on my tongue, you know it completely, O LORD. Search me, O God, and know my heart; test me and know my anxious thoughts. See if there is any offensive way in me, and lead me in the way everlasting.

–Psalm 139:1-4;23-24

He who conceals his sins does not prosper, but whoever confesses and renounces them finds mercy.

–Proverbs 28:13

When I kept silent, my bones wasted away through my groaning all day long. For day and night your hand was heavy upon me; my strength was sapped as in the heat of summer. Then I acknowledged my sin to you and did not cover up my iniquity. I said, 'I will confess my transgressions to the Lord'—and you forgave the guilt of my sin.

–Psalm 32:3-5

✎ **Based on what you read in these three passages, why should we confess and not keep resentments?**

_____

_____

You may have written something like this: Keeping resentments is not good for us because God knows all of our thoughts anyway. Keeping things inside us can cause us physical discomfort and can sap our energy. We will find compassion when we confess our resentments.

Face Your Compulsions

✎ **The compulsive behaviors I am working on are:** _____

_____

Below describe how you managed these compulsive behaviors yesterday.

_____

Work on Turning Points

Now, read again the third turning point that you've been working on during this unit.

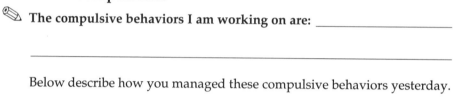

Turning Point 3
I will take an honest moral inventory of my life.

Complete your moral inventory and share it with your selected safe person. If you are participating in a Heart-to-Heart group, share your inventory with another person before the seventh meeting. If you do not complete the moral inventory or if you do not share it with another person, plan to go to the meeting anyway. Don't let compulsive perfectionism stand in the way of this important growth step.

➤ **Say aloud three times this unit's Scripture memory verse.**

_____

Notes
[1]Based on Exodus 20:1-17.
[2]Keith Miller, *Sin: Overcoming the Ultimate Deadly Addiction* (San Francisco: Harper and Row, Publishers, 1987), 179-180.

UNIT 7

Empowering

In this Unit you'll work on—
Turning Point 4
I will share my moral inventory
with another trusted person.

The Upward Cycle: An attitude of OPENNESS accompanied by the action of ASKING leads to EMPOWERING.

WHY LANCE TAUGHT SUNDAY SCHOOL

Lance felt bad about himself because of painful effects from his past. He had an overwhelming desire to be liked. A church leader he admired asked him to teach teen-age boys in Sunday School. Lance worked diligently to be a good Sunday School teacher. He called the members of his class weekly to bring a greeting to them. He took them out to the movies often. He visited them at their schools. Lance was very busy with his class of youth—not because he wanted to serve God or to be an example of God's love to his class but because he needed to be accepted. He thought doing a good job would make him gain acceptance with the church leader who recruited him. What does Lance need in his life? (Read more about him on page 116.)

Why you will find this unit useful

As you complete your moral inventory, you will become more aware of areas in which you need to grow. This week you will work on developing a clearer understanding of the power you need to overcome your character defects. You will examine your willingness to accept the help that God offers. You will look at several kinds of power that you will need as you seek to continue your recovery process.

The Power of Accepting Help	The Power to Take One Step at a Time	The Power of Knowing Who You Are	The Power to Show Love	The Power of Admitting Your Weakness
DAY 1	DAY 2	DAY 3	DAY 4	DAY 5

This week's memory verses

Now to him who is able to do immeasurably more than all we ask or imagine, according to his power that is at work within us, to him be glory in the church and in Christ Jesus throughout all generations, for ever and ever! Amen.

–Ephesians 3:20, 21

DAY 1

Today's Objective:
You will evaluate your willingness to accept help when you need it.

The Power of Accepting Help

Connecting with the Cycle of Recovery

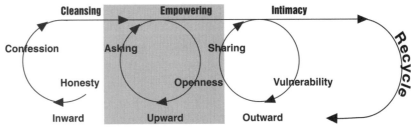

An attitude of openness to God accompanied by the action of asking God for help leads to the discovery of God's power to change for the better.

We need to ask for God to help us work on our character defects. In this stage of the growth process, we start by developing an attitude of openness to God. Asking God for help is one way we develop this openness. This week, let's think about where openness and asking God for help will take us.

Identifying the Cycle of Pain

Doing it my way

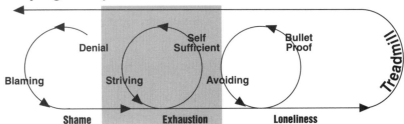

As humans we tend to say, "I'd rather do it my way." As adult children of dysfunctional families, we may have an even more intense need to deal with things by ourselves. Here's a childhood scenario that can lead to an "I'll do it myself" attitude: As a child you learn about trust. From your family you learn the most powerful lessons about trust. You need someone to put food on the table. You need consistency—someone who will be the same person each day. You need people on whom you can depend. When you have a parent who is emotionally dysfunctional, you learn to count on uncertainty. As part of that uncertainty you may not know which parent will come home at night. Will it be the dad who is kind and affectionate, or will it be the drunken man who is emotionally distant or who is filled with rage?

When behavior was OK one day and brought abuse the next:

_____

_____

_____

_____

_____

The uncertainty may result from a lack of consistent family policies. On one day one particular way you behave is acceptable. On another day, your parent explodes with anger or emotionally abuses you for the same behavior. In the margin box describe a time in which a particular behavior was OK one day and brought abuse the next.

Besides feeling uncertain, you may decide that your family does not work right. Without ever knowing the word "dysfunctional," you may decide that if you want to get things done, you will have to do them yourself. You begin to create your own certainty by controlling your life. You learn that when you depend on the people you need most, they often let you down. You learn to be independent. Rather than waiting to see if someone else will come through, you come through for yourself.

Situations in which you must depend on others make you uncomfortable. You try to avoid such situations, but you cannot avoid them entirely. If you must depend on someone else, you will try to control that individual. You learn obvious ways as well as subtle ways to control. Without even realizing what you are doing, you build a lifestyle that depends on as few people as possible and that controls as many people as possible.

Catherine's story

Catherine grew up in a family where she could not trust her parents to be consistent. As an adult, Catherine became a manager in her company. She often found herself in challenging situations that she didn't know how to tackle. Instead of seeking the advice of experienced co-workers who offered their help, Catherine chose the "go-it-alone" route. She tried to avoid depending on anyone else. Because of her unhealthy independence, she made many hurtful mistakes as she dealt with people on the job.

Catherine did have to depend on certain people, so she controlled them. Catherine depended on Thelma, an artist that worked in her office, to design brochures to publicize the department's work. Catherine gave Thelma conflicting instructions, frequently changed deadline dates, and held off until the last minute giving Thelma the information she needed for her planning.

✎ **Go back to the previous paragraphs about the "I'll-do-it-myself" attitude. Underline any words or phrases that you feel describe you.**

To move ahead in your recovery, you can confront the issues of control and unhealthy independence. In your relationships with other people you need interdependence—a balance of independence and dependence. In your relationship with God, you can learn dependence. The crucial question this week is, "Are you ready to depend on God in your struggle with your compulsions and character defects?"

You may have played the game of compliance with God. Compliance is a substitute for obedience and is a form of control. You play this game when you go through the outward motions of obeying God while inwardly working to stay in control.

Catherine at church

Catherine in the above illustration was an active member of her church. She sang in the choir, taught Sunday School, and served on a church committee. Many people thought of Catherine as deeply spiritual. Many people asked her to give her testimony. Outwardly Catherine looked very devoted to God, but she would not look objectively at herself. She refused to see that her painful past was causing her to hurt others with her controlling behavior and was causing her to cut herself off from the help of God and others.

✎ **Have you used God as a cover for making your own rules? ❏ Yes ❏ No Have you used your faith as a means of controlling the people around you? ❏ Yes ❏ No Or, have you openly rebelled against God—another way of trying to do it yourself? ❏ Yes ❏ No If you answered yes to any of these questions, explain your answer.**

_____

_____

_____

The end result of an independent life in which you must be in control is EXHAUSTION! At some point a part of you says, "I can't deal with this load any more. I am tired."

Letting Others Assist

On the night before Jesus died, He washed His disciples' feet. In those days, people wore sandals. The roads were dusty. One of the jobs of a servant was washing the feet of people who entered the house. Read the following Bible passage that describes an incident from the evening before the crucifixion of Jesus.

Jesus knew that the Father had put all things under his power, and that he had come from God and was returning to God; so he got up from the meal, took off his outer clothing and wrapped a towel around his waist. After that, he poured water into a basin and began to wash his disciples' feet, drying them with the towel that was wrapped around him.

When Peter refused help

He came to Simon Peter, who said to him, "Lord, are you going to wash my feet?"

Jesus replied, "You do not realize now what I am doing, but later you will understand."

"No," said Peter, "you shall never wash my feet."

Jesus answered, "Unless I wash you, you have no part with me."

"Then, Lord," Simon Peter replied, "not just my feet but my hands and head as well!"

Jesus answered, "A person who has had a bath needs only to wash his feet; his whole body is clean. And you are clean, though not every one of you." For he knew who was going to betray him, and that was why he said not every one was clean.

When he had finished washing their feet, he put on his clothes and returned to his place. "Do you understand what I have done for you?" he asked them. "You call Me 'Teacher' and 'Lord,' and rightly so, for that is what I am. Now that I, your Lord and Teacher, have washed your feet you also should wash one another's feet. I have set you an example that you should do as I have done for you. I tell you the truth, no servant is greater than his master, nor is a messenger greater than the one who sent him. Now that you know these things, you will be blessed if you do them."

–John 13:3-17

Jesus took the attitude of a servant and washed His own disciples' feet. Peter said no. Jesus told Peter that if he were not willing to receive this act of service, he could not have a part in what Jesus was doing. This incident in Jesus' life has at least two important messages. It directs us to serve other people with a spirit of humility. Second, it also directs us to receive help from other people. Peter said no to the act of service Jesus offered. Jesus told him that receiving was as important as giving.

Receiving—as important as giving

Letting others help is an issue of trust. When you accept help from someone else, that person may not do a task in exactly the way you would have done it. This is also true of accepting help from God. Accepting help may mean

We can't do it alone

admitting that you cannot do it alone. This is an issue of pride. You and I need God's help to overcome our compulsions and character defects. We cannot do it alone. Are you willing to let God help you?

✎ **Do you struggle with accepting help from others? Why?**

_____

_____

Are you willing to let God help you with your character defects?

_____

Have you gone through the motions of accepting God's help without really doing so? If yes, describe what you did.

_____

_____

One person answered like this: I struggle with accepting help from others because I feel embarrassed when I don't have all the answers myself. When I lost my job, friends came to me with suggestions and leads about places where positions were available. As I look back, I realize I was rude to them because I wanted to seem like I was in control. Refusing to accept their help set me back in my job search and as a result caused my family to suffer. I now realize that those people who offered to assist were part of God's provision for me. I had prayed for God to help me and had gone through the motions of accepting His help, yet I turned my back on the people He sent to minister to me.

Face Your Compulsions

✎ **The compulsive behaviors I am working on are:** _____

_____

Below describe how you managed these compulsive behaviors yesterday.

_____

_____

Work on Turning Points

Your assignment is to finish sharing your moral inventory before this group meeting. Review the work you have done thus far on the moral inventory. Have you been honest with yourself? Do you need to add some comments? At this group meeting you'll report on how you shared your moral inventory.

✎ **Begin to memorize this unit's memory verses, Ephesians 3:20-21. Underline words or phrases that bring you comfort.**

The Power to Take One Step at a Time

Today's Objective:
You will work on appreciating small positive changes in your life.

Avoid Thinking in Extremes

Adult children of dysfunctional families often think in extremes. For example we may think, "I want to be perfect. Right now I am a complete failure." We tend to minimize our accomplishments and maximize our failures.

This extremist thinking conflicts with (or destroys) a spiritually and emotionally healthy lifestyle. Sometimes you will make giant leaps in your recovery. Much of your growth may occur, however, in small, day-by-day steps. If you minimize the value of the small positive steps toward wholeness, you will hinder your healing.

Stop Living with Negative Expectations

You express hope by letting yourself believe that things are getting better. Hope means you are vulnerable. Being vulnerable means others can hurt you. You have been hurt too many times. Believing that things are getting better is frightening. We more easily can assume the worst. Living within a cloud of negative expectations feels like home.

Catherine's pledge

After she began participating in a support group, Catherine began to realize how growing up in a home with untrustworthy parents caused her to be a master controller. She decided that with God's help, she wanted to recover from that past, and she vowed to try sincerely to break some of her unhealthy patterns. With people in her office and others, she vowed to stop controlling with her chaos—she tried to be more precise with directions and deadlines.

Then one day Catherine slipped up. She assigned a project to her staff—then two days later, after her staff was halfway finished, Catherine changed all the requirements of the project. Her assistant manager confronted her with her conflicting directions. Catherine felt devastated. "I'm failing at this recovery business; I'll never get it right," she moaned to herself. She was unwilling to give herself credit for the small steps of progress she had made.

Part of the empowering you seek is the power to see and acknowledge small steps of progress. God can help you acknowledge the good that is happening in your life. Let go and let Him give you clear vision.

Seek balance in how you view things. Learn to catch yourself when you are minimizing or maximizing.

✎ **List some things you minimize that should not be minimized.**
    Examples: the pain of my childhood, my accomplishments

_____

_____

_____

_____

✎ **List some things you maximize that should not be maximized.**
Examples: my failures, the possibility of failure

_____

_____

_____

➤ Ask God to help you see your progress even when it occurs in small steps.

Face Your Compulsions

✎ **The compulsive behaviors I am working on are:** _____

_____

Below describe how you managed these compulsive behaviors yesterday.

_____

_____

Can you identify emotions you are feeling before you engage in these behaviors—for example, when you are tired, sad, lonely? Below write your response.

_____

Work on Turning Points

Take some time to continue finishing your moral inventory. If you need help, contact your group facilitator.

✎ **In the margin write this unit's memory verses three times.**

Today's Objective:
You will discover the power that grows out of understanding and accepting yourself.

The Power of Knowing Who You Are

Serving from a Clear Identity

Reread the account from John's Gospel of Jesus washing His disciple's feet from page 112. From the passage we learn that Jesus had a sense of timing about what He was doing. He knew that God had a plan for His life. He was living out that plan. John 13:3 says, "Jesus knew that the Father had put all things under his power, and that he had come from God and was returning to God."

He acted out of a sense of power from God. He acted out of a clear sense of identity because of His relationship with His Heavenly Father.

Acting from His self-awareness and acknowledgement of the power of His Heavenly Father, Jesus performed an act of service for His disciples. What Jesus did differs greatly from many of the acts people do in the name of Christian service. Outwardly we may serve others for the cause of Christ, while inwardly we serve to earn self-worth.

Think of the radical difference between helping someone because we want to feel good about ourselves versus helping someone else because we have a strong sense of personal identity as Jesus did. The person who helps someone in an attempt to earn self-esteem is not sure who he or she is. This giving to get says, in effect, "I need something back from you. I have helped you. Now you help me." Those who serve others because of a strong sense of personal identity find that service enhances their self-esteem. However, they will give primarily not to create an identity for themselves, but rather give to express the fullness of their identity in their Heavenly Father.

Lance's story

Lance believed he was no good because of some pain in his past. He had an overwhelming desire to be liked. A church leader he admired asked him to teach teen-age boys in Sunday School. Lance worked diligently to be a good Sunday School teacher—not because he wanted to serve God or to be an example of God's love to his class but because he thought doing a good job would impress the church leader who recruited him.

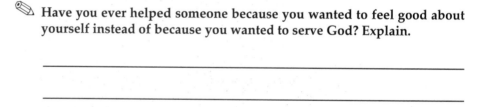 **Have you ever helped someone because you wanted to feel good about yourself instead of because you wanted to serve God? Explain.**

_____

_____

Serving others simply to enhance my self-esteem has the sting of control attached.

Jesus gave of Himself as He washed the disciples' feet. He did not have an ulterior motive. He was not trying to manipulate His disciples. Serving others simply to enhance my self-esteem has the sting of control attached. "I need you to respond to my helping a certain way so I can be a whole person," it says.

Submitting yourself to God's power and letting Him go to work on your character defects means letting God help you discover who you are. As you discover who you are and as you decide whom you want to be, you can learn a new way of giving to others. You can learn to give not as a means of controlling others but simply as a way of sharing who you are in Christ. In this life we never will be able to operate from 100 percent pure motives, but we can learn a basic purity of heart in what we do. The greatest power in the world is the power to be like Jesus. Jesus served others out of the fullness of His identity in the Father. God will help you to be like Jesus. You can decide to receive that help.

Face Your Compulsions

The compulsive behaviors I am working on are: _____

_____

Below describe how you managed these compulsive behaviors yesterday.

_____

_____

Can you identify emotions you feel before you engage in these behaviors—for example, when you are tired, sad, lonely? Write your response below.

_____

Work on Turning Points

Continue finishing your moral inventory. Remember, the goal is to finish sharing your moral inventory with another person by this group meeting.

➤ **Pray for each member of your Heart-to-Heart group by name today. Ask God to help you to be open to His power.**

DAY 4

Today's Objective:
You will discover some ways in which God's power can help you to show love to other people.

I tell you the truth, anyone who has faith in Me will do what I have been doing. He will do even greater things than these, because I am going to the Father.
John 14:12

The Power to Show Love

Learning to Love Like Jesus Loved

Reread from page 112 the account from John's Gospel of Jesus washing His disciples' feet. The greatest power in the world is the power to be like Jesus. As we read about Jesus washing the feet of His disciples, we realize that He possessed a great power to show love to others. "Having loved His own who were in the world, He now showed them the full extent of His love" (John 13:1).

The disciples were special people in Jesus' life. He wanted to show them just how much He cared about them. Judas Iscariot was among those whose feet Jesus washed. Jesus knew that Judas was going to betray Him, but He washed his feet anyway. Jesus knew that Peter was going to deny Him three times, but He washed his feet anyway. Jesus knew that when He was arrested, His disciples would run away, but He washed their feet anyway.

Jesus expressed His love for the disciples by doing something a servant normally would do. Read the verse appearing in the margin about what Jesus said not long after this incident. Jesus told us as His followers that we could show love just as He did on the night He washed His disciples' feet.

✎ **Check the following statement(s) that is true about learning to love like Jesus loved.**
   ❑ We only show love to the people who we know will love us back.
   ❑ Only perfect people can show love like Jesus did.
   ❑ We show love to others in hopes that what we do for them will keep them from hurting us.
   ❑ If we want to have the greatest power in the world, we will strive to be like Jesus.

We can love people like Jesus did even if we have great pain in our lives. We can love people like Jesus did even if we've only just begun to correct harmful patterns in our lives. We don't have to do big, showy things for people to love like Jesus did. The things we do for people in the name of Jesus won't necessarily stop others from hurting us. We do things for people because being Christlike is the greatest power in the world. The first three statements in the previous exercise are false; the last one is true.

Let Him start to work

Do you want to have the power to love people as Jesus did? Are you ready to let God begin working on your character defects? Don't wait until you are perfect to let God start loving people through you. Let Him start now.

Face Your Compulsions

 The compulsive behaviors I am working on are: _____

_____

Below describe how you managed these compulsive behaviors yesterday.

_____

_____

Can you identify emotions you are feeling before you engage in these behaviors—for example, when you are tired, sad, lonely? Write your response below.

_____

Work on Turning Points

Continue completing your work on your moral inventory and finish sharing it with another person. Complete this work before this group meeting.

 In the margin write what this week's Scripture memory verses mean to you.

Today's Objective:
You will describe the power that comes from being honest about your need for help.

The Power of Admitting Your Weakness

The Law of Vulnerability

When Jesus washed His disciples' feet, He was vulnerable. He was acting like a servant. He was the leader, but He took a vulnerable role with those under His leadership. The ultimate picture of vulnerability is Jesus on the cross. He became completely vulnerable so that He might fully express God's power and love. At first, the cross looked like the world's greatest defeat. Jesus had talked about life. Now He was dead. Jesus had healed the sick. Now He was silent. Jesus had challenged the religious leaders. They seemed to have triumphed, but in three days He proved them wrong. The cross became the decisive act of the greatest victory in the history of the world. As Jesus had become ultimately vulnerable, the greatest exercise of God's power had occurred.

Give Him your struggles

The Law of Vulnerability still applies. As you give your weakness and your brokenness to God, you find a new strength. The cross symbolizes the importance of vulnerability. God calls you to give Him your weakness. Give Him your character defects. Give Him your struggles. When you are weak, and when you acknowledge that weakness, you claim His power.

✎ **What do you need to do to become more vulnerable before God? Be specific.**

_____

_____

_____

Do you think it is possible to be vulnerable and strong at the same time? Explain your answer.

_____

_____

_____

You may have answered something like this: To become more vulnerable before God, I need to give up my belief that I can make people like me by doing things for them. I need to allow Him to become the source of my self-worth instead of believing that my accomplishments can provide that source. In the process of being vulnerable in that way, I actually gain strength because I allow God to be the source of my strength.

Face Your Compulsions

✎ **The compulsive behaviors I am working on are:** _____

_____

Below describe how you managed these compulsive behaviors yesterday.

_____

_____

Can you identify emotions you feel before you engage in these behaviors—for example, when you are tired, sad, lonely? Write your response below.

_____

Work on Turning Points

Now, read again the fourth turning point that you've been working on during this unit.

> ### Turning Point 4
> I will share my moral inventory with another trusted person.

Complete your moral inventory and share it with your selected safe person. At this Heart-to-Heart group meeting, you will be asked to share with the group about the time you spent with your selected safe person. To repeat our earlier reminder: Go to your group meeting even if you have not completed the moral inventory or shared it with another person.

Be sure your listener understands his or her role—to listen and affirm—not to solve problems or to give instructions. Allow yourself plenty of time for sharing—an entire morning or afternoon would be ideal. Invite God to be present in the session. Remember that an element of confession exists to what you are doing. Remember also that this is a time to share your victories and strengths. Allow yourself some quiet time alone after you share. Consider this as a milestone of cleansing and starting over in your life.

Next week you will begin working on Turning Point 5: *I am ready to let God change the way I think and act.* Are you ready to begin working on this?

UNIT 8

In this Unit you'll work on—
Turning Point 5
I am ready to let God change the way I think and act.

Openness

The Recovery Cycle: An attitude of OPENNESS accompanied by the action of ASKING leads to EMPOWERING.

THE PRICE OF PLEASING

Because she grew up with little attention focused on her needs, Juanita wanted the people with whom she worked to like her. Company policy did not allow employees to receive gifts from their clients, but Juanita didn't want the president of her client company to get mad at her, so she accepted when he presented her a gift certificate to a restaurant.

Because Juanita accepted this gift, she later had difficulty being impartial when she had to choose between this company and another one for a contract. (Read on page 130 about what Juanita and others can do when they struggle with spiritual battles such as how to be ethical in business dealings.)

Why you will find this unit useful

This week as you work on Turning Point 5, you will examine your level of availability to God. You will examine your attitude about authority figures. You will evaluate how your attitude about authority figures affects your ability to receive God's help in dealing with your character defects. You also look at the issue of spirituality. Are you open to spiritual things? Are you open to the presence of God? Do you allow God to lead you? Do you welcome God's power in your life?

Open to Authority Figures	Open to the Presence of God	Open to the Leadership of God	Open to the Power of God	Open to What Kind of God?
DAY 1	DAY 2	DAY 3	DAY 4	DAY 5

This week's memory verse

We have not received the spirit of the world but the spirit who is from God, that we may understand what God has freely given us.

–1 Corinthians 2:12

DAY 1

Today's Objective:
You will examine your response to authority figures and consider how your attitude about authority figures affects your attitude toward God.

Open to Authority Figures

Identifying the Cycle of Pain

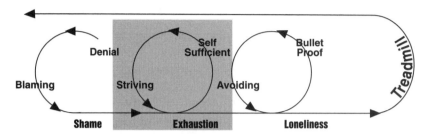

The first authority figures you encountered were your parents. How your parents exercised authority over you strongly affects your view of authority. If your parents were reasonably consistent and worthy of trust, you had a good foundation for learning to trust authority figures. If one or both parents were addicted to a substance, practiced a compulsive behavior, or simply lacked parenting skills, this damaged your view of authority figures.

Your teachers in school and other community leaders also shaped your view of authority figures. Your parents further shaped your view of authority by the manner in which they spoke in the home about authority figures. Family members with low self-esteem may lash out at community leaders as a way to express their own insecurity. Other dysfunctional families regard authority figures as super-human beings—far beyond the reach of ordinary people like you and yours.

Growing up in a dysfunctional environment may have robbed you of opportunities to express the frustrations you felt in dealing with authority figures in your life. For example, you may have felt tremendous anger toward your parents with no permissible avenue of expressing that anger. You may have transferred to other authority figures the anger you felt toward your parents.

Janet's story

Janet grew up in a family that expressed no emotions. She never remembers hearing her parents tell her that they loved her or that they were proud of her. If she tried to express anger or disappointment, her parents punished her. When she was an adult, she had great difficulty working with supervisors. Janet saw any rule that her supervisors made as a rule to be challenged.

Her boss required employees in her work area to work evenings during the last week of every month. Because she recoiled at any acts of authority over her, Janet refused to stay at work past 5 p.m. on the nights she was supposed to work late. Because she repeatedly violated this policy, Janet got low ratings on her performance review. This angered Janet so much that she quit her job. All of this occurred because Janet turned on authority figures the anger she felt at her parents.

Turning Point 5 states: *I am ready to let God change the way I think and act.* Authority figure issues may block you from letting God change the way you think and act. God is the ultimate authority figure. Turning Point 5 brings us back to the issue of surrender. Do you have authority-figure issues that make it difficult for you to let God change the way you think and act?

✎ **Below is a list of some authority figure issues. Check the box beside the authority issues that apply to you.**

❑ Ambivalent feelings toward authority.
I want to be close to you, but I am afraid of you.
❑ Fear of authority figures: *People with power always hurt me.*
❑ Assumptions about authority figures: *Authority figures look out for themselves and no one else. Authority figures don't have time for me. Authority figures cannot be trusted to keep their promises.*

Making Progress in Viewing God

The exercise below is one that you worked on in an earlier unit. Complete this exercise again to see if you have made progress in your view of God.

✎ **Re-evaluate your view of God. Begin by reading the Bible passage at left. This passage lists the fruit of the Holy Spirit. God exists as Father, Son (Jesus), and Holy Spirit. Therefore, the fruit of the Spirit are attributes of God. Look below at the list of fruit of the Spirit. Circle the traits that describe your heartfelt view of God. Notice that we ask you to describe your "heartfelt" view as opposed to what you have been taught or what you think you are supposed to believe.**

But the fruit of the Spirit is love, joy, peace, patience, kindness, goodness, faithfulness, gentleness and self-control.
Galatians 5:22-23

| Love | Joy | Peace | Patience |
| Kindness | Goodness | Gentleness | Self-Control |

If these attributes do not represent your heartfelt view of God, you are having trouble acknowledging the true nature of God. Take a few minutes to remind yourself of the nature of God. Say aloud:

God is loving.	God is joyful.	God is peaceful.
God is patient.	God is kind.	God is good.
God is gentle.	God is in control.	

Face Your Compulsions

✎ **The compulsive behaviors I am working on are:** _____

_____

Below describe how you managed these compulsive behaviors yesterday.

_____

Can you identify emotions you are feeling before you engage in these behaviors—for example, when you are tired, sad, lonely? Below write your response.

_____

Work on Turning Points

➤ **Take a few minutes to meditate on your level of openness to God's working in your life.**

Open to the Presence of God

Connecting to the Recovery Cycle

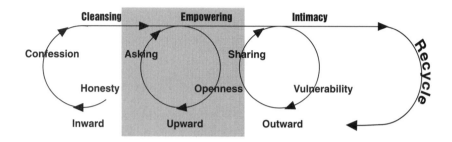

Today's Objective:
You will be challenged to heighten your awareness of the presence of God.

Being ready for God to work in your life means being open to His presence. God is present all of the time whether or not you acknowledge it, but you can choose whether you will be willing to become sensitive to His presence. This aspect of recovery is a quest for spirituality. For some people, spirituality means the same thing as unpleasantness. They believe that to be spiritual is to be sour and dour. I reject the idea that spirituality consists of self-righteousness, moralistic pride, and guilt-riddled living.

What does it take to be a spiritual person? Spirituality begins with an attitude. Spiritual people cultivate an attitude of openness to spiritual things. That is pretty simple, isn't it? Spiritual people are open to the presence of God.

Where can I go from your Spirit? Where can I flee from your presence? If I go up to the heavens, you are there. If I make my bed in the depths, you are there. If I rise on the wings of the dawn, if I settle on the far side of the sea, even there your hand will guide me, your right hand will hold me fast. If I say, 'Surely the darkness will hide me, and the light become night around me,' even the darkness will not be dark to you; the night will shine like the day, for darkness is as light to you.
Psalm 139:7-12

God is everywhere. The psalmist affirms it in the verses appearing at left. Some people cannot find God regardless of where they go. Others find God wherever they are. Place them in the depths of the deepest, most depressing crisis, lock them in a dark little room and throw away the key, put them wherever you will, and somehow they will find a way of sensing the presence of God.

Spiritual people are open to the presence of God. They seek Him. They are ready to believe that He is present. They believe that they can discover Him. They have their spiritual sensors on. They are ready to see Him active and at work in their lives.

Many of us are not open to God's presence. We have built a wall around ourselves. We have difficulty trusting. We have difficulty letting go. We are self-sufficient.

Have you ever been in the same room with someone who was not available to you? This person may have talked with you, but you were aware that the person simply was going through the motions of relating. You can be where God is but still be unavailable to His presence.

You can be where God is but still be unavailable to His presence.

If you want to be spiritual, start with an attitude. Remember that a spiritual person is someone who is open to the presence of God. Work on sensing the presence of God.

We have not received the spirit of the world but the spirit who is from God, that we may understand what God has freely given us.

1 Corinthians 2:12

Where can I go from your Spirit? Where can I flee from your presence?

Psalm 139:7

✎ **Engage in a quiet time right now. Avoid thoughts like, "I will do it later when I can plan for it." Stop now and focus your thoughts on being available to the presence of God. Start by reviewing this week's memory verse in 1 Corinthians and reviewing Psalm 139:7, both appearing in the margin. Continue by asking God to help you sense His presence. After five to ten minutes, write your feelings in the space we provide below.**

My response to this quiet time: _____

_____

_____

_____

Face Your Compulsions

✎ **The compulsive behaviors I am working on are:** _____

_____

Below describe how you managed these compulsive behaviors yesterday.

_____

Can you identify emotions you are feeling before you engage in these behaviors—for example, when you are tired, sad, lonely? Below write your response.

_____

_____

Can you identify any connection between your compulsive behavior and the material you studied today? Below write your response.

_____

_____

Work on Turning Points

➤ **Take a few minutes to meditate on your level of openness to God's working in your life.**

➤ **Stop and pray for each member of your Heart-to-Heart Group by name.**

➤ **Repeat aloud from memory three times this unit's Scripture memory verse, 1 Corinthians 2:12.**

DAY 3

Today's Objective:
You will examine some areas in which you need the leadership of God.

Open to the Leadership of God

Today's lesson will focus on the ways we need God's leadership in our lives.
• We need God's leadership in recovery.
• We need God's leadership in determining values.
• We need God's leadership in making decisions.
• We need God's leadership in developing relationships.
• We need God's leadership in facing crises.

We Need God's Leadership in Recovery

Being ready for God to go to work in your life means being open to His leadership. This aspect of recovery is a quest for spirituality. Spiritual people are open to the presence of God, and they are open to the leadership of God.

Soren Kierkegaard once told this parable about a certain rich man who bought a team of excellent, faultless horses. His own coachman was somewhat inept and undisciplined, but the rich man hoped that the quality of these fine horses would offset this. After a few months, it was impossible to recognize the once-proud horses. They were dull and drowsy—their pace inconsistent, their stamina gone. They developed strange quirks and bad habits. So the rich man called the King's coachman who knew horses. After he drove the horses for a month and they were familiar with his voice, they held their heads high, their eyes were bright and their pace beautiful. The capacities and possibilities were there all the time. It all depended on whose voice they heard directing them.[1]

So it is with you and with me. The question is, "Whose voice are you listening to?" The voice you listen to determines your pace. The voice you listen to determines how you hold your head and how you feel about yourself.

 Whose voice do you hear giving the primary direction in your life?

❑ God   ❑ Employer
❑ Parents   ❑ Neighbor
❑ Friend   ❑ Self
❑ Spouse   Other _____

Spiritual people are open to God's leadership. They want to hear His voice as He speaks. They listen to His voice above the voices of all other people.

We Need God's Leadership in Determining Values

We need God's leadership in determining the **values** that guide our lives. A good starting point for value development is the Ten Commandments. Review the values the Ten Commandments describe.
1. Put God first.
2. Put God in a place by Himself that no other person or thing can have.
3. Honor the name of God. Whenever you hear or use the name of God, remember that it is a very special word and treat it with respect.
4. Set aside a special day of the week to express your respect and worship of God.
5. Treat your parents with dignity.

value—a principle or quality intrinsically desirable (Webster's)

6. Treat all human life as sacred.
7. Honor marriage vows, your own and those of others.
8. Respect other people's property.
9. Speak the truth.
10. Find and appreciate the good in what is yours and not just in what belongs to somebody else.

Jesus summed up the Law and the Prophets when He said, "Love the Lord your God with all your heart and with all your soul and with all your mind and with all your strength," and, "Love your neighbor as yourself" (Mark 12:30-31). We need God's leadership in determining our values. We do not simply pull our values out of the air. We need God's help as we ask, "What values are eternal?"—what principles do we live by that really count to God? In the margin box describe the values that are eternal in your life. You may have written something like this: I strive to keep other people or other things from mattering more to me than God does. I try to treat my parents with dignity by not expecting more emotional support from them than they're capable of giving.

We Need God's Leadership in Making Decisions

Decisions are not easy. We live in a complex world. On a recent trip to Chicago, I obtained a map when I rented a car. The map seemed pretty simple. It showed a few main roads, rivers, and other important landmarks. Once I was on the freeway, however, things were not as simple as they looked on the map. The map did not show many roads that I passed. Sometimes the sun glared into my eyes while I was driving. At other times a driver behind me followed a few feet from my rear bumper and honked his horn. Sometimes I drove in darkness, and I could not see the necessary road signs. A few times I was lost and had no idea where I was in relation to any position on my map.

Life is like that. Life is not simple. We need God's leadership because no one has a road map with all the answers clearly spelled out. No simple blueprint says, "This is the way everything is going to be." Through the Bible we have clear guidelines from God about how we should live, but we do not have exact written instructions for every situation. We need God's present involvement in our decision-making process. We need help in applying biblical values and in making right decisions.

✎ If we can read the Bible for God's guidelines for our lives, why do we need Him to be involved in our daily lives?

_____

_____

Life can take many turns that are not always clear cut. If we stay tuned to His leading in our lives, we will be more likely to make the right decision when we do not find exact written instructions for all of life's instances.

We Need God's Leadership in Developing Relationships

We need God's leadership as we develop relationships with our spouses, friends, children, and co-workers. All these relationships are complex.
For example, look at the marriage relationship. When we get married,

The values that are eternal in my life are—

_____

_____

_____

_____

_____

No simple blueprint

especially when we are young, no one can tell us anything. We know what we want. We believe we know each other. We love each other. That is all that matters. After 12 months, we start admitting, "This is not as easy as we thought it was going to be."

Look at parenting. As a society, we are so busy and so committed to work and a million other different things that many of us spend only a minimal amount of time in active parenting. Many parents are trying to rear children without possessing even the most basic parenting skills.

Many men in our society have been taught and have accepted the idea that emotional closeness is a feminine trait. Many men are lonely for friendship.

Life is complex. I cannot deal with my relationships by myself. I need help. I need God's leadership. In the margin box describe one relationship in which you believe you need God's help.

We Need God's Leadership in Facing Crises

We all face crises in life. Some crises are developmental. When we get married, when we have children, when our children go away to school, when they move away from home, and when our parents start to get older, we experience developmental crises.

Several years ago while I attended a church picnic, I received a message that my mother had been taken to the hospital emergency room in my hometown. My sister told me that our mother might not live through the day. I caught the next available plane so I could be with my mom. She surprised the doctors and was better by the next day, but several weeks later she died after a long and painful struggle. In that experience I had questions. I had fears. I felt inadequate. I felt helpless, but I was not alone. I did not know all the answers, but I sensed the leadership of God at a point of crisis in my life.

You will face crises in your life—not just the developmental crises that occur but unexpected things as well. You cannot avoid facing crises in your life.

Spiritual people are open to the presence of God and to the leadership of God. At left read what Paul prayed for the Colossian Christians. That is what we need. We need the knowledge of what God's will is, and we need to be able to follow His leadership. The Russian writer Dostoevsky said that the difference between people and ants is that people have the ability to change the paths on which they walk.[2] We do not have to live tomorrow as we lived yesterday. With God's leadership we can change, and our lives can be better.

✎ **List three areas of your life in which you are becoming ready to follow God's leadership.**

1. _____

2. _____

3. _____

Here are examples of answers others have given: I am becoming ready to

---

> **I need God's help with this relationship—**
>
> _____
>
> _____
>
> _____
>
> _____

For this reason since the day we heard about you, we have not stopped praying for you and asking God to fill you with the knowledge of his will through all spiritual wisdom and understanding.

Colossians 1:9

follow God's leadership as He helps me learn how to be a better friend to others. I am ready to follow those in leadership as I learn to set aside feelings about my parents when I relate to my boss.

Face Your Compulsions

✎ **The compulsive behaviors I am working on are:** _____

_____

Below describe how you managed these compulsive behaviors yesterday.

_____

Can you identify emotions you are feeling before you engage in these behaviors—for example, when you are tired, sad, lonely? Write your response below.

_____

Can you identify any connection between your compulsive behavior and the material you studied today? Below write your response.

_____

Work on Turning Points

✎ **Are you ready to follow God's leadership in the areas of compulsive behavior in your life?**

_____

➤ **Stop and pray, asking God to help you to learn to trust Him more.**

Open to the Power of God

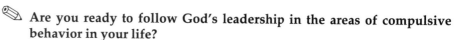

Spiritual Power

Becoming available to God means developing an openness to God. The quest for openness to God is a search for spirituality.

Spiritual people are open to sense the presence of God.

Spiritual people are open to receive the leadership of God.

Spiritual people are open to being channels for the power of God.

Today's Objective:
You will examine your feelings about God's power.

For our struggle is not against flesh and blood.

Ephesians 6:12

Read what the Scripture at left says about the spiritual battles we fight. Here are some examples of these battles:

A spiritual battle occurs when you make a decision about whether you will be ethical in your business dealings. Because she grew up with little attention focused on her needs, Juanita wanted the people with whom she worked to like her. Company policy did not allow employees to receive gifts from their clients, but Juanita didn't want the president of her client company to get mad at her, so she accepted his present of a gift certificate to a restaurant. Because Juanita accepted this gift, she later had difficulty being impartial when she had to choose between this company and another one for a contract. Juanita struggled with a spiritual battle.

Daily struggles

Howard grew up in a shame-bound family. As an adult, he reacted to this shame-bound situation by trying to see how shameless he could act himself. He had difficulty controlling his sexual urges, and he slept with several women in violation of his marriage commitment to his wife. Howard struggled with a spiritual battle when he made these decisions.

Gary knew some gossip he heard about George wasn't true. His conscience told him to speak out and correct the misinformation, but he didn't want to take an unpopular stand with his peers, who didn't like George. It was easier for Gary to continue to repeat the lie. A spiritual battle occurred in Gary's life when he made the decision about lying or telling the truth.

 Go back to the previous three paragraphs on spiritual battles. Underline phrases that represent things that you believe keep you locked in spiritual battles.

You may have underlined such phrases as *grew up with little attention focused on her needs, wanted the people with whom she worked to like her, see how shameless he could act himself, didn't want to take an unpopular stand with his peers, easier to continue to repeat the lie.*

The one who is in you is greater than the one who is in the world.

1 John 4:4

We are not strong enough to win this spiritual battle by ourselves. We can win only if we bring in reinforcements. Spiritual people are open to the power of God. To be spiritual is to say, "God, I can't do this by myself. I am powerless. I am not strong enough, but with your strength I can." This is a form of brokenness. Read the Scripture at left about the strength that we have to fight spiritual battles. If you have received Jesus Christ into your life, you have within you a divine power source for this spiritual battle.

Face Your Compulsions

 The compulsive behaviors I am working on are: _____

_____

Below describe how you managed these compulsive behaviors yesterday.

_____

_____

Can you identify emotions you are feeling before you engage in these behaviors—for example, when you are tired, sad, lonely? Below write your response.

_____

Can you identify any connection between your compulsive behavior and the material you studied today? Below write your response.

_____

_____

Working on Turning Points

➤ **Take a few minutes to meditate on your level of openness to God's working in your life.**

✎ **List three areas of your life in which you need God's power. Be open to including addictive/compulsive behaviors.**

1. _____

2. _____

3. _____

✎ **Write three times in the margin this unit's Scripture memory verses, 1 Corinthians 2:12.**

DAY 5

Today's Objective:
You will think about the nature of God.

Other things God is not—

_____

_____

_____

Open to What Kind of God?

Getting to Know What God Is Not

This week we have been working on developing an openness to God. We have thought about the importance of being open to God's presence, His power, and His leadership. Turning Point 5 describes our goal this week: *I am ready to let God change the way I think and act.* Are you ready to give God your compulsions, your addictions, your fears? Take some time to think again about the nature of God. Be clear on who God is as you make the decision to let Him go to work in you.

• God is not a manipulating God.
• God is not a condemning God.
• "For God did not send his son into the world to condemn the world but to save the world through him" (John 3:17).
• God is not a dysfunctional parent.

In the margin box write some other things that God is not. You may have written something like this: God is not someone who turns His back on me because of shame in my life. God is not someone who bases His love for me on my performance.

Getting to Know Who God Is

- God is the Lord God, the Everlasting Father, the Son Jesus Christ, the Holy Spirit. He is three but one.
- God is love.
- God sent His Son Jesus Christ to show His love to humanity. Jesus died on the cross. He was innocent, but He died on the cross with the weight of your sins and mine upon His back.
- God is a tender shepherd.
- God is forgiving.
- God is gentle.

Other positive attributes of God—

_____

_____

_____

_____

_____

In the margin box list some other positive attributes of God. You may have written something like this: God loves me regardless of what occurred in my past. God cares about me individually. God is there when I need Him. God doesn't change even when circumstances around me change.

Face Your Compulsions

✎ **The compulsive behaviors I am working on are:** _____

_____

Below describe how you managed these compulsive behaviors yesterday.

_____

_____

✎ **Can you identify emotions you are feeling before you engage in these behaviors—for example, when you are tired, sad, lonely? Write your response below.**

_____

Turning Points

Now, read again the fifth turning point that you've been working on during this unit.

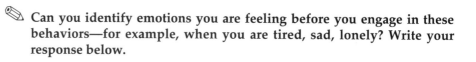

Turning Point 5
I am ready to let God change the way I think and act.

➤ **Take some time to meditate on your level of openness to God's working in your life.**

Notes
[1]King Duncan, "Bits and Pieces," _Dynamic Preaching_, June, 1989, Vol. IV, No. 6, (Knoxville: Seven Worlds Publishing, 1989), 12-13.
[2]G. Curtis Jones, "Breaking the Patterns," _1000 Illustrations for Preaching and Teaching_ (Nashville: Broadman Press, 1986), 286.

In this Unit you'll work on—
Turning Point 6
I ask God to remove the
defects in my character.

Asking

The Recovery Cycle: An attitude of OPENNESS accompanied by the action of ASKING leads to EMPOWERING.

DON'T ASK; MANIPULATE

As a child, Joey manipulated his parents by avoiding eye contact with them. Instead of speaking up when he needed attention, Joey irritated his parents by refusing to look at them. "Why do you look away when I try to talk to you?" his mother begged. Joey learned that this technique was one way of getting his parents' attention that he needed.

As an adult, he manipulated by using the same tactics. At work he deliberately avoided eye contact with his boss. Joey found that doing this caused his boss to pay more attention to him because he was puzzled about why Joey acted this way. Read page 135 to see what Joey needed in his life.

Why you will find this unit useful
Adult children of dysfunctional families tend to do a poor job at making direct requests for the things they need. In this unit you will learn some of the reasons why you may have trouble communicating your needs to others. We will challenge you to develop the skill of making direct requests to God and to other people when you need help.

The Importance of Asking	Asking God for Guidance	Asking God for Strength	Recognizing How God Answers	Giving God Your Short-comings
DAY 1	DAY 2	DAY 3	DAY 4	DAY 5

This week's memory verses
Ask and it will be given to you; seek and you will find; knock and the door will be opened to you. For everyone who asks receives; he who seeks finds; and to him who knocks, the door will be opened.

–Matthew 7:7-8

DAY 1

Today's Objective:
You will consider the importance of making direct requests when you need help.

You trusted and you expected, and someone let you down.

The Importance of Asking

Identifying the Cycle of Pain

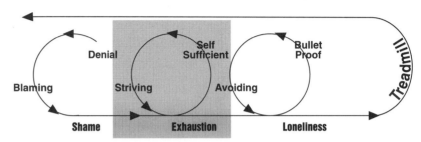

Don't Ask; Do It Yourself

A dysfunctional family focuses on the needs of addictive/compulsive parents rather than on nurturing the children in the family. This does not mean that the parents do not love the children. It does not mean that the parents never do anything to help the children. It means that nurturing the children takes a back seat to meeting the emotional needs of an addictive adult who is stuck in a childlike emotional state.

Children of dysfunctional families are survivors. At an early age, they learn that they must take care of themselves.

Perhaps you learned to take care of yourself. You learned to think, "If it is going to be done for me, I must do it myself." You learned to provide for your own needs. You learned that counting on someone else to do what you need done causes pain. You trusted and you expected, and someone let you down.

At some point you decided that not asking at all was better than asking and getting little or nothing. You became more and more independent, and in the process, you became more and more emotionally isolated.

Don't Ask; Manipulate

Perhaps control and manipulation were the standard modes of operation in your home. Anyone who got what he or she needed in your family used these two accepted means. You watched and learned to play by the family rules. You mastered the skills of codependency. You learned how to ask in less direct ways. You learned to get through manipulative giving.

Sherra manipulated by sulking. Instead of telling her mother she needed to spend time with her, Sherra got her mother's attention by looking sullen. As an adult, Sherra continued to react in this manner. Instead of telling her boss that she felt overloaded with work and asking her boss to reprioritize some of her projects, Sherra gave her boss the silent treatment.

Joey manipulated by avoiding eye contact. Instead of speaking up for his needs, Joey irritated his parents by refusing to look at them. "Why do you look away when I try to talk to you?" his mother begged. Joey learned that this technique was one way of getting his parents' attention. As an adult, he manipulated by using the same tactics. At work he deliberately avoided eye contact with his boss. Joey found that doing this caused his boss to pay more attention to him because he was puzzled about why Joey acted this way.

✎ **How did you respond to your family of origin?**
- ❏ I learned not to ask and to do for myself.
- ❏ I learned to ask indirectly—to manipulate others to get what I needed.
- ❏ Other _____

Don't Ask; Suffer Alone

Besides not asking for what you need, you may have stopped making any direct statements about your needs. Somewhere along the way, you started to wonder, "Why doesn't anyone see that I am hurting inside?" If you could have verbalized the question, the answer would have been, "People don't know you are hurting because you don't tell anyone."

A rule of dysfunctional families is "Hide the pain." Members of severely dysfunctional families feel shame for their dysfunctional nature. "If we all act like everything is OK, maybe other people will think everything is OK." If you bought into that message, you learned to look OK when things were not OK inside you. You became a master at hiding your inner pain. Now, you don't even think about it. You don't even realize that you can be hurting deeply and yet never let it show outwardly.

You learned to look OK when things were not OK inside you.

People know what you tell them and what you show them. A few perceptive people may see through your false front, but don't be surprised if no one knows how much you are hurting inside.

Connecting with the Recovery Cycle

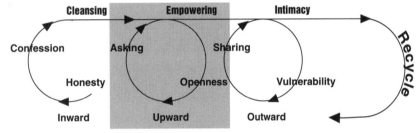

God affirms the value of asking. God knows your spirit, your heart, and your emotions, but He asks you to ask Him for help. See what the verses appearing at left say about this.

Ask and it will be given to you; seek and you will find; knock and the door will be opened to you.

Matthew 7:7

You do not have because you do not ask God.

James 4:2b

Asking means admitting that you need help. This may not be an easy admission. As a child, the thought that you depended on one or more adults who in some major areas of life were not dependable frightened you. To survive you learned to believe you needed no one else. Asking means you are willing to receive help. Trust is the underlying issue. If I don't ask anyone for help, I won't be disappointed. I won't get hurt. If I ask for help, I might get an outright no. Worse, I might get a yes followed by another disappointing failure to follow through.

> Recovery involves learning to ask for help.

You had no choice about who your parents were. Perhaps you were forced to trust someone who was not worthy of that trust. Now, you can make choices.

You can learn to sense how trustworthy a person is. You can choose not to trust people who do not show evidence of trustworthiness. You can decide to trust people who prove worthy of your trust.

Not a magic lamp

Decide if you are willing to trust God. You may feel that He has let you down. You may believe that you cannot trust Him because He permitted you to experience pain. You still may be seeing God through the memory of your parents' behavior. Let God be God. He is full of love. He is worthy of trust. He invites you to ask Him to meet your needs. God's invitation to ask is not a magic lamp by which you may have any wish granted. God's invitation to ask is your opportunity to get to know a loving God who seeks to guide you in the right direction and to provide for your deepest needs. God will not always say yes to your requests. He always will answer you with loving concern.

✎ **What is one thing you could ask God for now? Are you willing to ask? Are you willing to accept His answer—whatever it is?**

_____

_____

Ask God for one thing today.

✎ **What is one thing you need to request from someone else? Whom should you ask? Are you willing to risk this request?**

_____

_____

Face Your Compulsions

✎ **The compulsive behaviors I am working on are:** _____

_____

Below describe how you managed these compulsive behaviors yesterday.

_____

Can you identify emotions you are feeling before you engage in these behaviors—for example, when you are tired, sad, lonely? Below write your response.

_____

Work on Turning Points

➤ Take a few minutes to meditate on your level of openness to God's working in your life. Are you willing to ask God to help you change your behavior?

➤ Begin to memorize this unit's Scripture memory verses, Matthew 7:7-8. Write them in the margin three times.

DAY 2

Asking God for Guidance

Today's Objective:
You will work on asking God to give you guidance in your decision-making.

We Need God's Wisdom and Guidance

When We Determine Values

You will have difficulty working on your character defects if you are uncertain about what is right and what is wrong. Many people would say, "What is right is what feels right to you." What feels right to you is important when you buy clothes, but it is not an adequate test in determining values.

Character building requires a foundation upon which to build. Are you willing to accept the concept that what is right in your life will be based on what God calls right? How do you find out what God calls right? The Bible is the source. Below is a sample of some basic values the Bible teaches.

1. The most important thing is to love God and show Him you love Him.
2. You should not worship anything other than God.
3. Love other people.
4. Love yourself.
5. Be honest.
6. Learn to forgive.
7. Avoid bitterness.
8. Share with others.
9. Do not judge other people.

 What other basic Bible values would you add to the list above?

_____

The Bible does not specifically address every single issue. For example, the Bible does not say anything about smoking cigarettes, but it does say that your body is the temple of God and should be treated with respect. When the Bible does not address an issue directly, you may seek biblical principles to help you determine values.

When We Make Decisions

We need God's wisdom and guidance when we are making decisions. "Should I change jobs?" "Should I let my kids _____?" "Which option should I choose?"

Life is full of decisions. The decisions you make determine the outcome of your life. Opening the Bible before you make every decision is not always feasible. Committing yourself to knowing the basic teachings of the Bible leads to a thought process that is shaped by biblical truth.

Your inner guide

God has given the Holy Spirit to those who accept Jesus. The Holy Spirit is your inner guide. He will help you as you make decisions. The key is learning to sense the leadership of the Holy Spirit. We run the risk of playing games here. You easily can credit the Holy Spirit for your own decisions. Be careful that you do not blame God for decisions you make without seeking His guidance.

When We Develop Relationships

We need God's wisdom and guidance when we make decisions. Recovery means moving beyond destructive relationships. We can experience healing in the area of relationships. We may need to suspend or end some relationships. Adult children of dysfunctional families often hold on to relationships when they should let go. Sometimes they let go when they should hold on.

We need God's help in developing relationships. Sometimes, a problem in a relationship may respond only to prayer. You may say, "God, I have done everything I can. Help!"

When We Face Crises

Sometimes life caves in. You feel alone, out of control, helpless. Jesus said that those who hear and practice His words are like a man who built his house on a rock. When a great storm came, the rain fell and the wind beat against his house, but it stood firmly (Matthew 7:24-25). When you face the storms of life, Jesus can help you to remain stable.

We Must Decide to Ask for God's Help

In each of these areas, asking for God's help is your choice. You must decide to let God guide you. God's leadership is not always immediately clear. Keep listening. Go on the best information you have. He will guide you.

✎ **List four areas of your life in which you need God's guidance.**

1. _____

2. _____

3. _____

4. _____

Put a star by the area in which you believe you need God's guidance the most.

Face Your Compulsions

✎ **The compulsive behaviors I am working on are:** _____

_____

Below describe how you managed these compulsive behaviors yesterday.

_____

_____

Can you identify any connection between your compulsive behavior and the material you studied today? Below write your response.

_____

Work on Turning Points

➤ Take a few minutes to meditate on your level of openness to God's working in your life. Are you willing to ask God to help you change your behavior?

➤ Review this unit's Scripture memory verses as they appear on page 133. Underline words or phrases that have the most meaning for you.

DAY

3

Today's Objective
You will work on asking God to give you strength to develop your character.

Asking God for Strength

God Always Says Yes When . . .

When you ask God for something, you cannot always assume the answer will be yes. You may ask God for some things that would harm you. As a loving parent, God sometimes says no. When you ask God for strength to do the right thing, He always will answer yes.

Read the following Bible passage as a promise from God.
No temptation has seized you except what is common to man. And God is faithful; he will not let you be tempted beyond what you can bear. But when you are tempted, he will also provide a way out so that you can stand up under it.
–1 Corinthians 10:13

How does it make you feel when you realize that God will not let you be tempted beyond what you can bear?

_____

_____

God desires to provide you with spiritual strength to do the right thing. As a follower of Jesus, you have the Holy Spirit inside you. The Holy Spirit is your divine power source. He will give you strength to say no to temptation. He will help you say yes to what is right. When you ask God to remove your shortcomings, He will not turn a deaf ear to you. He will help you.

Your compulsive behaviors have a compelling call. If you cannot hear their call now, be assured you will hear it again. Your compulsions are stronger than you are by yourself. You need reinforcements. You need God's power as you face your compulsions. When you ask God for power to overcome your compulsions, He will not ignore you. Be patient. Growth takes time.

Kimberly's story

Kimberly's compulsion was that of being involved in an inferior relationship. She was involved in a dating relationship that was harmful to her. On one hand Kevin, the man she dated, flattered her and told her she was beautiful and capable; on the other hand he only seemed interested in using her to help him achieve and was insensitive to her needs.

In recovery Kimberly realized that she needed to free herself from this harmful relationship, but her addiction to Kevin's flattery and attentions kept her from making the break that she needed for her healing. Kimberly realized that her compulsion was stronger that she was by herself. She prayed for God's power to help her overcome her compulsion.

At first Kimberly was frustrated when she didn't feel free instantly from her compulsion. She expected God to deliver her immediately from the pain of this situation. Growth occurred slowly. First God began to put other people in her path so that Kimberly would develop healthy relationships. Then He helped her develop the ability to set boundaries—she learned to alter her route so that she would not encounter Kevin and be forced into unhealthy conversations with him.

Then He helped her acquire some wholesome volunteer activities so that Kimberly found worth in genuinely helping others instead of being used in a codependent relationship with Kevin. In looking back, Kimberly saw that God was not ignoring her but was putting building blocks to recovery in her life.

Sometimes you may not be open to His help. Sometimes, you will slip. Don't give up because you fail. You are not alone. God is with you. Perhaps you know these things in your mind, but you do not believe them in your heart. Are you willing to trust that God is going to give you the strength you need?

✎ **Are you ready to ask God to remove your shortcomings? Yes ❏ No ❏ If you answered yes, describe in the margin box some areas of your life in which you need to ask God for strength.**

Face Your Compulsions

✎ **The compulsive behaviors I am working on are:** _____

_____

Below describe how you managed these compulsive behaviors yesterday.

_____

_____

Can you identify any connection between your compulsive behavior and the material you studied today? Below write your response.

_____

_____

Work on Turning Points

➤ **Take a few minutes to meditate on your level of openness to God's working in your life.**

➤ **Pray for each member of your Heart-to-Heart group by name today. Ask God for something you need.**

➤ **Say aloud three times this unit's Scripture memory verses.**

I need to ask God for strength in these areas—
_____
_____
_____
_____
_____

DAY 4

Today's Objective
You will examine some of the ways God offers leadership.

Recognizing How God Answers

How Does God Speak?

Turning Point 6 states: *I ask God to remove the defects in my character*. Asking God to help me with my shortcomings means I am willing for Him to go to work in my life. God will help me change by leading me as I make decisions, determine values, and develop relationships. God will give me extra strength to say no when appropriate and yes when appropriate.

Hearing God speak can be a complicated endeavor. God usually does not speak in an audible voice. Sometimes, I may confuse other voices with God's voice. I even may put God's name on my own wishes. I may say that I'm following God as a cover to justify doing what I want to do.

God Speaks Through the Bible

The Bible is God's Word. In the Bible I can find principles by which to live. I can hear God speaking to me through the Bible. As an adult child of a dysfunctional family, I may need to re-learn how to read the Bible. Part of my own recovery has been discovering that I gravitate toward the difficult sayings in the Bible. If I hear one passage that reminds me of God's love for me and another passage in which I am challenged to try more diligently to be good, I will remember the passage that challenges me to try more diligently and will minimize the passage about God's love. This is not a conscious decision, but it is a powerful emotional process. Something about my childhood conditioned me to hear the things that challenge me and to minimize things that support me.

Hearing all that God says

Recovery means learning to hear everything that God says—the supportive and the challenging aspects of His truth.

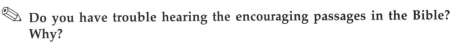 **Do you have trouble hearing the encouraging passages in the Bible? Why?**

_____

_____

Your relationship with your parents shaped much of your view of God. If your parents consistently modeled unconditional love, you had an easier time sensing God's unconditional love for you. If your parents did not give you a sense of being blessed, or if the blessing they gave you was conditional, you now may have a difficult time sensing God's blessing on you.

Let God speak. Listen to all He has to say. Don't confuse His voice with some inner voice of pain from the past.

God Speaks Through Other Believers

The Church is the body of Christ. The followers of Christ often are His messengers. God may speak to you through another Christian. You may find help in dealing with your character flaws through the loving advice and support of another believer.

Codependency may tell you to listen to everyone. Codependency may mean that you assume anyone else's opinion is better than yours and that you should run in whatever direction someone tells you to run. Hearing God speak through other believers means learning to be selective about whom you listen to. Not every believer speaks with equal accuracy. Part of recovery is developing the skill to assess the reliability of the advice you receive.

Learning to be selective

✎ **Name some Christians through whom God has spoken to you.**

_____

Name some Christians to whom you should listen more. _____

_____

God Speaks Through Circumstances

With a heart that is open to God and a mind that sincerely seeks God, you can sense His leadership in the things that happen to you. Be careful about interpreting what you see. Sometimes you can interpret circumstances to fit what you want to be true. At the same time God may speak powerfully through events.

Sometimes you interpret circumstances to fit what you want to be true.

✎ **Describe a time when God spoke to you through circumstances.**

_____

_____

_____

How Does God Empower?

When you ask God to remove your shortcomings, you can expect Him to lead you and to empower you. As a follower of Christ, you have the Holy Spirit living inside you. The Holy Spirit is your power source. The Holy Spirit will give you the strength to say no when you need to say no. He will help you to say yes when you need to say yes. The Holy Spirit is working within you to make you more like Christ. The Holy Spirit will remind you of what is true and what is right. The Holy Spirit will help you to follow in the steps of Jesus.

You never will achieve perfection in this life. However, your life in Christ is meant to be an experience of upward growth and maturing. You will move with forward and backward steps, but with His help the forward steps will far outnumber the backward steps.

✎ **What is the greatest obstacle you face in making yourself available to God's power?**

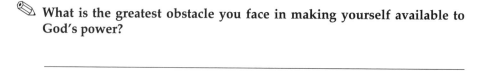

_____

Here are examples of some answers others have given: My greatest obstacle is difficulty trusting in Him after so many people in my past proved untrustworthy. My greatest obstacle is my belief that others' opinions of me are more important than is God's unconditional love for me. My greatest obstacle is my fear of change: my whole lifestyle is built around my harmful patterns; I'm scared about what will happen if I start working on some of those patterns. Regardless of what you listed as an obstacle, that obstacle is not too big for God to help you overcome.

Face Your Compulsions

✎ **The compulsive behaviors I am working on are:** _____

_____

Below describe how you managed these compulsive behaviors yesterday.

_____

_____

Can you identify emotions you are feeling before you engage in these behaviors—for example, when you are tired, sad, lonely? Below write your response.

_____

Can you identify any connection between your compulsive behavior and the material you studied today? Below write your response.

_____

Work on Turning Points

➤ **Take a few minutes to meditate on your level of openness to God's working in your life. Are you willing to ask God to help you change your behavior?**

Giving God Your Shortcomings

Now Is the Time to Ask for God's Help

You have learned some of the ways that your childhood has affected who you are today. Hopefully, you have confronted the pain of your childhood. Hopefully, you have made significant progress in making peace with your past.

Now, you are facing the present. Understanding how you got where you are is one thing; changing your present behavior is another. You may find that working on the present is more difficult. Changing your behavior is difficult, but with God's help, the change is possible.

Today's Objective
You will work on implementing Turning Point 6.

Larry's story

After participating in a support group, Larry understood that growing up in a home with an alcoholic, distant father and a compulsive, critical mother impacted him significantly. He knew that his past was a major source of pain in his life. He also knew that his past caused him to hurt others when he withdrew from them and refused to communicate directly with them. He knew that his desire to avoid being distant like his father kept him from setting boundaries on his children's misbehavior. Even though Larry realized these patterns harmed him and others, he struggled to change his present behavior. "I've been this way too many years," Larry said about his reluctance to make changes. "I'd have too much difficulty changing now."

✎ Can you identify with Larry? Can you by now easily identify the source of the pain in your past but hesitate when you think about changing the way your past affects your behavior? Below describe your feelings about this matter.

_____

_____

_____

God is available

God is available to help you change if you are willing to let Him. If you are willing, the next step is to identify the behaviors that you need to change. Review your moral inventory.

✎ Using the moral inventory, make a list of five character flaws that you need to change. Use the space below to write the list.

List the character flaws that need the most work. Your list does not need to be comprehensive. Let God work on whatever character flaws come to mind for your list. Do not be concerned about making a perfect list.

My Character Flaws

1. _____

2. _____

3. _____

4. _____

Face Your Compulsions

✎ The compulsive behaviors I am working on are: _____

_____

Below describe how you managed these compulsive behaviors yesterday.

_____

_____

Can you identify emotions you are feeling before you engage in these behaviors—for example, when you are tired, sad, lonely? Below write your response.

_____

Work on Turning Points

Now, read again the sixth turning point that you've been working on during this unit.

> ### Turning Point 6
> I ask God to remove the defects in my character.

✎ Will you now begin asking God to remove the character flaws listed on the previous page? Using Turning Point 6 as a guide, write a prayer that expresses your feelings.

_____

_____

_____

_____

_____

_____

Intimacy

The Outward Cycle: An attitude of VULNERABILITY accompanied by the action of SHARING leads to INTIMACY.

A ONE-WAY RELATIONSHIP

Barry sincerely wanted to build a close friendship with Glen. Glen confided about his personal struggles at his work and about family issues Glen was working to resolve. Barry wanted to talk confidentially to Glen about similar matters, but when Glen began to ask Barry personal questions, Barry pulled away. He insinuated that he could not trust Glen. Glen felt hurt because he believed he had been open with Barry and had, during the course of their relationship, proved himself trustworthy. Unresolved issues of trust from Barry's family of origin stood in the way of a close friendship developing between the two men. (Read more on page 148 about what Barry needed in his life.)

Why you will find this unit useful

Loneliness occurs when a person is emotionally isolated from other people. Adult children of dysfunctional families live with barriers to emotional intimacy. This week you will discover that learning to be emotionally close to other people is an essential part of spiritual and emotional health. This unit begins the Outward Cycle. You have been challenged to look inward and upward. Now the challenge is to reach outward to other people. In this unit you will learn some reasons why emotional intimacy is difficult for adults who grew up in dysfunctional families. You will examine some inadequate substitutes for emotional intimacy. You will learn about the type of honesty that is the essential foundation for emotionally intimate relationships, and you will be challenged to seek God's help in moving toward a commitment to emotional closeness with other people.

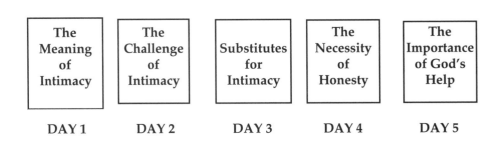

The Meaning of Intimacy	The Challenge of Intimacy	Substitutes for Intimacy	The Necessity of Honesty	The Importance of God's Help
DAY 1	DAY 2	DAY 3	DAY 4	DAY 5

This week's memory verse

But if we walk in the light, as he is in the light, we have fellowship with one another, and the blood of Jesus, his Son, purifies us from all sin.

–1 John 1:7

DAY 1

Today's Objective:
You will discover the meaning of emotional intimacy.

The desire to be intimate stems from the fact that we are made in God's image.

The Meaning of Intimacy

Connecting with the Recovery Cycle

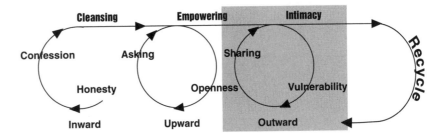

We feel a certain sense of incompleteness that can be lessened only when we experience relationships with others. In an intimate relationship we are free to acknowledge and express our basic needs to belong and to be significant. In an intimate relationship we can be honest about the fears and doubts that plague us. We feel a warmth that encourages us and enables us to let down our barriers. In an intimate relationship we believe we can share and listen. We feel as though God has given us the gift of another person. As a result God can become very real to us.

As humans we have a need to belong—a need for emotional connections with other people. We want to be intimate with other human beings. This desire stems from the fact that God makes us in His image. God created humans to have fellowship with Him. We, being made in His image, desire fellowship or intimacy with other people.

This week we will study these five special dimensions of intimacy:
• Intimacy means being yourself.
• Intimacy means trust.
• Intimacy means acceptance.
• Intimacy means being relaxed.
• Intimacy means an unspoken bond.

Intimacy Means Being Yourself

Evie's story

From her support-group study, Evie learned that she had acquired the hero role in her family of origin. Her father drank away all his earnings, so her family was very poor. Evie was the first member of her family to attend college. Evie's success in her job brought her family much pride. She was determined to succeed in removing the blight on the family name. As a result, Evie over-identified with her role in her job. She never let anyone see her as a real person outside the role of super-successful professional woman. This proved to be a barrier to intimacy with friends. Evie wanted to have close relationships with others, but she was unable to let her guard down and to let people relate to her outside her role.

An intimate relationship involves the feeling that you can be yourself with the other person. You can take off masks that you are wearing. You have a sense that others will accept you even though you are not putting your best foot forward. You can let your guard down. You feel safe to be you.

Intimacy Means Trust

Barry's story

Barry sincerely wanted to build a close friendship with Glen. Glen confided in Barry about his personal struggles at his work and with his family. Barry wanted to talk confidentially to Glen about similar matters, but when Glen began to ask Barry personal questions, Barry pulled away. He insinuated that he could not trust Glen. Glen felt hurt because he believed he had been open with Barry and had, during the course of their relationship, proved himself trustworthy. Unresolved issues of trust from Barry's family of origin stood in the way of a close friendship developing between the two men.

You build an intimate relationship on trust. You trust the other person to let you be yourself. You trust this person to be honest with you. The trust is mutual. You both are willing to take risks—to know and to be known.

✎ **Review the stories of Evie and Barry in the previous two sections on intimacy. Have you ever experienced the fear of being yourself or experienced the lack of trust like these paragraphs describe? If so, explain below.**

_____

_____

_____

Intimacy Means Acceptance

Lee's story

Lee was politically active in his community. His friend Jason, with whom he had attended college, worked for an employer who took public stands on issues. The stands he took opposed some political views Lee defended strongly. That Jason would work for a boss who held such opinions offended Lee. Jason wanted to be close friends with Lee and believed that the two of them could disagree on certain issues without harming their friendship. Because he grew up in a dysfunctional family, Lee was determined to control. He believed he only could be friends with Jason if Jason criticized his boss and came over to Lee's way of thinking.

An intimate relationship is an accepting relationship. This does not mean that you and the other person always agree on everything. It means that you accept who the other person is and what the other person has to say. You receive it. You hear it. You may express disagreement, but you do so with love. You may encourage this person to change, but you do so with the understanding that your relationship does not hinge on the change.

Intimacy Means Being Relaxed

Joyce's story

Joyce wanted her friendship with Tina to be one in which she could share day-to-day events in her life. If her son won an award at school, Joyce wanted to call Tina and tell her the news. If she and her family went on an enjoyable vacation, she wanted to call Tina and describe it to her. If she felt anxious about her mother's health problems, she wanted to confide in Tina about it. But Joyce began to notice that her conversations with Tina were one-sided.

Although Joyce shared openly with Tina, Tina's conversations in return were stilted and forced. The easy, relaxed, open sharing that occurred easily for Joyce was a struggle for Tina. Because of painful issues in her past, Tina was unable to relate except in a stilted, almost programmed way. She could talk with Joyce about a certain few safe topics, but she couldn't practice the kind of easy, intimate sharing that Joyce demonstrated.

A climate of acceptance

An intimate relationship has a relaxed quality about it. People take off masks. They put aside roles. They accept each other. They express affirmation. All of this adds up to a relaxed atmosphere in the relationship.

✎ **Review the stories of Lee and Joyce in the previous two sections on intimacy. Have you ever experienced a barrier to intimacy because you could not accept someone or because you could not relax? If so, explain below.**

_____

_____

_____

_____

Intimacy Includes an Unspoken Bond

An unspoken bond holds an intimate relationship together. The bond grows out of a sense that this relationship has something special about it.

✎ **Review the characteristics of an intimate relationship that we have described in this day's reading. Make a list of your past and present relationships that met or presently meet these criteria for intimacy.**

Past relationships: _____

_____

_____

Present relationships: _____

_____

_____

Don't give up if you haven't experienced intimate relationships. With God's help, you can!

We hope you identified several relationships in the past and present that you believe meet these criteria. If this type of relationship hasn't been possible for you, however, don't give up. With God's help, the material you've already studied in this book plus the information on the remaining pages can help you experience the most intimate relationships that you have ever known.

➤ **Stop and pray, thanking God for any relationships you've already had that meet this criteria. Ask Him to help you learn how to improve in this area or to start developing more intimate relationships.**

Face Your Compulsions

 The compulsive behaviors I am working on are: _____

_____

Below describe how you managed these compulsive behaviors yesterday.

_____

_____

Can you identify any connection between your compulsive behavior and the material you studied today? Below write your response.

_____

 Begin to memorize this unit's memory verse, 1 John 1:7. In the margin write what this verse means to you.

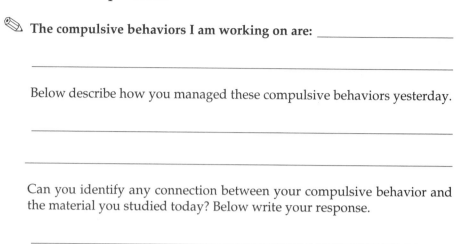

DAY 2

Today's Objective:
You will discover why intimacy is especially difficult for adult children of dysfunctional families.

Intimacy is built on honesty. The dysfunctional family is in denial.

The Challenge of Intimacy

Identifying the Cycle of Pain

Intimacy involves mutual trust and sharing. Intimacy implies that each family member should be the focus of attention some of the time. A dysfunctional family focuses its attention on an addictive/compulsive family member. By its very nature the dysfunctional family does not create an atmosphere that makes intimacy happen.

Intimacy includes the open sharing of feelings in an atmosphere of acceptance. A dysfunctional family places limits on the expression of feelings. Intimacy means you can talk about the private matters of your soul. A dysfunctional family discourages its members from discussing privately the obvious problems in the family.

Intimacy communicates an acceptance of the other person as he/she is. Members of dysfunctional families fall into survival roles. Children begin to act out roles that contribute to the needs of the unhealthy family system.

In an intimate family the members emotionally nurture each other. A dysfunctional family fails to provide adequate nurture for the emotional needs of developing children. Intimacy is built on honesty. The dysfunctional family is in denial.

To help you remember the difference between intimacy and the characteristics of a dysfunctional family that represent barriers to intimacy, go back to the four paragraphs you just read. Underline with one line key words or phrases that represent traits of intimacy. Then underline with two lines key words or phrases that describe barriers to intimacy found in dysfunctional families.

For traits of intimacy you may have underlined *mutual trust and sharing, open sharing of feelings, atmosphere of acceptance, emotionally nurture each other, honesty, talk about private matters.* For barriers to intimacy you may have underlined *focuses attention on addictive family member, limits on expression of feelings, survival roles, fails to provide nurture, denial.*

Keeping your distance

By its very nature, a dysfunctional family is not conducive to intimacy. When you have grown up in a dysfunctional family, intimacy will not feel normal. Keeping your emotional guard up will feel normal. Keeping your emotional distance from others will feel normal. Holding your deepest feelings inside and sharing them with no one else will feel normal.

Becoming emotionally intimate with another person may threaten you because you feel you must pay back any kindness extended to you. Rather than be indebted to others, you may choose to remain isolated.

✎ **Has today's material given you a better understanding of why intimacy is difficult for you? Below write your thoughts about this.**

_____

_____

_____

If appropriate, list two things about your family of origin that cause you to have a difficult time being emotionally intimate with other people.

1. _____

2. _____

Some possible answers for the last question might include: In my family of origin all attention was focused on my mother's eating disorder. We children were expected to pretend that nothing was amiss in our family; therefore, I learned never to show my feelings, and that affects my adult relationships with others. Or, in my family of origin I took on the clown role—I believed that if I kept people laughing, they wouldn't notice the pain that we were in because of my father's scrapes with the law. That role kept others from accepting me as I really was—a hurting individual. I didn't grow up learning to accept people as they are; therefore I tend to want to accept people today only if I can change them.

Face Your Compulsions

✎ **The compulsive behaviors I am working on are:** _____

_____

Below describe how you managed these compulsive behaviors yesterday.

_____

_____

Can you identify any connection between your compulsive behavior and the material you studied today? Below write your response.

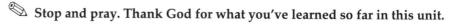

➤ **Work on memorizing this unit's Scripture memory verse. Write it in the margin three times.**

✎ **Stop and pray. Thank God for what you've learned so far in this unit.**

<table>
<tr><td rowspan="6">

DAY

3

Today's Objective:
You will learn to recognize inappropriate substitutes for emotional intimacy.

You may reserve your thickest emotional armor for those times you are with your spouse.

</td><td>

Substitutes for Intimacy

Substituting Imitations for Intimacy

When someone close to you hurts you, you may seek substitutes for intimacy. The following paragraphs describe some of these substitutes.

Sexual Encounters Are Not Necessarily Intimate
Moving from one sexual relationship to another is a way to avoid emotional intimacy. This lifestyle focuses on adrenaline, hormones, and conquest, not emotional intimacy. Emotional intimacy means staying around long enough to know a person well. Emotional intimacy means listening. Emotional intimacy means closeness—not sex.

Moving from one surface sexual relationship to another can be a response to the fear of knowing and being known. It is a means of staying in control and staying hidden.

Marriage Does Not Automatically Create Intimacy
Being married does not necessarily mean you experience emotional intimacy. A married couple may live together and still be out of touch emotionally. You may reserve your thickest emotional armor for those times you are with your spouse. Marriage potentially is the closest of all relationships; therefore it can be the most threatening to you if you fear intimacy.

The Church Is Not Automatically an Intimate Place
The church offers great hope for intimate relationships because it seeks to follow the pattern set in the New Testament where the norm was open, honest sharing. The New Testament Church was not perfect, but it did experience a closeness among its members that does not appear to be typical today.

As churches reclaim the New Testament call to small-group sharing and confession, they may rediscover an intimate fellowship built around small groups, but you cannot assume that because you are involved in a church, you are guaranteed emotionally intimate relationships with other people.

We do not mean for these statements to speak of the church in a disparaging way. We merely are trying to take a realistic look at how to discover emotional intimacy. The church offers the best potential community setting for cultivating honest and emotionally intimate relationships, but those relationships do not occur automatically.

</td></tr>
</table>

✎ **Based on what you've just read about intimacy, check below which of the following statements are true.**

❑ 1. Sexual intercourse does not necessarily produce intimacy.
❑ 2. Intimacy occurs only in a relationship with the member of the opposite sex.
❑ 3. Marriage does not automatically guarantee intimacy.
❑ 4. People who are members of the same church automatically are close to one another.
❑ 5. A husband and wife can live together and still be out of touch emotionally.

Sexual intercourse or a relationship with the opposite sex do not guarantee intimacy, nor does marriage or church membership assure it. Husbands and wives can be married for years yet keep great emotional distance between each other. The true statements in the list were 1, 3, and 5.

Substitutes that Don't Look Like Intimacy

Isolation

Avoiding being hurt

Believing that you never can succeed at intimacy, you may choose to isolate yourself emotionally. In other words you may choose a lifestyle that keeps you emotionally distant from other people. You have been hurt. You do not want to be hurt again. Trying to get close to other people is too risky. You decide to isolate—to build your own emotional castles and live in them.

Work
An addiction to work can be a substitute for intimacy. While you work, you don't feel the loneliness. Your work is your companion. The people with whom you work relate to you based on the guidelines of the work you do. These relationships feel safe because they have built-in boundaries. When you go home, you face your intimacy problem.

Other Addictions
Any addictive behavior can be a substitute for intimacy. As with work, other addictive behaviors can make the pain of emotional loneliness go away—but only temporarily.

✎ **What substitutes have you found for intimacy?**

_____

_____

What would it take for you to let go of these substitutes?

_____

_____

Are any of these substitutes for intimacy related to the compulsive behaviors you have been working on in this group?

_____

Some people become overly absorbed in their hobbies or in sports—not as a way to add interest to their lives but because stamp-collecting or gardening or TV football represent ways to avoid spending time building intimate relationships. Some parents substitute over-involvement with their children as a way to avoid intimacy with spouses or friends. Letting go of these substitutes requires honesty and courage, but with God's help, it can be done!

Face Your Compulsions

✎ **The compulsive behaviors I am working on are:** _____

_____

Below describe how you managed these compulsive behaviors yesterday.

_____

_____

➤ **Pray for each member of your Heart-to-Heart group by name today. Thank God for the closeness of your group. As needed pray that your group members will develop further emotional intimacy.**

DAY 4

Today's Objective:
You will learn that honesty is the foundation for emotionally intimate relationships.

The Necessity of Honesty

Honesty Is the Mainspring for Intimacy

Robert L. McDonald, author of *Intimacy: Overcoming the Fear of Closeness*, wrote, "If you view intimacy's dimensions as the finely synchronized movements of the parts of a watch, honesty would be the mainspring."[1] If you want to make intimacy a reality in the important relationships of your life, you must come to grips with what being honest means.

One of the traits of adult children of dysfunctional families is, "Adult children . . . lie when it would be just as easy to tell the truth."[2] When I first started reading about adult children, I quickly identified with most of the traits except this one. I was compulsively honest in ethical matters. Now I understand how this trait applied to me. Let me tell you a story to illustrate.

A Personal Experience

In grade school we had separate boys' and girls' physical education classes. One day when the girls' class was in the gym and the boys were outside, a friend of mine mischievously asked me if I would let him sit on my shoulders while he looked through the window into the girls' gym. Even though I normally would avoid anything I thought was wrong, I agreed. I was staring into a solid door while he was peering into the window. I'm still not sure what was wrong with his looking through the window, but I do remember that a sudden loud whack and a severe pain on my bottom interrupted our joint venture. My friend quickly jumped off my back and ran. I turned to see a smirking teacher walking off with his wooden paddle in his hand.

I hurt physically and emotionally. I walked away and sat on a curb. I felt like crying, but I didn't. My friend David Templeton sat beside me. "What's wrong?" he asked. "Nothing," I replied. "You look like something is bothering you," he said. "No, I'm fine." He asked me again. I gave the same answer.

I hurt physically from the swat with the paddle. My pride was hurt. I was scared. My dad had told me that if I ever got a whipping at school, I would get a worse one at home.

Hiding feelings

I did not talk to anyone about what happened. I didn't talk to David, who wanted to help. I did not talk about it with my parents. I already had learned to be dishonest about my feelings. This dishonesty kept me from letting a friend encourage me. I hid a part of my life that I could have shared.

> Intimacy is based on emotional as well as ethical honesty. It starts with honest communication about how you feel.

➤ **Describe a time in which you have avoided sharing a painful incident with someone because your family of origin taught you to be dishonest about your feelings.**

_____

_____

Blame and Shame Block Honesty

When you grow up in a shame-inducing environment, blame is a big issue. "Whose fault was it?" is the first question when something goes wrong. In a healthy environment, people explore cause and effect as ways of making sure things go better next time. In a dysfunctional environment, the issue is making sure my self-esteem is protected when blame for an incident is assigned. If I am stuffing my feelings, I can use blame to unload a whole range of unexpressed feelings. A child who spills his milk may collect weeks of unexpressed anger from other family members when the milk hits the table.

Self-protecting distortion

A child learns to wiggle out of these kinds of situations. If he knows he cannot win when he shares what really happened or how he actually feels, he may decide to say something else—something to avoid blame—to shift the focus away from his offending act. When a whole family is living this way, reality becomes distorted. Family members describe events through a filter of self-protecting distortion. After a while, the simple process of saying exactly what happened or exactly how one feels is not even considered. Family members are not clear on what actually did happen in a given situation.

✎ **Which of the ways described above did your family members use to deal with blame?**
❑ The cause-and-effect method—studying what occurred to make sure things occurred differently next time
❑ The finger-pointing method—making sure they identified the culprit

Below describe how this occurred in your family.

_____

_____

Let Boundaries Guide Expressions of Honesty

You may be tempted to move from being honest with no one to telling everyone everything that has happened to you and everything that you feel. You may switch from a practice of keeping things to yourself to a practice of uncontrolled honesty.

Don't overreact. Lying is wrong and unacceptable. Do not lie, but be careful in the decisions you make about sharing what you feel. Emotional honesty does not mean you tell *everyone* everything you feel. It does not mean you must be compulsively driven to share every failure with every person who will listen. It does mean you will find selected safe people with whom you can share. It means you will be honest with people your actions hurt.

Learning to Say "I'm Sorry"

When you hurt someone, you need to speak to that person. The circle of confession should be as wide as the circle of offense. Next week you will begin work on Turning Point 7: *I am willing to share my struggles and weaknesses with selected safe people. I will ask forgiveness of the persons I have harmed.*

Part of your recovery process is addressing damaged relationships. Start by admitting your responsibility to the people you have hurt. Stop making excuses. Stop blaming others. Take responsibility for what you have done. Many events are complex in terms of who caused what. Don't get bogged down in trying to decide if something was 40 percent your fault or 50 percent your fault. Learn to say "I'm sorry for my part of the pain."

Deciding When to Share Yourself

Do not give dogs what is sacred; do not throw your pearls to pigs. If you do, they may trample them under their feet, and then turn and tear you to pieces.
Matthew 7:6

Honesty does not mean you share all of yourself with everybody. Read the verse appearing in the margin. You would be foolish if you gave jewelry to pigs or a Bible to dogs. Not everyone can understand the information you might share. Not everyone will treat with care what you share. The old, unhealthy way of thinking says, "Trust no one. Keep things to yourself." You may be tempted to swing like a pendulum and say, "Trust everyone!" That too is dangerous. Some people are more trustworthy than others are. You can learn to sense a person's safety level with some degree of accuracy. You will make some mistakes, but you also will find the rewards of personal emotional closeness with other people.

Find AST's with SSP's

One aspect of spiritual and emotional recovery is finding SSP's—Selected Safe People with whom you can share. Another skill is learning the skill of determining AST's—Appropriate Sharing Times with SSP's.

✎ **What steps do I need to take to be more honest—**

about communicating what happened? _____

_____

about my feelings? _____

_____

about wrongs I have done? _____

_____

➤ **In the margin box list the names of some people you believe you can trust. Then stop and pray, thanking God for those individuals.**

Face Your Compulsions

✎ The compulsive behaviors I am working on are: _____

_____

Below describe how you managed these compulsive behaviors yesterday.

_____

Can you identify any connection between your compulsive behaviors and the material you studied today? Below write your response.

_____

I can trust these people—

_____

_____

_____

_____

DAY 5

Today's Objective:
You will be challenged to seek God's help as you move toward a commitment to emotional intimacy.

Jennifer's story

The Importance of God's Help

Getting in Touch

But if we walk in the light, as he is in the light, we have fellowship with one another, and the blood of Jesus, his Son, purifies us from all sin.

—1 John 1:7

A personal relationship with Jesus Christ paves the way for intimacy with other people. However, being a follower of Christ does not mean that emotional closeness occurs automatically. If you grew up in a dysfunctional family, you probably live with barriers that make emotional intimacy difficult for you. "Walking in the light" with Christ means being in touch with Him. It means seeking to obey Him. A person easily can get caught up in religious busyness while missing the full impact of the spiritual power Jesus offers.

Jennifer had every night of her week tightly scheduled with some church-related activity. When she wasn't attending a Bible study, she was meeting with her church committee or attending choir practice. Friends had a difficult time finding Jennifer at home because of her many church activities. The pastor knew he could call on Jennifer if a church member needed to be picked up at the airport or if he needed her to visit someone in the hospital. On the surface, Jennifer seemed to be totally immersed in serving the Lord. In reality, however, Jennifer believed that if she stayed busy doing religious activities, she wouldn't have to stop to really get in touch with God—to hear His will for her. Jennifer had participated in a support group in which she realized that some unresolved issues in her life were keeping her from serving God effectively. In her support group she studied about how God wants people to take off their masks and be honest. Jennifer was afraid to do that, so she just added more activities to her already busy schedule.

✎ **Have you ever been so busy doing church work that you failed to stop and get in touch with God and with people? Describe your situation.**

_____

_____

Therefore confess your sins to each other.
James 5:16

The Bible teaches us to be honest. See the verse appearing at left on this subject. Early Christians confessed their failures and needs to each other. Too often we have chosen a watered-down faith. When we have shared with other believers, we have filtered out anything that is too painful or too embarrassing. Many outsiders to the church sense this and decide to look elsewhere for an atmosphere of honesty.

Here are some steps you can take to get in touch with God and with people.
1. Make certain you have invited Jesus to forgive you and to live inside you as the leader of your life.
2. Be sure your day-to-day fellowship with Jesus is up to date. Are you spending some time each day thinking about Him and asking Him what He expects of you? Are you telling Him your needs?
3. Ask God to help you begin living with a new level of honesty in your life.
4. Ask God to put you in touch with people who will model the honesty and emotional closeness you desire in your life.
5. Ask God to show you some people with whom you can be honest.

✎ **Go back to the five steps you just read. Circle the number beside the step that you believe will be the most difficult one for you to accomplish. Ask God to help you as the tackle these five steps.**

Face Your Compulsions

✎ **The compulsive behaviors I am working on are:** _____

_____

Below describe how you managed these compulsive behaviors yesterday.

_____

_____

➤ **Say aloud three times this unit's Scripture memory verse. Stop and pray, asking God to make the message of this verse real in your life.**

Notes
[1]Robert L. McDonald, M.D., *Intimacy: Overcoming Fear of Closeness* (Old Tappan, New Jersey: Fleming H. Revell Company, 1988), 38-39.
[2]Janet Geringer Woititz, *Adult Children of Alcoholics* (Pompano Beach, Florida: Health Communications, 1983), 4.

In this Unit you'll work on—
Turning Point 7
I am willing to be vulnerable
with selected safe people.

Vulnerability

The Outward Cycle: An attitude of VULNERABILITY accompanied by the action of SHARING leads to INTIMACY.

A FEAR OF LOOKING WEAK

Chuck seemed always to be buying new clothes while his wife Christine felt she was stuck with the same wardrobe year after year. Christine wished that just once, she could go out on a shopping spree after payday, but she believed that she should set aside that wish. Appearance seemed to be more important to Chuck's job than it was to her role as a full-time homemaker. Christine thought she should ignore her needs in deference to Chuck. She thought if she spoke up and Chuck refused, she would look weak. She wasn't sure she wanted to make herself that vulnerable. What did Christine need in her life? (Read more on page 166.)

Why you will find this unit useful

As an adult child of a dysfunctional family you probably have a difficult time being vulnerable. Someone took advantage of your tender vulnerability when you were a child. As a result you learned to be tough and to be on guard. Now you are hyper-vigilant—always on the lookout, always ready for a crisis. Such protection requires you to build walls. These walls protect you from some forms of pain, but they also can shut out love and joy. To experience wholeness, you must learn to be vulnerable. This unit will help you discover the importance of vulnerability and will challenge you to take some steps toward becoming vulnerable in a healthy way. One step toward vulnerability is a willingness to admit when you have been wrong. We will challenge you to complete Turning Point 7, which involves making a list of people you have wronged. In this unit you will learn about boundaries. Boundaries provide personal safety without shutting out love and joy. Boundaries are essential for healthy vulnerability.

Vulnerable Is Not an Easy State	Vulnerable Means Being Like Jesus	Vulnerable Does Not Mean Weakness	Vulnerable Does Not Mean Doormat	Vulnerable Means Admitting Mistakes
DAY 1	DAY 2	DAY 3	DAY 4	DAY 5

This week's memory verse

And being found in appearance as a man, he humbled himself and became obedient to death—even death on a cross!

–Philippians 2:8

Vulnerable Is Not an Easy State

Today's Objective:
You will learn some reasons why vulnerability is difficult for adult children.

A foundation stone

Connecting with the Recovery Cycle

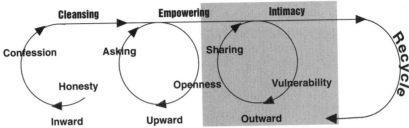

No one should be vulnerable all the time. The key to developing a positive vulnerability in your life is understanding that some situations are safe and others are not. Some people are safe and others are not. Some people are safe some of the time and unsafe at other times.

Vulnerability is one of the foundation stones upon which we build healthy relationships. To build meaningful relationships, we must learn when to trust. Dysfunctional families do a poor job of helping children develop clear guidelines about when to trust and when not to trust.

Identifying the Cycle of Pain

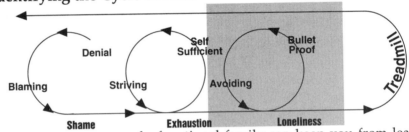

Here are some ways a dysfunctional family can keep you from learning healthy vulnerability:

You Could Not Trust the People You Most Needed to Trust.
If one parent is addicted and the other parent is taking care of the addict, the children will have trust issues with both parents. Both parents are caught in the addictive system. They are not emotionally available in a consistent way. They may be emotionally available on some occasions but not on other occasions. In extreme cases, they may always be unavailable at an emotional level.

When parents consistently cause emotional pain, children develop ways of protecting themselves. They learn that in their family—the environment capable of the most intimate relationships possible—they must maintain their guard. If it is not safe to be vulnerable at home, they reason, then it must not be safe anywhere. In the margin box describe one way you learned to keep your guard up.

Here are responses that some people have written: I kept up my guard by always being too busy to let anyone get close to me. I kept up my guard by never letting on that I was hurting, even when my best friend got the part I wanted in the play.

You Received No Clear Guidelines on When to Be Vulnerable.

When parents alternate between nurture and emotional abandonment, our confusion is compounded. I never could predict when my father would get drunk. I could see no identifiable pattern. I looked for warning signs. For a while, in my childlike reasoning, I thought that he got drunk whenever he got a new car. Later, he got drunk at a time that made my theory seem incorrect. Once while drunk, he was explaining why he had taken the first drink. He kept repeating the explanation, "The bottle was so pretty." Was that what made him drink—seeing a bottle that looked pretty? I could not figure out what triggered his drinking. If I could have predicted it, I would have known when to be vulnerable and when to protect myself. His drinking binges always came out of nowhere and had a shocking impact. The only response I knew was to maintain some level of emotional guard at all times.

You Were So Vulnerable that Showing It Was Dangerous

Another aspect of growing up with an addicted parent is living with a high level of emotional pain. If you show the pain, someone outside your family will ask you what is wrong. The person will be asking you to speak about the unspeakable. You will be forced to betray your family.

The no-talk, no-show rule

You have learned the "no talk" rule. You understand the "no show" rule, too. The "no show" rule means that you don't show your feelings—especially your hurt. To you, "vulnerable" is another word for "stupid." To you, only stupid people expose themselves to pain they can avoid. You learn to wear emotional armor.

✎ The previous paragraph said that people from dysfunctional families liken "vulnerable" to "stupid", but in reality why are you unwise *not* to be vulnerable? Below write your answer.

_____

_____

_____

You may have written something like this: If I'm never vulnerable, I may end up making myself physically ill by holding inside all my feelings and never sharing them with anyone. I may make some stupid mistakes because I try to solve my own problems and don't avail myself of the advice of someone with expertise. I may deprive myself of some healthy friendships and thus may end up offending someone who desired to be my friend.

You Tried to Break the Pattern and Got Hurt

One day you meet someone from outside your family who seems worthy of your trust. Outwardly, this person seems very different from the family members who have hurt you. What you do not realize is that you have picked up on some hidden signals that tell you this person is like the people in your family when it comes to processing emotions. You are not conscious of these hidden signals. You are conscious of being attracted to this person. Something feels right. You swing from total emotional isolation to total vulnerability. You have little experience in trusting, but when you trust, you go all the way. Maybe it is a friendship. Perhaps it is a dating relationship. Maybe it is a marriage.

You do not realize it, but this person has a hidden emotional dysfunction. You sense it, and it makes you feel at home, but you are not consciously aware of it. In your family of origin, dysfunctional emotional relationships felt normal. Now you have been attracted to someone who communicates an emotional undercurrent that makes you "feel at home."

It happened again!

Eventually, you get hurt. Besides the pain of the disappointment in the relationship itself, you are hurt in another way. Your resolve not to trust has grown stronger. "See, it happened again," you tell yourself.

✎ **Have you been drawn into other dysfunctional relationships outside your family of origin? List examples below indicating what drew you into the relationship and how it has affected your willingness to be vulnerable. You may need to use additional sheets of paper for this.**

_____

_____

Here are some answers that one person wrote to this question: I was drawn into a friendship with another person who, like me, was an adult child of an alcoholic. This person was open and friendly, unlike people in my family who were reserved and emotionless. He had not processed any issues in his life, so he related in hurtful ways. When I tried to talk about subjects that were anything more than surface, he seemed to back off from me. When he was having difficulty at work and I tried to give him some advice, he treated me rudely. Eventually I felt that this relationship which seemed to have such potential at the outset was hurting me more than helping.

Face Your Compulsions

✎ The compulsive behaviors I am working on are: _____

_____

Below describe how you managed these compulsive behaviors yesterday.

_____

_____

Can you identify emotions you are feeling before you engage in these behaviors—for example, when you are tired, sad, lonely? Below write your response.

_____

Work on Turning Points

➤ Turn to the Reconciliation Worksheet in the back of the book to see the format you will use for your list of people you have wronged. Begin thinking about the people who need to be on your reconciliation list. Stop and pray, asking God for guidance.

DAY 2

Today's Objective:
You will discover the vulnerability of Jesus and will be challenged to follow His example.

Strength, not weakness

But I, when I am lifted up from the earth, will draw all men to myself.

John 12:32

Vulnerable Means Being Like Jesus

Jesus Lived a Vulnerable Life

The biblical writer Paul explained that Jesus' coming to earth was an act of vulnerability. He came from the presence and power of God the Father to the humility and helplessness of a baby born in a manger. Here's what Philippians 2:5-8 says about this act: "Your attitude should be the same as that of Christ Jesus: Who, being in very nature God, did not consider equality with God something to be grasped, but made himself nothing, taking the very nature of a servant, being made in human likeness. And being found in appearance as a man, he humbled himself and became obedient to death—even death on a cross!"

Jesus chose to become vulnerable. He removed Himself from His place in heaven to come to the earth as a baby. What is more vulnerable than a baby? A baby cannot go where it wants to go. Somebody else has to meet a baby's every basic need. Jesus came to earth in a vulnerable form. He became a baby—crying, hungry, and helpless. His very entrance into Bethlehem was a mark of extreme vulnerability.

Jesus Showed His Vulnerability

Specific things that happened during Jesus' life point to His lifestyle of vulnerability. Jesus made Himself vulnerable to the disciples. He had come to change the world. He had come to show humanity the identity of God. The disciples were slow to understand His mission. His whole ministry hung in the balance of how His disciples responded to his ministry. Jesus could have said, "I'm not going to depend on these men. I am going to do it by Myself." He trusted them, and in that trusting He made Himself vulnerable to them.

When Jesus heard that His friend Lazarus had died, He wept. He knew that He was going to bring Lazarus back to life, but He felt the sadness of the moment. He was strong, but He could cry and let others see Him cry. He was vulnerable.

The Gospel writers tell us on several occasions that Jesus was tired. He was God but in human form. In becoming a man He became subject to exhaustion. The tiredness of Jesus points to His willingness to be vulnerable.

Jesus permitted His enemies to arrest Him. He was humiliated. He was whipped and later nailed to the cross. He chose to say yes to this form of death. He knew it was what He was supposed to do, and He chose to do it.

Jesus turned the cross into the ultimate symbol of vulnerability. Read the verse appearing in the margin to see what He said about this. The cross has great drawing power. When we see Jesus on the cross, we see vulnerability. We see Him stripped of everything, not just His clothes, but His very life and His dignity. It is all gone. A power greater than anything I have ever seen or known draws me to the cross. The cross is a horrendous thing, and yet it draws me to it. What is it that draws me to the cross? It is love—the sacrifice of Jesus for me. It is His vulnerability—the pain He was willing to feel and experience for me.

✎ **Based on what you just read about Jesus's vulnerability, check below the statements that are true.**

❑ 1. Jesus could have done His earthly work on His own but decided to make Himself vulnerable by trusting the disciples.
❑ 2. Jesus showed His vulnerability by letting others see Him express the human emotion of sadness.
❑ 3. The thought of the love that Jesus showed for humanity on the cross turns Jesus' act of vulnerability on the cross into a symbol of power and not of weakness.

Jesus' vulnerable acts of trusting the disciples, letting others see Him express sadness, and dying on the cross all were means of drawing people to Himself. His exhaustion did not dilute the impact of His message; it showed that He was doing what He came to earth to do. All the statements in the above exercise are true.

He became obedient to death—even death on a cross.

Philippians 2:8

Jesus was vulnerable. He was the strongest man in the world, but He was vulnerable. He was vulnerable not because somebody forced Him to be, but because He decided to be vulnerable. Read Paul's words appearing in the margin. Though He was vulnerable, Jesus was strong. He wept at Lazarus' death, but then He brought Lazarus back to life. He was tired at times, but He overcame the limitations of the physical world. He was put to death on the cross, but He turned the cross into a victory.

Jesus taught us the power of vulnerability. Vulnerability is a choice. Vulnerability does not mean you are afraid to assert yourself. Jesus was assertive, but He also was vulnerable. Are you willing to follow the example of Jesus in this aspect of His life?

✎ **Are you willing to be like Jesus in the area of vulnerability? What would you need to change in your life to do this?**

_____

_____

Face Your Compulsions

✎ **The compulsive behaviors I am working on are:** _____

_____

Below describe how you managed these compulsive behaviors yesterday.

_____

Can you identify emotions you are feeling before you engage in these behaviors—for example, when you are tired, sad, lonely? Below write your response.

_____

_____

Work on Turning Points

 Review the Reconciliation Worksheet in the back of the book. Continue thinking about the people who need to be on your reconciliation list. Also, what are you willing to do this week to express vulnerability toward selected safe people? Ask God for guidance.

 Begin learning this week's Scripture memory verse, Philippians 2:8. Write it three times in the margin.

Today's Objective:
You will learn the difference between vulnerability and weakness.

Vulnerable Does Not Mean Weakness

Vulnerability Versus Weakness

The idea of vulnerability may cause you to react negatively because it sounds a lot like something you have been trying to get away from: WEAKNESS! If you have struggled with letting people walk over you and if you have had little or no assertiveness in your life, the challenge to be vulnerable may sound like the worst possible option for you.

People who are codependent frequently engage in an unhealthy form of passiveness. Here are some of its marks:

1. I don't know what I want.
2. I am not sure I have a right to want anything.
3. When I want something, I cannot ask for it directly.
4. If someone else wants something, I must ignore my needs.

 Can you identify with any of the four statements above? Which ones? Why?

_____

_____

_____

An act of choice and strength

If you are working to free yourself from the web of codependency, a call to vulnerability may repulse you because it sounds too much like the unhealthy emotional pattern that has characterized your life. Vulnerability does not mean the same thing as weakness. Vulnerability is an act of choice and strength.

Codependency says, "I don't know what I want; therefore, I will make what others want a priority in my life." Vulnerability is a choice to let your feelings, your needs, and your wants show. It is a willingness to be open to a person in a way that permits emotional closeness. Such openness may result in emotional pain and disappointment because the other person may choose not to respond to your needs. You know this risk, and knowing the risk, you choose to become vulnerable.

Codependency says, "I don't have a right to want anything." You exercise vulnerability within the context of understanding that you have needs and

*Letting someone know what you
need and want means
taking off masks.*

wants and that having needs and wants is normal. Vulnerability means that you will let another person know you with the awareness that knowing you means knowing your needs and wants. Letting someone know you in that way means taking off masks. It means risking rejection.

Codependency says, "When I want something, I cannot ask for it directly." Vulnerability is not being silent about needs. It is being willing to share a need and know that someone may choose to say yes or no to your request.

Jesus taught us the power of vulnerability.

Codependency says, "If someone else wants something, then I must ignore my needs." Vulnerability means being sensitive to the needs of other people while being honest about my own needs. Vulnerability means working together in a relationship to set priorities for meeting needs. I may not get everything I want. I may not be able to give the other person everything he or she wants. It is a matter of give and take which involves some degree of risk, but it is not a matter of automatically denying my own feelings whenever anyone else has a need.

For example, Chuck seemed always to be buying new clothes while his wife Christine felt she was stuck with the same wardrobe year after year. Christine wished that just once, she could go out on a shopping spree after payday, but she felt that she should set aside that wish since appearance seemed to be more important to Chuck's job than it was to her role as a full-time homemaker. Christine thought she should ignore her needs in deference to Chuck. She thought if she spoke up and Chuck refused, she would look weak.

In studying about codependency, however, Christine learned that she actually looked weak when she failed to speak up for her needs. When she mustered her courage and told Chuck that she wanted to buy a new dress next payday, Chuck was genuinely shocked.

Chuck thought Christine had given up caring about her appearance after their last child was born. Her weakness about *not* speaking up eventually could have had some serious implications for their marriage in the long run if Chuck continued to perceive that Christine was refusing to care for her appearance.

The fact that Christine expressed her wishes didn't negate the fact that Chuck needed an ample wardrobe in his job, but the two of them were able to map out a plan whereby the needs of both husband and wife were met. Christine's decision to become vulnerable by expressing her needs led to growth in her marriage.

As a follower of Christ, I frequently will make a conscious choice to place the needs of others above my own needs, but when I do so it should be a choice that grows out of my willingness to be loving, vulnerable, and sacrificial, not a codependent drive to deny the needs that actually are present in my life.

✎ In your own words, write a sentence that describes the difference between vulnerability and codependent passiveness.

_____

_____

Face Your Compulsions

✎ The compulsive behaviors I am working on are: _____

_____

Below describe how you managed these compulsive behaviors yesterday.

_____

_____

Can you identify emotions you are feeling before you engage in these behaviors—for example, when you are tired, sad, lonely? Below write your response.

_____

Work on Turning Points

➤ Continue to work on the Reconciliation Worksheet in the back of your book. What amends will you need to be make? Stop and pray, asking God to guide you as you study about making amends.

✎ Continue to memorize this unit's Scripture memory verse. In the margin write what this verse means to you.

➤ Pray for each member of your Heart-to-Heart group by name today. Pray that each person in your group would learn to be vulnerable.

DAY 4

Today's Objective:
You will learn how to develop boundaries.

Vulnerable Does Not Mean Doormat

What Are Boundaries?

Vulnerability and boundaries go together. You might think that being vulnerable means having no boundaries and letting anyone do whatever he or she wants to you. Actually vulnerability will not work without boundaries. Boundaries are limits you place on how other people relate to you.

You have a right to set boundaries. Abusive behavior violates boundaries. If you grew up in a dysfunctional family, family members may have violated certain boundaries. You may have believed that you had no right to have boundaries. Try saying aloud, "I have a right to set boundaries for my life."

Physical Boundaries

We see a simple illustration of a boundary in what occurs when you stand too close to someone. If you are talking to someone who has healthy physical boundaries and move to within one inch of that individual's face, he or she will step back. He or she will step back because you have violated that person's physical boundary. This physical boundary is an invisible circle around a person that says, "Do not come any closer without my permission." Boundaries flex depending on the situation and the person involved. If the same person's two-year-old child is one inch away from him, he may choose to pull the child closer in a warm hug.

Losing the sense of self-protection

If someone abused you physically when you were a child, you may have lost the sense of protecting or even having physical boundaries. You may be willing to let other people violate your physical boundaries by hurting you physically. You even may accept such behavior as normal. Physical boundaries are a way of saying, "I have a right to say what happens to my body. I have a right to say what is painful to me and to stop it."

Sexual Boundaries

Sexual boundaries are your limits on what happens to you sexually. Having sexual boundaries means you can say what you permit and what you don't permit in terms of your own sexual involvement with another person.

Powerless over one's body

People who have been sexually abused sometimes lose a sense of having the right to give or to deny others permission to be involved with them in a sexual way. For example, they may not even be aware that an individual on a date has a right to say, "I really enjoy our relationship, but I plan to wait until after I'm married to have sexual intercourse."

Perhaps when you were a child, someone touched you in an inappropriate sexual manner. At first you did not understand what was happening. You did not know what to do. As the behavior continued, you felt trapped, and you probably were trapped. You lost the sense of power over your body. The imprint stuck. You began to think of yourself as a person who had to say yes whenever anyone wanted to be sexually involved with you. You did not know you had right to say, "Stop that. I will not let you touch me in that manner."

After a while, you may have added another problem to the absence of sexual boundaries. You may have become addicted to the sexual behavior which at first you could not refuse. In this case two issues are occurring in your life. The first issue is re-establishing sexual boundaries. The second issue is breaking an addictive pattern of behavior. Another possible response to sexual abuse is an inability to experience a healthy sexual relationship in marriage.

 Go back to the above paragraphs on physical and sexual boundaries. Underline statements that indicate what a person would say to establish physical and sexual boundaries in his or her life.

Emotional Boundaries

What will you let other people do with your emotions? Will you freely permit them to use rage to control you? Will you let someone use pity to repeatedly manipulate your feelings and your behavior? Will you cave in under the shame another person imposes upon you? These are examples of emotional boundary violations.

You have the right to your own feelings. Emotional enmeshment occurs when you begin to live someone else's feelings. Think about how a trailer connects to a car. The brake lights on the trailer are connected to the car so that when the driver presses the brake, not only do the brake lights on the car illuminate, the brake lights on the trailer light up as well. The brake lights on the trailer are slaves to the brake lights on the car. Emotional enmeshment means being the brake lights on the trailer. When the other person is sad, you are sad. When the other person is happy, you think you are happy.

Slavery to others' emotions

Trevor was a slave to the emotions of his elderly mother. If he arrived at her home to find her full of self-pity, he was miserable the rest of the day. Even though his mother had plenty of opportunities to get out of the house and socialize with others, she refused to do so. Instead she turned a guilt trip on Trevor by criticizing him for taking his children to the movies instead of spending time with her. Trevor became like the brake lights on the trailer to his mother. His mood swings that were parallel to his mother's mood swings were beginning to have an effect on his marriage.

You have the right to emotional autonomy. You act appropriately when you empathize with others when you choose to do so. Empathy by choice is not the same thing as emotional enmeshment. You can experience life as a free-standing individual. You can stand up for your rights. You can state your position. You can have your own feelings.

Spiritual Boundaries
Some people violate spiritual boundaries by using religion to control and to intimidate. A healthy spiritual life means a daily walk with Christ in which we sense God's love and forgiveness. The Bible contains warnings that should produce a healthy fear in us. The Bible tells us that we should feel godly sorrow for some things we do. However, the message of the Bible is that God in His very essence is love. God forgives when we repent of our sins. God offers us hope. When religion loses sight of God's love and forgiveness and speaks only of shame and fear, spiritual boundaries have been violated. When a child's spiritual boundaries are violated, that child may have difficulty responding to the message of God's love.

A shame-and-fear religion

The Pharisees of Jesus' day violated people's spiritual boundaries. They heaped religious rules on people. They worried about sin, but they could not recognize the love of God even when they were eye to eye with Jesus.

 You just read about four types of boundaries—physical, sexual, emotional, and spiritual. With which boundaries do you still struggle?

_____

 Stop and pray, asking God to help you learn to establish boundaries.

How Do Boundaries Differ from Walls?

Boundaries are flexible. Walls are rigid. Boundaries are like filters that determine what I permit to enter my life. Boundaries are selective. Walls are barriers that not only block out pain but also joy.

Filtering what enters

When your boundaries are damaged, walls may seem like the only alternative. You need some way to protect yourself. With walls you shut out feelings and people. Sometimes the energy required to keep the walls up is too great. You get lonely behind the walls. In a moment of weakness, the wall falls down. What enters is a gamble. If you had boundaries, you could filter what enters your life. With the temporary collapse of your wall, inappropriate people and/or feelings enter. You get hurt again. The wall goes back up.

How Do Boundaries and Vulnerability Go Together?

Boundaries help you to be selective about vulnerability. Living without boundaries is not vulnerability; it is self-destructive, sick, and painful. Boundaries mean I can decide when and where and with whom I will be vulnerable. Granted, I do not ever have complete control over my vulnerability; that is part of being human. However, with boundaries I can help determine the direction of my life and relationships. I can decide who gets close and who does not get close. With walls, no one gets close. With boundaries I may decide what hurts and say no to it. I can discern what is right and what feels good to me and encourage it.

With walls, no one gets close.

In dealing with his mother, Trevor had two choices—he could put up a wall or institute a boundary. Putting up a wall would have sounded like this: "Mother, your demands on me are ruining my life. You'll never see me around here again." Or perhaps Trevor would have put up his wall in a passive way. He simply would stop going to his mother's house with no explanation. Either way he would be acting irresponsibly.

✎ **Below describe why putting up a wall could be self-destructive in Trevor's life.**

_____

_____

One person responded to this activity this way: In his anger Trevor could miss the fact that his mother might get sick and genuinely need his attention. This could leave a permanent scar on his life if something happened to his mother because of his neglect.

✎ **Below describe how Trevor might respond to his mother if he were to institute healthy boundaries in the situation.**

_____

_____

Doing all you can within limits

Trevor could decide that he would not allow his mother's self-pity to affect him. He could give her schedules of seniors' groups or church activities that she might enjoy and could arrange for her transportation. If she refused to participate, Trevor could recognize that he was not responsible for her choices. He could tell her the days he could visit her and days he would not be available. Through this, Trevor would communicate to his mother, "This I will do. This I won't do." In this way Trevor could feel that he had acted responsibly toward his mother without depriving his family of his presence.

What are two things you need to do to become vulnerable in a healthy way?

1. _____

2. _____

Face Your Compulsions

 The compulsive behaviors I am working on are: _____

_____

Below describe how you managed these compulsive behaviors yesterday.

_____

_____

Work on Turning Points

 Continue working on the Reconciliation Worksheet in your book. Do you blame someone for your compulsive behavior? What are you willing to do to express vulnerability toward selected safe people?

DAY 5

Today's Objective:
You will work on Turning Point 7, "I am willing to be vulnerable with selected safe people."

Don't create more pain

Vulnerable Means Admitting Mistakes

One form of vulnerability is admitting my mistakes. When I hurt people and do not acknowledge the pain I cause them, I build walls in these relationships. I destroy emotional intimacy by repeatedly hurting someone without confession or restitution on my part.

Turning Point 7 states, "I am willing to be vulnerable with selected safe people. I will make a list of the people I have wronged." Making amends does not mean you must undo all the wrong you have done. That would be impossible. Making amends means you attempt to bring healing to the relationships that you have injured. You tell the person you are sorry. If you have said unkind things, you apologize. If you broke promises, you talk about it. You may need to do some symbolic act. A gift might be appropriate. You may need to return something that you took.

Avoid getting into a compulsive attempt to relive your life–to undo every ounce of pain you caused. No one can do such a thing. Ask God to help you know what restitution you need to make. Do not be overwhelmed by having unrealistic expectations that you can undo all the wrong you have done.

Avoid creating more pain in your attempt to make amends. Mary approached Linda and said, "For years I hated you. I am sorry. I ask your forgiveness." Linda never thought things were not OK with Mary. Mary approached her to bring healing to the relationship, but Linda did not know the relationship was broken. In this situation, Mary caused pain while she was attempting to make amends.

✎ **Below describe how Mary could have made amends more effectively without causing additional pain.**

_____

_____

Mary would have done better to simply confess to God that she hated Linda. She could have made amends without ever telling Linda that she hated her. She could have taken some positive actions without ever mentioning the negative feelings that Linda did not know about anyway. Sometimes the problem is in the open, and we should address it directly. At other times a more subtle approach may be best. Making amends should not create new pain. It should bring a healing of existing pain and brokenness.

Face Your Compulsions

✎ The compulsive behaviors I am working on are: _____

_____

Below describe how you managed these compulsive behaviors yesterday.

_____

_____

Can you identify emotions you are feeling before you engage in these behaviors—for example, when you are tired, sad, lonely? Below write your response.

_____

Work on Turning Points

Now, read again the seventh turning point that you've been working on during this unit.

> ### Turning Point 7
> I am willing to be vulnerable with selected safe people.

✎ **Use the Reconciliation Worksheet to complete your list of the people you have wronged. Ask God for guidance.**

UNIT 12

In this Unit you'll work on—
Turning Point 8
I will share my feelings and my failures with selected safe people.

Sharing

The Outward Cycle: An attitude of VULNERABILITY accompanied by the action of SHARING leads to INTIMACY.

> ## PUTTING FEET TO HIS WORDS
>
> Charlie did not trust Bob, so he spread rumors about him. He gossiped about him in hopes that Bob would have trouble at work. He achieved his goal; co-workers began snubbing Bob because of the things Charlie told them. Later Charlie learned that the stories he told others about Bob were untrue. He also got to know Bob better and realized that Bob was a decent, honorable person and not a threat as Charlie first believed.
>
> In recovery Charlie learned that his reaction to Bob had grown out of trust issues from Charlie's childhood. Charlie realized he had caused Bob great harm. He asked for Bob's forgiveness, but he went beyond just saying, "I'm sorry." Charlie went to each person to whom he had gossiped and told them that he had spread false information. Then he used his influence at work to get Bob appointed to a significant committee. Charlie's amends went beyond mere words–he put feet to his words and went out of his way to try to restore Bob's good name.
>
> (On page 185 read more about how making amends like Charlie did can bring healing in our lives.)

Why you will find this unit useful

We want to achieve emotional intimacy as part of our quest for recovery and healing. To reach this goal we cultivate an attitude of vulnerability. Being vulnerable means we selectively choose to risk being hurt by others because we know such vulnerability is a part of a trusting relationship. We learn to make good choices about relationships. The desired outcome is emotional intimacy. The attitude to cultivate is vulnerability, but we need more than an attitude. We must take steps to share ourselves with others to experience emotional intimacy. This week we will explore the action of sharing as it relates to your emotional and spiritual recovery. You will be challenged to make some contact with the persons on your reconciliation list with a goal of moving toward healing in these relationships.

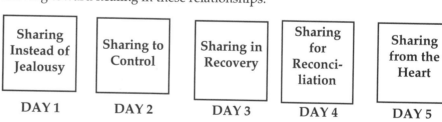

Sharing Instead of Jealousy	Sharing to Control	Sharing in Recovery	Sharing for Reconciliation	Sharing from the Heart
DAY 1	DAY 2	DAY 3	DAY 4	DAY 5

This week's memory verse

Give, and it will be given to you. A good measure, pressed down, shaken together and running over, will be poured into your lap. For with the measure you use, it will be measured to you.
                                                                        –Luke 6:38

Sharing Instead of Jealousy

Identifying the Cycle of Pain

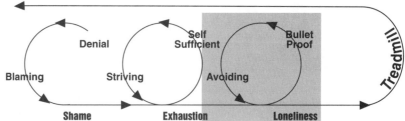

Today's Objective
You will learn how the losses you experienced in a dysfunctional family may lead to a lifestyle of jealousy.

Think about this story: "Two shopkeepers were bitter rivals. Their stores were directly across the street from each other, and they would spend each day keeping track of each other's business. If one got a customer, he would smile in triumph at his rival. One night an angel appeared to one of the shopkeepers in a dream and said, 'I will give you anything you ask, but whatever you receive, your competitor will receive twice as much. Would you be rich? You can be very rich, but he will be twice as wealthy. Do you wish to live a long and healthy life? You can, but his life will be longer and healthier. What is your desire?' The man frowned, thought for a moment, and then said, 'Here is my request: Strike me blind in one eye!' "[1]

This man stood face to face with a fantastic opportunity to share of himself with others, but he chose a very unwise and selfish alternative.

When you grow up in a dysfunctional family, you may not realize how much other families struggle. You imagine problem-free family living in their homes. What they seem to have intensifies your pain.

Haves and have nots

You grow up in emotional isolation. You see others who receive emotional nurture. You work to get for yourself what someone gives them freely. A part of you commits to rise above your situation. You work to achieve goals. Perhaps you succeed. Maybe you fail. Either way, you learn to look at other people as "OK" and yourself as "not OK." They are the "haves." You are the "have not."

This inner attitude can be so strong that even when you reach your goals, you still may feel that you are less a person than others are. You maintain this feeling by minimizing your accomplishments and maximizing others' attainments. You never stop to commend yourself for your last achievement.

At one level you simply long to feel happy inside. At another level you feel jealous about the good fortune of others. You are different. You never can be like them. You never can have what they have. At least that is how you feel. You may live on the same street and make as much money as those you envy, but long ago you learned to feel inferior.

Rick's story

Rick knew that his friend Michael was going on a business trip to Switzerland. Rick was jealous because he always had wanted to visit that country. He felt inferior because Michael had the opportunity. When Michael left for his trip, Rick never told him goodbye or wished him a good time. When Michael returned, Rick hardly spoke to him. Michael told Rick he'd like to take him to lunch and share with him about his trip. Rick replied rudely to Michael, "I don't think I'd be interested, thanks." Rick couldn't congratulate Michael on his good fortune because he was consumed with jealousy and inferiority.

Several months later Rick got a chance to go to Switzerland on a church trip. At last, he thought, I'll do something that makes me happy. On his trip to Switzerland Rick saw the same parts of the country Michael did. He took basically the same trip as Michael did, but when he returned home, he didn't feel the happiness that he desired. He still felt inferior to Michael.

 Have you ever been in this kind of situation where jealousy and feeling inferior kept you from rejoicing over someone else's joy? Below describe how this affected you.

_____

_____

Depriving you of joy

You may have answered that you wanted to rejoice over a friend's promotion but couldn't because jealousy ate away at you. You may have attended a relative's vocal performance, but because envy consumed you, you slipped away without congratulating her on a job well done. Regardless of what kind of situation you described, your jealousy deprived you of an opportunity for intimacy that could have brought you joy if you had allowed it.

Jealousy Blocks Sharing
Sharing yourself with others is difficult when the feeling consumes you that no matter how much you have, others always have more. Giving is difficult when you believe that what you have to share has no worth. Outwardly, you may appear selfish. Inwardly, you feel impoverished.

Jealousy and Blame Work Well Together
Dysfunctional families major on blame. "Whose fault was it?" is a major question in the dysfunctional family. Jealousy and blame go hand in hand. You can blame the people you envy for the emotional pain you feel.

Jealousy Is Like a Tumor
Outwardly, jealousy seems like a way to assert your rights and to protect yourself. Actually, jealousy is a deadly boomerang that destroys your energy for spiritual and emotional health. Jealousy keeps you from facing the truth about yourself. What is your responsibility for the pain that has occurred in your relationships?

Which of three byproducts of jealousy you just reviewed do you experience most often? Write your answer in the margin box.

Do you really have to be the greatest person in the world? As a child you may have felt like you only had two alternatives: (1) disappear in the whirlpool of emotional pain your family created, or (2) rise to the top of the ladder and fight off anyone who tries to unseat you.

Another alternative exists. You can be an emotionally healthy and happy person who does some good and makes some mistakes. You even can learn to admire others who excel. You can learn to congratulate winners. You can learn to feel like a normal person. You can learn to congratulate yourself for your significant achievements.

> **How jealousy affects me—**
>
> _____
>
> _____
>
> _____
>
> _____

Face Your Compulsions

✎ The compulsive behaviors I am working on are: _____

_____

Below describe how you managed these compulsive behaviors yesterday.

_____

_____

Can you identify any connection between your compulsive behavior and the material you studied today? Below write your response.

_____

Work on Turning Points

Does jealousy keep you from sharing your feelings and failures with selected safe people? ❑ Yes ❑ No

Of what are you jealous? _____

_____

Of whom are you jealous? _____

_____

➤ Begin to memorize this unit's Scripture memory verse, Luke 6:38. In the margin write the verse in your own words three times.

Sharing to Control

Today's Objective
You will discover how sharing of yourself with others can be a cover for controlling behavior.

Adult children of dysfunctional families may share for a variety of wrong reasons. In today's lesson we'll discuss these reasons. These reasons can be–
• Sharing to Gain Control
• Sharing to Become Invulnerable
• Sharing from Low Self-Esteem
• Sharing Instead of Asking for Help
• Sharing to Avoid Intimacy
• Sharing Out of Fear of an Angry God

Sharing to Gain Control

Sometimes nice people are controlling people. An adult child who assumed a family role such as "the hero," or "daddy's little princess" does not permit himself/herself to be "bad." He/she must be nice. Nice people don't take. They give. Nice people share. Nice people do what others want them to do.

The person who thinks this way has to find some release. When I pretend that my individual needs do not exist, I live in denial. If I cannot permit myself to address my needs directly, I will find a way to address them indirectly. I will find a way to get what I need while I pretend that I don't need anything.

Sacrificing values

I will learn ways of quietly getting from others while I obviously give a great deal to them. One of my recurring messages may be, "After I have done so much for you, how could you be unwilling to do this one little thing for me?" The problem is that the "one little thing" may be a big thing to the person I am addressing. It may involve sacrificing values, priorities, or even identity. I expect you to sense my needs even though I do not clearly voice them to you. When I live this way, I will wonder why so few of my needs are met .

 Go back to the previous three paragraphs. Underline words or phrases that you believe describe some of the ways you share to gain control.

Jesus told a story about the judgment. In the story two types of people appear. The first group of people receive praise from Jesus. He says, "For I was hungry and you gave me something to eat, I was thirsty, and you gave me something to drink" (Matthew 25:35). They reply, "When did we see you hungry and feed you, or thirsty and give you something to drink?" (Matthew 25:37) They were surprised that they had done something to help Jesus. Jesus replies, "I tell you the truth, whatever you did for one of the least of these brothers of mine, you did for me" (Matthew 25:40). Jesus was not saying that we earn admission to heaven. Entrance into heaven results from receiving God's grace through faith. Jesus was saying that a mark of true faith is that His followers give unselfishly to others. The people's faith was evident in the way they had responded to Jesus—with no thought of giving to gain a reward.

Jesus tells the second group of people to depart from Him. He says they saw Jesus in need and did not respond. The people in this group reply, "When did we see *You* (author's italics) hungry or thirsty or a stranger . . . and did not help you?"(Matthew 25:44) They seemed to say, "Jesus, if we had known it was You, we certainly would have stopped to help."

Some people give to get. Giving to get is one characteristic of codependent living. The codependent person says, "I don't have a right to have needs. I exist to meet other people's needs." Another part of the codependent person says, "Help! I am hurting inside. Perhaps, if I try harder, if I give more, then others will give me what I need."

Dysfunctional families feel out of control. The child emerging from such a family makes a silent promise, "Whatever I do, I never will let others control me this way again." Staying in control is a priority. One way to control people is to give to them—to obligate them. When I have given you what I think you need, then I may be able to use shame and guilt to control your behavior. When I live this way, my gifts have hooks on them. After one of these hooks has caught you, you learn to be wary of my gifts. You put up your guard, and emotional intimacy is a few steps further away.

 Below describe a time you gave in order to get something back.

_____

_____

Perhaps your answer to the question was something like Sheila's. She told her support group this story: "I helped my friend find a job because I knew her family was financially strapped. I did this because I thought this would make her indebted to me. Then she would pay more attention to me because she felt obligated to me. She won't dare turn me down because of how I helped rescue her." Sheila certainly understood about hooks and how to use them.

Sharing to Become Invulnerable

If I give myself to you sacrificially, you will have a difficult time criticizing me. You may be angry with me at times, but I can expect you to remember how much I have done for you. If you do criticize me, I can move into a martyr role. "Poor me. I have done so much for you. Look what I get for it." I count on my martyr responses to push you back into enough shame and guilt to make you realize how much you owe me. If these techniques work, I have made myself invulnerable to your criticisms. I also have made the possibility of emotional intimacy even more remote.

A martyr role

✎ Sheila's friend Betsy appreciated what Sheila had done for her, but she also started growing irritated with Sheila when she made so many demands on her. Below write what you think might happen if Betsy expressed her feelings of irritation to Sheila.

_____

_____

Sharing from Low Self-Esteem

I may not be aware of how my behavior manipulates. I may feel that I do not have a right to ask for help. I learned this concept in my family of origin. An addictive parent was the focus of our family. All other needs took a back seat. Such self-loathing is not what Jesus taught. Before He was crucified, Jesus took the attire of a servant and washed the disciples' feet (John 13). He acted from strength, not weakness. He served the disciples out of a clear sense of who He was. He did not give to get but gave out of the fullness of who He was.

Jesus served the disciples out of a clear sense of who He was.

Sharing Instead of Asking for Help

If I have learned that I could not ask someone to meet my emotional needs, I will seek other ways to ask for help. One method is doing for others what I wish someone would do for me. I even may hope subconsciously that after I perform an act of kindness, the recipient will ask what I want in return. If that person asks me, I still may be unable to ask for what I need.

✎ After reading the previous three paragraphs about sharing, check which one of the following statements is true.

    ❑ 1. Jesus washed His disciples' feet because He was weak.
    ❑ 2. In an addictive family children learn to speak up for what they need.
    ❑ 3. A person who manipulates others always knows exactly what he/she is doing.
    ❑ 4. If someone asks me what's wrong, I likely will be unable to tell them.

Identifying my feelings and speaking up for what I need is very difficult for a person from a dysfunctional family. That person much more easily can share in hopes of getting someone to do something nice in return. The last statement was true; the rest were false.

Sharing to Avoid Intimacy

I may take a job—volunteer or paid—that is based on giving to others. This may be a volunteer task at church. Ironically, this may be an unhealthy substitute for emotional closeness with significant people in my life. I may get closer to the people I help in my job than I am to my own family. Being close to my family is frightening and difficult to control. So much possibility for pain exists there. Instead I will build another kind of closeness within a controlled framework of professional or volunteer help to others.

Sheila tried to lose herself in church work. That ensured that she had little time at home to remind her of how she lacked closeness with her family. Have you ever lost yourself in church work or any other kind of seemingly worthwhile activity for the wrong reason? If so write in the margin box to describe the situation.

Sharing Out of a Fear of an Angry God

If I confuse God with an angry controlling parent, I may give of myself because I am afraid not to do so. The Bible teaches us to fear God in terms of respecting Him. The Bible also teaches that perfect love casts out fear (see 1 John 4:18.) A healthy relationship with God is based on love, not on fear.

Realizing that she shared of herself because she feared an angry God is what caused Sheila to become aware that she needed to work on past issues in her life. Sheila heard a speaker talk about how a person's relationship with parents affected that person's perception of God. Sheila realized that as a child she did good deeds because she was terrified of her parents and was a "good" child out of fear of them. This prompted her to study why she was serving in her church and doing other good deeds for people. As she learned that God's love was not based on her performance, she began to study more closely some of the other reasons behind her sharing with others, This experience launched Sheila into a whole new way of relating to people.

Face Your Compulsions

✎ The compulsive behaviors I am working on are: _____

_____

Below describe how you managed these compulsive behaviors yesterday.

_____

_____

_____

Times I've done a worthwhile activity for the wrong reason—

_____

_____

_____

_____

There is no fear in love. But perfect love drives out fear, because fear has to do with punishment. The one who fears is not made perfect in love.

1 John 4:18

Can you identify any connection between your compulsive behavior and the material you studied today? Below write your response.

_____

Work on Turning Points

✎ **Do you give in order to control others?**

If yes, list three examples: _____

_____

_____

Who are the people this behavior has hurt? _____

_____

How does this affect your ability to share your feelings and failures with selected safe people?

_____

_____

✎ Write in the margin three times this unit's Scripture memory verse.

DAY 3

Today's Objective
You will learn some guidelines for sharing in the context of a recovery lifestyle.

Sharing in Recovery

Connecting with the Cycle of Recovery

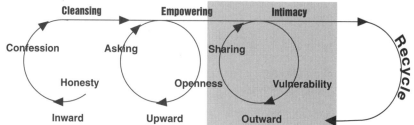

Cleansing · Empowering · Intimacy
Confession · Asking · Sharing
Honesty · Openness · Vulnerability
Inward · Upward · Outward
Recycle

Sharing of yourself in recovery starts with knowing how to take care of your own emotional needs. As a Christian, this idea may frighten you. You are committed to following the example of Christ who gave of Himself in service to other people. The idea of taking care of yourself may sound as if you are selling out on your faith. Take time to understand what sharing of yourself in recovery means. You are able to more effectively help other people when you have learned to identify and respond to your own needs.

Sometimes the Pendulum Swings

During the early stages of recovery, people who know you may think you are self-centered. If you have lived a codependent lifestyle in which you always

Those who know you may not see your move toward emotional health as positive.

said yes to everything someone asked you to do, a shift toward sensing your own needs will seem radical to those who know you. They have learned to depend on your codependency. At first they may not see your move toward emotional health as positive. At times even you may wonder if you have become a selfish person.

Dave's children had him on a string. At 8:30 every night—just as Dave was about to relax for the first time that day—his children approached him with their lists. "Dad, I just remembered that I need a new package of pencils for class," or "Please run to the store and get this t-shirt for me. I just HAVE to have it," they'd say, night after night. Dave promised himself he'd be a good dad since his own father never was around to help him. No matter how tired he was, Dave always denied himself and said yes to their requests.

How I've dealt with my family's reaction—

_____

_____

_____

_____

_____

In recovery Dave learned that he needed to start thinking about himself as well. He told his children that from now on, he would buy school supplies only on weekends–except in the event of extreme emergency. He learned to set boundaries by telling children to write their needs on a list he posted on the refrigerator. Dave's children were horrified. They depended on his codependency. Dave had taken a move toward emotional health, but his children saw this as selfish. They wondered what had happened to good old reliable Dad. When they complained, Dave wondered if he truly had become selfish in his effort to meet his own needs for relaxation at the end of the day.

✎ Have you discovered this happening to you as you have begun your recovery journey? Have you discovered that as you've set boundaries family members have accused you of being selfish? In the margin box describe how you've dealt with the situation.

Keep in mind the dangers of continuing in the role of codependent helper. These dangers, which you will read about below, are:
• Codependent helpers burn out.
• Codependent helpers engage in denial.

Codependent Helpers Burn Out
In the early stages of my personal recovery, I had to face the fact that if I continued to live without being sensitive to my own emotional needs, I would reach a point of being unable to function. I could not go on the way I had been living. If I burned out, I would be unable to help anyone.

Codependent Helpers Engage in Denial

If I cannot admit how I hurt, I may not be able to see how you hurt.

People who deny their own needs can offer only a shallow kind of help to others. If I am blind to many of my basic needs, I may not be able to see your needs very clearly. If I cannot admit how I hurt, I may not be able to see how you hurt.

Sometimes the Pendulum Does Not Swing Back

Individuals who begin the process of spiritual and emotional recovery usually move into a "taking-care-of-me" stage. This swing away from just taking care of others is a natural adjustment that should lead to a balanced lifestyle of nurturing oneself, caring for others, and even self-sacrifice. However, some people get stuck in the "taking-care-of-me" stage and do not move toward a healthy balance.

Forgetting to be tactful

In recovery Natalie realized that she had spent much of her life living out the "Little Princess" role. In her family of origin she tried to be her mother's perfect child in an effort to divert some of the family's shame because of a neglectful father. As she processed these issues Natalie realized that she had spent much of her life never speaking up for her needs. This had caused difficulties in her marriage and in other relationships.

When Natalie began making mid-course corrections, the pendulum swung too far in the other direction. Natalie became so self-centered that she forgot to be tactful. Many of her remarks hurt those around her. In recovery she alienated many friends because she didn't understand about achieving the proper balance in her life.

 Have you discovered this happening to you as you have begun your recovery journey? Have you discovered that in your effort to set boundaries you've occasionally gone overboard and been hurtful or rude? In the margin box describe how you've reacted.

As you begin speaking up for your needs, you may tend to do whatever you do in the extreme. Remember that balance is possible and commendable. You can learn to be aware of your own needs while you still are sensitive to the needs of others.

Sharing in the Present Tense

Is it possible to be in recovery and to be a giving person? Yes! This is one of the aims of recovery. Are self-sacrifice and recovery compatible? Definitely!

> Helping others because I feel worthless is a crippling kind of self-sacrifice. Helping others because God has helped me is biblical.

When I discover God's love at the deepest part of myself, I learn that God values me. God made me and knows my needs. He says my needs are important. As I let God nurture me, I discover a greater wholeness. From that wholeness, I may choose to give of myself. I make this choice not because I am worthless. I make this choice not because I am perfect. I make this choice to give myself to others because I recognize my brokenness and God's love and power in my life. I choose to surrender. I choose to serve.

Here are some important points about sharing of myself. We'll read more about them in this lesson.
- Don't wait until you are perfect before you share.
- Don't wait until you have all you need before you share.
- When you share, share to give.
- When you share, share your heart.

Don't Wait Until You Are Perfect Before You Share
Beware of the attitude which says, "When I get everything straightened out, then I will share. When I get all these problems solved, then I can give to others." Do not wait for everything that is wrong in your life to be fixed before you start to help others. Recovery is a process. You can share yourself while that process is in progress.

> ## How I've overreacted in my recovery—
>
> _____
>
> _____
>
> _____
>
> _____
>
> _____

Don't Wait Until You Have All You Need Before You Share

Recovery is not meant to point you toward a self-centered lifestyle.

You will wait forever if you wait until all your needs are met to begin sharing. A basic aspect of spiritual wholeness in Christ is the fact that you become stronger as you minister to others. Recovery is not meant to point you toward a self-centered lifestyle. Part of recovery is learning to share with others.

When You Share, Share to Give

Codependent giving carries hidden motives and unseen hooks. Learn the simple act of sharing for sharing's sake. Learn to give without expecting anything back. Share yourself because that's who you are in Christ. Share yourself because Christ has made you a person of worth.

When You Share, Share Your Heart

People who share only *things* are lonely people. Learn to share your heart. Don't share it with just anyone. Evaluate the risk level when you share your heart. Sometimes you will choose to take a risk, but be aware of what you are doing. You must be willing to be vulnerable. Let another person know you and see you as you are. Share your pain and your joy.

✎ **After you read the previous four paragraphs about sharing, check which of the following statements is true:**

❏ 1. Sharing is good for me because it guarantees that someone will give me something in return.
❏ 2. I can have joy only when I share material items.
❏ 3. I don't have to wait until I'm whole to begin sharing.
❏ 4. All my needs must be met before I can share.

We can share starting right this minute; we don't have to wait until one of those "if-only" moments to achieve a perfect time when sharing can begin. We can share of ourselves—our time, our undivided attention, our affirmations, our interest—with others; these gifts of ourselves don't cost a nickel and mean far more than do material goods. Giving because of what we can get does not represent sincere sharing. The correct answer to the exercise you just worked is statement 3.

Face Your Compulsions

✎ **The compulsive behaviors I am working on are:** _____

_____

Below describe how you managed these compulsive behaviors yesterday.

_____

_____

Can you identify any connection between your compulsive behavior and the material you studied today? Below write your response.

_____

_____

Work on Turning Points

✎ **List three things you need to change about the way you share of yourself with other people.**

1. _____

2. _____

3. _____

Who have you hurt by this behavior? _____

_____

What do you need to do to make amends? _____

_____

➤ **Pray for each member of your Heart-to-Heart group by name. Ask God to teach each person about sharing of themselves.**

✎ **In the margin write this week's Scripture memory verse. In the verse underline the words or phrases that mean the most to you.**

DAY 4

Today's Objective
You will write a plan for implementing Turning Point 8, "I will share my feelings and my failures with selected safe people."

Sharing for Reconciliation

What Reconciliation Requires

An attitude of vulnerability combined with the action of sharing leads to emotional intimacy. For almost three weeks we have worked on the outward cycle of recovery. We seek meaningful emotional contact with other people. We have learned about the importance of becoming vulnerable. We are discovering that we can learn to share in a healthy way.

An important part of developing emotional intimacy with others involves addressing the hurts we have caused in other people's lives. Remembering and thinking about the pain you have caused others is painful in itself. You may be inclined to avoid thinking about it at all. "What good will it do?" you ask. You may fear the wave of shame and guilt that occurs when you think about the way you have hurt others. Facing the pain you have caused others is part of recovery. Ignoring the pain you have caused others is a form of denial.

Denying the pain you have caused others creates an emotional weight that you carry all the time. It hinders the building of positive self-esteem. It adds to the difficulty of dealing with other aspects of your past. It feeds an unhealthy attitude that says you are "less than" and unworthy. From a spiritual perspective, unresolved relationships with other people hurt your fellowship with God. Jesus taught us to make peace with people as we make our peace with God.

Part of the challenge of Turning Point 8 is to seek reconciliation with the people we have wronged. Reconciliation sometimes calls for making amends.

Here are some things to remember about making amends.
- Making amends is not salvation by works.
- Making amends is not rewriting history.
- Making amends is not manipulation.
- Making amends involves some risks.

Making Amends Is Not Salvation by Works
Making amends does not mean that you cancel out the wrong you have done. It does not mean you atone for your sins. Jesus already has died for your sins. Making amends means that your move toward reconciliation is more than just a mental attitude. Perhaps making amends means giving a present or taking someone to lunch. It may mean repaying a loan or giving some of your time.

Making amends means that your move toward reconciliation is more than just a mental attitude.

Charlie did not trust Bob, so he spread rumors about him. He gossiped about him in hopes that Bob would have trouble at work. Co-workers began snubbing Bob because of the things Charlie told them. Later Charlie learned that the stories he told others about Bob were untrue. He also got to know Bob better and realized that Bob was a decent, honorable person.

In recovery Charlie learned that his reaction to Bob grew out of trust issues from his childhood. Charlie realized he had caused Bob great harm. He asked for Bob's forgiveness, but he went beyond just saying, "I'm sorry." Charlie went to each person to whom he had gossiped and told each one that he had spread false information. Then he used his influence at work to get Bob appointed to a significant committee. Charlie's amends went beyond mere words—he went out of his way to try to restore Bob's good name. As you read these descriptions, some people to whom you need to make amends may come to mind. In the margin box write their initials.

Some people to whom I need to make amends–

_____

_____

_____

Making Amends Is Not Rewriting History
Making amends does not mean you will attempt to erase the wrong you have done. You cannot change the past. You can initiate healing in relationships. In each situation, decide what is appropriate. Some of your past behavior may have legal implications. Be honest. Do what is right. Seek God's leadership. Get advice from a trusted friend who understands Christian values and the recovery process.

If you went to one extreme, you would try to put everything back to exactly where it would have been if you never had hurt anyone. That is impossible. If you went to another dangerous extreme, you would minimize the harm you caused and do little or nothing concrete to rectify what you had done.

Charlie would have erred if he had told Bob he was sorry but dismissed the harmful effects of his gossip. Many times people feel bad about ways they have hurt others but deal with those wrongs simply by ignoring the situation. Amends involves more than just an "ignore-it-and-it-will-go-away" attitude.

✎ **Can you think of a time when you knew you had wronged someone but wanted to minimize the harmful effects of that wrong? Below describe that situation.**

_____

_____

Making Amends Is Not Manipulation

Make certain you do not try to manipulate as you make amends. Charlie could have apologized to Bob and make amends for the wrong reasons. He could have decided to make amends to manipulate Bob to do something nice for him–the giving-in-order-to-get mentality that is common among adult children of dysfunctional families–not because doing so was necessary for his own healing and spiritual health or because it would ease Bob's pain. For the amends to be effective Charlie needed to make sure Bob knew that he expected nothing in return but forgiveness and goodwill.

Making Amends Involves Some Risks

Some people with whom you consider making amends may be emotionally dangerous people. You may fear that such people will take advantage of you if you reach out to them.

Do not give dogs what is sacred; do not throw your pearls to pigs. If you do, they may trample them under their feet, and then turn and tear you to pieces.

Matthew 7:6

In Matthew 7:6 Jesus warned us not to cast pearls to swine. Pigs don't appreciate fine jewelry. Some people do not have the emotional and spiritual sensitivity to respond appropriately when you make amends. Seek God's direction. Don't use this as an excuse, but realize that some people are not ready to hear what you might want to say in the way of making amends.

For example Bob might have believed that even though making amends was the right thing to do, Charlie would use Bob's humbling of himself as a means to berate Bob—to give him the tongue-lashing he had been waiting to deliver to this co-worker who had ruined his reputation.

You cannot make people accept your gestures of reconciliation. If you have made a sincere attempt at reconciliation, you have done what you need to do. In the margin box write out the prayer that you will pray to God about this aspect of making amends.

Father, I pray that you'll help me to–

_____

_____

_____

_____

_____

_____

What I Needed from My Father

Sometimes my father apologized to me for being drunk. He would punctuate the apology by repeatedly saying that he loved me enough to die for me. He felt great shame about his drinking.

My father loved me very much, but he also hurt me by not being there emotionally. He hurt me by being unable to discuss the "elephant" in our house—his drinking. He hurt me when he was arrested more than once for driving while intoxicated. He hurt me when he stayed away from home while he drank and by his critical attitude toward people who were my heroes.

While I was in junior high school, my father became ill and almost died. It was a major turning point for him. He resolved to stop drinking. Our family became more active in church. He made several positive changes in his life. He supported me in many, many ways. Unfortunately, he did not have the benefit of a program of recovery. He experienced several relapses. I do not remember a time when he formally made amends to me. Many of his emotional issues remained powerfully present even after he quit drinking.

My father is deceased now, but I ask myself, What did I need to hear from my dad? What would have been sufficient in the way of amends? I know that I would not have expected him to change what already had happened.

I wish he could have taken me to lunch and said something like, "Today, I want to tell you I am sorry for all the years when I was drinking. I know you were hurt by it in ways that I cannot understand. I cannot change what I did, but I am sorry. I want you to know that you can always talk to me about this. It may be painful for me, but I am willing to do it. You can ask me any question. You can tell me how you hurt, and I will listen." If he could have said something like this, he would have given me a great blessing.

My father did bless me in many ways. He had told me he was sorry for the way he had lived, and I knew that he had resolved to live a better life with God's help, but I don't think he knew how to make amends. I still love him deeply. Thinking about what I needed from him helps me to understand how I need to act toward the people I have hurt.

Face Your Compulsions

✎ The compulsive behaviors I am working on are: _____

_____

Below describe how you managed these compulsive behaviors yesterday.

_____

Work on Turning Points

Be prepared to tell your group at least one of your plans for making amends.

➤ Say aloud from memory this unit's memory verse three times.

DAY 5

Today's Objective
We will challenge you to share from the heart.

Sharing from the Heart

Sharing from the Heart Means Simple Giving

A story about a man whose children kept appearing as he tried to read the evening paper illustrates the concept of sharing from the heart. "As he attempted to read the paper, he was constantly being interrupted by his children," the story goes. "One child came and asked for money for an ice-cream cone, and his father gently reached into his pocket and gave him the necessary coin. Another child arrived in tears. Her leg was hurt and she wanted her daddy to kiss the hurt away. An older son came with an algebra problem, and they eventually arrived at the right answer. Finally, the last and youngest of them all burst into the room looking for good old dad. The father said cynically, 'What do you want?' The little youngster said, 'Oh, daddy, I don't want anything. I just want to sit on your lap.' "[2] The youngest child knew about sharing from the heart.

The greatest act of sharing in all of history occurred when Jesus gave His life for us on the cross. He gave from the heart. He loved us from the deepest part of Himself. His love did not spring from fear. He was not trying to make

Himself feel worthy. He gave out of the fullness of who He was. He gave out of the strength He received from His Heavenly Father.

Here's what sharing from the heart means:

- Sharing from the heart means giving without complex motives of control and manipulation.
- Sharing from the heart means giving because you choose to give and not because someone is pressuring you to give.
- Sharing from the heart means being in touch with who you are and what you are feeling.
- Sharing from the heart is a flow of spiritual energy from you to another person.
- Sharing from the heart means dealing with past hurts and refusing to ignore or magnify them.
- Sharing from the heart means getting on with your life. It means refusing to be stuck in emotional pain from past mistakes.

In the margin box write one sentence that describes your commitment to share from the heart.

Face Your Compulsions

✎ **The compulsive behaviors I am working on are:** _____

_____

Below describe how you managed these compulsive behaviors yesterday.

_____

_____

Can you identify emotions you are feeling before you engage in these behaviors—for example, when you are tired, sad, lonely? Write your response below.

_____

_____

Work on Turning Points

Now read again the eighth turning point you've been working on during this lesson. Be prepared to discuss the work you have done on this turning point.

> **Turning Point 8**
> I will share my feelings and my failures with selected safe people.

A flow of spiritual energy

> **My commitment to share from the heart–**
> _____
> _____
> _____
> _____
> _____

Notes

[1] Thomas Lindberg, "Jealousy," *Leadership,* Fall Quarter, 1985 (Stevens Point, Wisconsin 1985), 76.

[2] King Duncan, *Dynamic Preaching,* July, 1989, Vol. IV, No. 7, (Knoxville: Seven Worlds Publishing, 1989), p. 19 citing Eric Ritz.

In this Unit you'll work on—
Turning Point 9
With God's help I will keep
working on my recovery.

Recycling

The Recovery Cycle: An attitude of BROKENNESS accompanied by the action of SURRENDER leads to RECOVERY.

WHERE DO I GO FROM HERE?

By the time Jeannette completed her written work on Unit 13 and completed her moral inventory, she understood that recovery does not occur in an instant. It is a process that will continue for the rest of her life. She learned some principles that she will use again and again.

Although she knew the process was not over, Jeannette felt a little confused about what she should do next. For months she had written in her *Moving Beyond Your Past* workbook daily. She had grown from the relationship with the person who heard her moral inventory and enjoyed the group support. This system no longer would be a regular regimen, and she wondered, "Where do I go from here?"

(Read on page 203 what Jeannette can do as an outgrowth of what she has learned in recovery.)

Why you will find this unit useful
This unit will help you develop a concept of an ongoing recovery lifestyle. Recovery is a continuing journey. You have taken an initial walk through each of the three cycles—inward, upward, and outward. This unit challenges you to develop a lifestyle that is sensitive to repeating these cycles as necessary. At times you will find yourself needing to repeat the upward cycle of openness, asking, and empowering. At other times, a new form of brokenness will call for the inward cycle of honesty, confession, and cleansing. Sometimes the greatest need for growth will be in the relational area—the outward cycle that calls for vulnerability, sharing, and intimacy. The cycles of recovery provide different entry points in initiating new levels of spiritual and emotional growth at various times in your life.

Looking Within	Living in Gratitude	Returning to the Inward Cycle	Returning to the Upward Cycle	Returning to the Outward Cycle
DAY 1	DAY 2	DAY 3	DAY 4	DAY 5

This week's memory verse
And we know that in all things God works for the good of those who love him, who have been called according to his purpose.

–Romans 8:28

DAY 1

Today's Objective
You will become aware of the need to monitor basic needs and feelings as you continue in recovery.

Have a plan for evaluating your personal growth.

Looking Within

How Long Does Recovery Take?

"Am I well yet?" "How long do I need to keep working on recovery?" We ask these questions in the early stages of our understanding of recovery.

Recovery is a life-long growth process. Recovery is a way of describing a facet of the growth that many of us need to experience as disciples of Jesus. People do not change easily the patterns of thought and actions they developed in a dysfunctional family of origin. You may make great progress in the way you think and act while you participate in a weekly share group, only to find that you have gone back to many of your dysfunctional ways of thinking and acting a few months later.

Crystal was ecstatic when she completed her support group sessions. She had learned how to identify her needs and how to speak up for herself. She had learned about her shame-based background and how that affected her current relationships. She had learned how to set boundaries and how to stop others from their abusive behavior. But a month after her sessions ended, Crystal felt devastated after she attended a family reunion. She was disappointed in some conversations she had that put her back in the child role. "I thought I was healed, but I really bombed it," Crystal said. "I totally forgot some things I learned in recovery."

Recovery needs constant reinforcement. One of the ways to insure continued progress in your personal recovery is to have a plan for evaluating where you are in several basic areas of personal growth. Later this week we will encourage you to develop a self-care plan designed to maintain the recovery principles you have learned.

Staying Aware of Your Needs

Denying our needs gets us into trouble. Knowing our needs and deciding to make personal sacrifices is one thing. Denying that we have certain needs while we live under tremendous emotional pain because of denial is another.

Wearing a mask

When you ignore the basic needs in your life, you wear a mask. You are pretending to be someone you are not. No one really can know you when you live like this. When you ignore your basic needs, you may be dangerously vulnerable to be used or abused by someone who can meet those needs in an inappropriate manner. Staying in touch with your basic needs is an important aspect of self-care.

Staying in Touch with Your Feelings

Knowing what you are feeling is basic to being alive. Knowing what you are feeling is the normal state for living. Being emotionally blank is not normal. Even after you have gained some basic experience in being in touch with your feelings, you easily can slip back into an unfeeling state. Your program of self-evaluation can include a plan for evaluating whether you are staying in touch with your feelings.

✎ Get some practice right now by reviewing the list of feelings below and marking any feelings that you have had during the last 24 hours.

aggressive	agonized	angry	apologetic
arrogant	ashamed	bashful	bored
cautious	cold	confident	content
curious	demure	determined	disappointed
disapproving	disbelieving	disgusted	distasteful
ecstatic	enraged	envious	exhausted
fearful	foolish	frustrated	grieving
grumpy	guilty	happy	hopeless
horrified	hot	hurt	hysterical
idiotic	indifferent	innocent	interested
jealous	joyful	lonely	loving
meditative	mischievous	miserable	obstinate
optimistic	pained	paranoid	prudish
puzzled	relieved	sad	satisfied
shocked	smug	surprised	suspicious
sympathetic	uncertain	undecided	vulnerable
withdrawn	anxious	blissful	confused

Identify what you've felt

Face Your Compulsions

✎ The compulsive behaviors I am working on are: _____

_____

Below describe how you managed these compulsive behaviors during the last 12 weeks.

_____

_____

What have you learned about the relationship between your emotions and your compulsions? Below write a description of a typical scenario of a particular emotional state followed by a particular compulsive response.

_____

_____

_____

Work on Turning Points

Working on your recovery means staying in touch with your needs.

✎ Make a list of some important needs in your life:

Physical: _____

Emotional: _____

Spiritual: _____

Other: _____

 In the margin write three things you can do each week to check whether you are staying in touch with your feelings.

DAY

2

Today's Objective:
You will consider the importance
of living a life characterized
by thankfulness.

Living in Gratitude

Recovery Includes Thankfulness

Thankfulness is an attitude of faith. Being thankful requires you to trust that God is at work in your life. The alternative to this attitude of faith is an attitude of cynicism. Cynicism assumes the worst about God and the world. Thankfulness is an attitude of dependence. Thankfulness cannot coexist with the "I'll-do-everything-by-myself" mentality. The alternative to this healthy dependence on God is control. If you have a problem with trying to control everything, you will have difficulty with thankfulness.

Thankfulness is an attitude of humility. Otherwise, it is not true thankfulness. The Pharisee prayed about himself, "God, I thank you that I am not like all other men—robbers, evildoers, adulterers—or even like this tax collector. I fast twice a week and give a tenth of all I get" (Luke 18:11-12). The Pharisee's attitude was not a healthy attitude of thankfulness.

Thankfulness Is Not Minimizing the Pain

Thankfulness is not minimizing the pain of your life. It is maximizing the good. Face the pain of your past. Being thankful does not mean denying reality. The pain of your past may make heartfelt thankfulness especially challenging for you. You may have learned to minimize your pain—glossing it over with a thin veneer of thankfulness. You may have become a spiritual parrot—expressing the thanks that others told you to express, but you do not feel. Recovery means facing the pain and cultivating a positive attitude.

Jarred had difficulty developing a prayer life. When his wife told him she hoped the two of them could pray together as a couple, Jarred resisted. He believed he had such a painful past that the act of being thankful would mean he was minimizing the pain that he had experienced.

 Have you ever refused to have an attitude of thankfulness because you believed that to do so would gloss over your pain? Below describe how you felt in this type of situation.

_____

_____

Looking your pain squarely in the face will help you progress in recovery. Don't deny it; admit it; work on it. But don't let your facing of past pain blind you to the good that occurs in your life every day. Be grateful for that good.

Thankfulness Is a Mark of Faith

And we know that in all things God works for the good of those who love Him, who have been called according to his purpose.

Romans 8:28

Do not be anxious about anything, but in everything, by prayer and petition with thanksgiving, present your requests to God.

Philippians 4:6

Thankfulness means claiming God's promise that He always is working for your good (see the first verse at left). It means trusting that good can spring from something that appears to be totally negative. Thankfulness means choosing to trust God in difficult times. As part of your self-care program for recovery, develop the habit of saying "thank you" to God. (See the second verse at left.) Look for the good. Highlight it. Thank God for it.

✎ **For what are you thankful today? Below list four things.**

1. _____

2. _____

3. _____

4. _____

Face Your Compulsions

✎ The compulsive behaviors I am working on are: _____

_____

✎ What are some specific situations that seem to set you up for compulsive behavior? Below indicate the type of compulsive behavior that usually follows this situation. Have you seen any changes in your response to these situations in the last few weeks? If necessary use additional sheets of paper for this exercise.

_____

_____

Work on Turning Points

✎ Do you have a problem with gratitude? If yes, how did this problem begin?

_____

_____

✎ What is one thing you can do today to begin cultivating an attitude of thankfulness?

_____

_____

✎ Begin to memorize this unit's Scripture memory verse, Romans 8:28. Write it in the margin three times.

DAY 3

Returning to the Inward Cycle

Today's Objective:
You will review some areas of personal behavior that you need to examine on a regular basis.

Watching for Compulsive Behavior

Compulsive behavior is a way of avoiding your feelings. Some areas of compulsive behavior are:

1. Addiction to alcohol and other drugs
2. Work addiction
3. Addiction to gambling
4. Addiction to overspending or spending too little
5. Addiction to cigarettes or other tobacco products
6. Compulsion to control others
7. Food addictions
8. Sex addictions (pornography, sex, romance)
9. Compulsive need to please people
10. Compulsion to rescue others
11. Dependency on harmful relationships
12. Exercise addictions
13. Addiction to compulsive religious activity (preoccupation with an outward set of religious guidelines rather than benefiting from the spiritual message)
14. General perfectionism
15. Compulsive cleaning
16. Shopping addiction
17. Compulsive busyness
18. Repetition—doing the same thing over and over the same way, so that the repetition almost becomes a ritual

Deal with underlying causes

Finding a way to escape pain you do not want to feel is a driving force of compulsive behavior. If you stop a compulsive behavior without dealing with the underlying emotional causes for the behavior, you are likely to substitute another form of compulsive behavior for the behavior you stopped.

A person can stop drinking and then become addicted to sex. A work addict may take a day off and eat compulsively all day. The underlying issue is "Find a way to stop the emotional pain."

Part of your ongoing recovery process is to be sensitive to compulsive behaviors in your life. Be honest about such behaviors. Ask yourself what feelings you are trying to avoid with these behaviors.

Force of habit

Another driving force behind compulsive behaviors is the force of habit. We did a certain thing yesterday and the day before that, and we feel compelled to do it today. With some behaviors, an actual physical addiction also may be present. Staying in your compulsive behavior can be a way of avoiding change. When you stay in your old behaviors, you don't have to make decisions about changing. You just follow your inner compulsions.

✎ **I still struggle with the following compulsions:**

_____

_____

When you feel pulled into a compulsive behavior, ask yourself what feelings you are trying to avoid. Work on feeling the feelings instead of running from them by acting compulsively. Talk to someone else if you need to do so. If your compulsive behavior is a strong addiction, you may need some help in stopping the cycle. Addressing the feelings behind the compulsion is not always enough.

Watching for Rebellious Behavior

Using an unsuspecting authority figure to work out your anger toward someone else is unhealthy.

We have studied the fact that many of us have problems with authority figures. Authority figures may represent our parents and may offer us easy targets for fighting unresolved battles from the past. Using an unsuspecting authority figure to work out your anger toward someone else is unhealthy.

Dexter and his employee, Tommy, got along well. But lately Tommy was rude and sarcastic to Dexter. Tommy rebuffed Dexter's acts of kindness to him. He also made cutting remarks when Dexter gave him an assignment on the job. Dexter was at wits' end to understand what was occurring with Tommy.

A friend who was in a recovery group helped Dexter with an explanation. Tommy was going through a divorce but had not yet told his father about this occurrence. Tommy's dad always had been critical of Tommy, and Tommy feared his dad's reaction when he broke the news to him. At work Tommy was not seeing Dexter as his boss but as his dad. Dexter was the unsuspecting victim of Tommy's anger at his father.

> **I've wrongfully taken my anger out on—**
>
> _____
>
> _____
>
> _____
>
> _____

Think about times in which you have been like Tommy and have taken out your anger on some unsuspecting authority figure. In the margin box write the initials of people on whom you have wrongfully taken out your anger.

If you find yourself giving someone a difficult time because he/she reminds you of someone else or some other situation, stop and think about it. What is this about? What relationship from the past are you trying to process? Deal with the relationship in which the problem started, not the one that reminds you of the problem relationship.

Part of recovery is learning to live without a chip on your shoulder.

You may have developed a habit of acting rebelliously. At first, your rebellious behavior involved acting out of inner pain; later it became a habit. It became a mark of your personality. Part of recovery is learning to live without a chip on your shoulder.

✎ **Do you still rebel against certain things?**

❑ When someone asks me to do something, I do the opposite.
❑ I don't like anyone to have authority over any part of my life.
❑ I must do what I want to do all of the time.
❑ Or _____

Checking for Compliant Behavior

While some of us rebel, others are compliant. Compliance can be a hidden rebellion. The hostility and anger are present, but we hold them inside. You may be frightened at the level of anger you know to be inside you. If the anger ever came out, who knows what would happen?

You are a person who does the right thing. Your unspoken rule is, "Other people get to make mistakes, but I don't. Other people can raise questions, but I can't. Other people can ask for help, but I can't. I'm the one who is supposed to help people. I'm not supposed to ask for help." A compliant person follows the rules but inwardly is full of resentment.

An angry but compliant person is a boiler under pressure. The anger will get out some way. It may make you sick. It may make you depressed.

Billie's story

Friends were horrified at all the misfortunes that happened to Billie and her husband. First Billie lost her job. Then the family moved to a new house, only to see it destroyed by fire. Then Billie's husband lost his job, too. When friends called to express their sorrow about these losses, Billie tried to minimize these events. Instead of expressing her anger, which friends believed she had every right to feel, Billie brushed off the occurrences and gave responses like, "Oh, it's not such a big deal." No one was surprised when Billie was hospitalized with severe gastrointestinal pains, which were symptoms of an ulcer. Holding in all her anger instead of expressing it in a healthy way had made her sick.

✎ **Why do you think Billie was reluctant to be honest about the anxiety she was feeling because of these circumstances? Have you ever been compliant and held hostility and anger inside? Describe below.**

_____

_____

Billie likely was terrified of what would happen if she ever confessed exactly how angry she was. After all, she perceived of herself as the compliant person who always did and said the proper thing. Billie also could have had an image of herself as the person who always consoled others in their misfortunes.

Compliance follows close behind a lack of heartfelt understanding of the grace of God. If I see God's love as conditional, I may choose compliance. If I understand that God's love is unconditional, I realize that He still will love me even when I make a mistake. In a surprising sort of way this gives me a new freedom to obey God.

Looking like I am good

Shame also is related to compliance. My shame tells me I must go through the motions "of looking like I am good" even when I am rebelling on the inside. I must play the part or else my shame will be more visible to everyone.

It may seem like a step backward, but for some of us obedience to God occurs after we finally admit we are not as good as we have been pretending to be. We have followed the rules while nurturing wrong in our hearts. When I become honest about what I truly am feeling, spiritual maturity can follow. God does not seek pretenders. He wants willing followers.

✎ **In what areas are you are compliant but resentful? Make a list.**

_____

_____

_____

Face Your Compulsions

✎ What are your plans for dealing with your compulsive behaviors after this group ends? Be sure to include these plans in your self-care program.

_____

_____

_____

Work on Turning Points

✎ What trigger events or attitudes—those occurrences, people, places, or things that cause an urge for us to return to our compulsive behavior—would tell you in future months that you need to move into the inward cycle of honesty, confession, and cleansing? Below make a list of these events or attitudes.

Example: I know that I need to connect with the inward cycle when I start yelling at my kids when I am angry about events at work.

_____

_____

_____

✎ What areas of personal behavior do you need to examine regularly?

Compulsive Behavior: _____

_____

Rebellious Behavior: _____

_____

Compliant Behavior: _____

_____

Self-Care Plan

Use the Self-Care Worksheet in the back of this book to work on your plan for self-care in recovery. We also will ask you to work on your self-care plan tomorrow and the next day.

➤ Pray for each member of your Heart-to-Heart group by name.

➤ Say aloud three times this unit's memory verse.

<table>
<tr><td>

</td></tr>
</table>

DAY 4

Today's Objective
You will learn the place of obedience in a lifestyle of recovery.

Returning to the Upward Cycle

Obedience as a Mark of Recovery

Obedience is not just for children and dogs. Learning to obey God is one of the crucial steps in the path to recovery from compulsive/addictive behavior and emotional pain.

Being obedient to God does not mean that you are subservient to everyone you meet. It means saying yes to God. Obedience is trusting God even when you don't know all the answers. Psychologists tell us that a mentally healthy person can tolerate uncertainty and change. Many people in mental institutions are people who cannot tolerate uncertainty and change. They must have the correct answers for everything even if they must create their own fantasy world of answers.

The ability to live with uncertainty also is a mark of spiritual health. Faith equips us to live with uncertainty. Faith means you can say yes to God even when you don't understand everything that is happening around you. Obedience is connected to faith. We are called to the obedience that comes from faith.

 Are you waiting for some special discovery before you can start trusting God? Describe what must happen for you to start trusting and obeying.

_____

_____

Obedience as an Expression of Love

Therefore do not let sin reign in your mortal body so that you obey its evil desires.

Romans 6:12

If you love me, you will obey what I command.

John 14:15

And this is love: that we walk in obedience to his commands. As you have heard from the beginning, his command is that you walk in love.

2 John 6

Consider two options for your life. One, you can turn sin or self-centeredness loose in your life. The Bible warns against such a lifestyle. See the Scripture appearing at left. Or, you can live a life of expressing love to God. How do you show love for God?

Jesus told us how to show love to God, as the second verse in the margin illustrates. The third explains further about obeying His commands as a way that shows love. What are His commands? Let's look at the concepts the Ten Commandments describe.

1. Put God first.
2. Put God in a place all by Himself.
3. Honor the name of God.
4. Set aside a special day to honor God each week.
5. Honor your parents.
6. Treat human life as sacred.
7. Honor marriage vows—yours and those of other people.
8. Respect other people's property.
9. Tell the truth.
10. Find and appreciate the good in what is yours rather than focusing your desires on what other people have.

Jesus summed up all the commandments by challenging us to love God with all our hearts, minds, and souls, and to love our neighbors as ourselves (Matthew 22:37,39). Another way of summing up what God expects of us is to say, "In each situation I will ask, 'What would Jesus do?'"

✎ **Is it difficult for you to associate obedience with love? Why?**

_____

_____

What misconceptions do you need to release before you can connect obedience with love for God?

_____

_____

Some people have answered these questions this way: I have difficulty associating obedience with love because my parents physically abused me when I did not obey. I need to release the misconception that God will "zap" me in anger the way my parents did when I'm disobedient before I can comprehend the fact that I obey God as a way to show love for Him.

Obedience as Gratitude for Forgiveness

We all have a sin problem. Keith Miller described sin as "our apparent inability to say no to our need to control people, places, and things in order to implement our own self-centered desires. We do this either with blatant power or through apparent weakness—for example, by making a thousand minute suggestions about how people should run their lives. We may believe in God and love Him a great deal, but at the essential level _we_ are in control— or struggling to be."[1]

God's solution

We all have a sin problem, but God has a solution. The first part of this solution is forgiveness. Jesus died on the cross so we could be forgiven. In Christ we find God's forgiveness.

The second part of the solution is obedience. Forgiveness is a gift. Forgiveness cannot be earned. Obedience is not an attempt to earn credits to merit forgiveness. Obedience is a loving response to a loving God who has forgiven us. Leave out forgiveness and you will live a life of guilt and shame. Leave out obedience and you will live a life that offends God and hurts people.

✎ **What are you most likely to leave out? Forgiveness or obedience? What are the results when you do?**

_____

_____

_____

_____

Face Your Compulsions

✎ The compulsive behaviors I am working on are: _____

_____

✎ What is the connection between your compulsive behaviors and your obedience to God?

_____

_____

Work on Turning Points

✎ How does obedience connect with the upward cycle of openness, asking, and empowering?

_____

✎ What do you need to do to check yourself to see if you need to work on the upward cycle?

Example: I know I need to connect with the upward cycle when I feel I am going through the motions of Christianity without feeling any spiritual power in my life.

_____

_____

Self-Care Plan

Use the Self-Care Worksheet in the back of this book to work on your plan for self-care in recovery. We also will ask you to work on your self-care plan tomorrow.

DAY 5

Today's Objective
You will examine some ways you can evaluate your relationships from the standpoint of recovery.

Returning to the Outward Cycle

Identifying Resentments

Codependency is a lifestyle that involves hiding your true feelings from other people and sometimes from yourself. One of the hidden feelings invariably will be anger. Hidden, smoldering anger becomes resentment. You feel helpless. You are afraid to be yourself. Authority figures are frightening. Life always has seemed out of control, and you resent it. You must face your anger. You must admit its presence. You must let yourself feel it. Feeling your anger does not mean you express it in ways that are destructive to yourself or to others. You can learn acceptable ways to express your anger. When you face your anger and the resentments it has fostered, you can experience cleansing. You can be emptied of the smoldering resentments that you feel toward other people.

Part of your self-care program involves checking for new resentments. When you believe you feel resentment toward someone, identify that resentment, name it, and work on it. Do you need to talk about it? Maybe you need to talk about it with the person toward whom you feel it. Maybe you need to discuss it with an uninvolved third party. If you are at fault, ask God to forgive you. If you can do so without hurting the offended person, ask that person's forgiveness. In the margin box list some of your current resentments.

Watching for Bitterness

Besides resentments toward other people, you may feel bitterness about life in general. The pain of your childhood may have planted seeds of bitterness. "Why did I have to hurt like that? Why couldn't I have had the nurture that others had?" you may ask.

Address the weight of bitterness from your past. Watch for new hints of bitterness. Bitterness can result from anger toward God. If you are angry with God, talk to Him about it. Don't let a negative, pessimistic viewpoint creep back into your life.

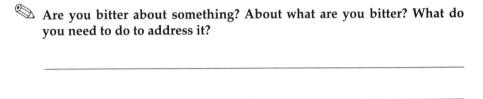 **Are you bitter about something? About what are you bitter? What do you need to do to address it?**

_____

_____

Admitting My Wrongs

Hopefully, you now have completed Turning Point 8, "I will share my feelings and my failures with selected safe people." You have dealt with the wrongs of the past. You have made amends to those you have hurt. You will hurt others in the future. You are human. You are not perfect. This does not mean you try to hurt others and use your humanity as an excuse. It means that when you hurt someone, you ask that person's forgiveness. You admit you were wrong. You say, "I was wrong. I am sorry."

When you hurt someone, you ask that person's forgiveness.

Can you think of someone you have hurt in the last week? What do you need to do to make amends?

_____

_____

Evaluating My Approachability

Check yourself for emotionally intimate relationships. Are you letting anyone get close to you emotionally? You may have taken giant steps in moving closer to other people, but you can slip back into old patterns. Someone will hurt you. You will be tempted to give up on emotionally intimate relationships. Keep working on letting yourself be vulnerable and accessible to selected safe people.

✎ **How are you doing on emotional closeness with your immediate family?**

_____

_____

✎ **Who are some new people you are permitting to know the real you?**

_____

✎ **What have you done lately to deepen the friendships you now have?**

_____

_____

Checking My Boundaries

We have learned the importance of being vulnerable. Being vulnerable does not mean having no boundaries. Remember the different types of boundaries:
- Emotional
- Physical
- Sexual
- Spiritual

You have a right to take care of yourself.

Recovery means establishing, rebuilding, and sustaining boundaries. Boundaries mean taking care of yourself. You have a right to take care of yourself. You have the option to walk away from abusive behavior.

If someone violates your boundaries, you can—
- Say no;
- Create more distance;
- Leave the room;
- Change the nature of the relationship;
- End the relationship if appropriate;
- Press charges if the behavior was illegal.

The momentum of your childhood will place continual pressure on you to drop your boundaries or to substitute walls for boundaries. The old way of thinking creates a pull.

✎ **What boundaries are difficult for you to establish?**

_____

_____

✎ **Who are some people who consistently violate your boundaries? What boundaries do they violate? What are you going to do about this violation? (Use a separate sheet of paper for this exercise.)**

Person	Boundary Violated	My Plan

Work on Turning Points

Here is the turning point on which you've been working this week.

Turning Point 9

With God's help I will keep working on my recovery.

Self-Care Plan

 Use the Self-Care Worksheet in the back of this book to complete your plan for self-care in recovery. Be prepared to tell the group about your plans.

On day 5 of week 1 in this study you prepared a list of statements describing what you would like your life to be like in a state of spiritual and emotional health. Review the list you wrote. Have you made progress since you wrote the list? Be prepared to discuss with the group your progress.

Where Do I Go from Here?

By the time Jeannette completed her written work on Unit 13 and completed her moral inventory, she understood that recovery does not occur in an instant. It is a process that will continue for the rest of her life. She learned some principles that she will use again and again. Although she knew the process was not over, Jeannette felt a little confused about what she should do next. For months she had written in her *Moving Beyond Your Past* workbook daily. She had grown from the relationship with the person who heard her moral inventory, and she enjoyed the group support. This system no longer would be a regular regimen, and she wondered, "Where do I go from here?"

Jeannette's feelings are common to those who complete their initial work in recovery. In this final day in *Moving Beyond Your Past*, we will share some suggestions about what next steps people in this situation can take.

Jeannette has learned that recovery is a lifelong task. After completing *Moving Beyond Your Past* she may have other emotional issues on which she is ready to work, or she may be ready to address discipleship issues from the foundation of emotional healing she gained through this study. She may choose to go through *Moving Beyond Your Past* again, or she may want to pursue other concepts in her growth. She may be ready to improve her understanding of God's will or her prayer life. If she is not already involved in a regular Bible study at her church, such as a weekly Sunday School class, she would find that regular focus on God's Word to be important in her life. She may want to learn to lead support groups in her church so she can share her growth experience with others, or she may want to talk to a church staff member about a way she can use her new understanding of and commitment to Christ to teach a Bible study or to serve the Lord in some other way in her church.

Beyond that, she could benefit from one of the following resources, all of which are written in the interactive format *Moving Beyond Your Past* uses. All of these books are intended for group study. All will enable individuals to continue their spiritual growth.

To build self-worth on the forgiveness and love of Jesus Christ:
• *Search for Significance* LIFE₍ᵣ₎ Support Group Series Edition. Helps individuals use the principles from God's Word to replace false beliefs that Satan teaches about themselves. (Houston: Rapha Publishing), product number 080549990; Leader's Guide, product number 080549989X.

To identify and replace codependent behaviors:
• *Untangling Relationships: A Christian Perspective on Codependency.* Helps individuals learn how to make relationships more healthy. (Houston: Rapha Publishing), product number 0805499733; Leader's Guide, 0805499741.

• *Conquering Codependency: A Christ-Centered 12-Step Process.* Helps persons whose lives are devastated by codependency to learn a Christ-centered 12-Step process toward recovery and to depend on God through Christ to restore them to spiritual and emotional health. (Houston: Rapha Publishing), product number 080549975X; Facilitator's Guide, 0805499768.

To understand God's will for your life:
• *Experiencing God: Knowing and Doing the Will of God.* Find answers to the often-asked question, "How can I know and do the will of God?" (Nashville: LifeWay Press), product number 0767390873; Leader's Guide, product number 0805499512

To help you know more about the Bible:
• *Step by Step Through the Old Testament.* This self-instructional workbook surveys the Old Testament, provides a framework for understanding and interpreting it, and teaches Bible background. (Nashville: LifeWay Press), product number 0767326199; Leader's Guide, product number 0767326202.

What next?

• *Step-by-Step Through the New Testament.* This 13-unit self-instructional workbook surveys the New Testament, provides a framework for understanding and interpreting the New Testament, and teaches Bible background. (Nashville: LifeWay Press, product number 0805499466; Leader's Guide, product number 0767326210.

To help you learn how to disciple others:
• *MasterLife: Discipleship Training.* This six-month in-depth discipleship process for developing spiritual disciples and leaders trains people to help carry out Christ's vision to make disciples of all nations. For more information write Adult Discipleship and Family Department, MSN 151, 127 Ninth Avenue, North; Nashville, TN 37234.

To help you learn to think the thoughts of Christ:
• *The Mind of Christ.* This course helps the person who is ready for a serious study of what it means to have the thoughts of Christ and to renew his or her mind, as Scripture commands. (Nashville: LifeWay Press), product number 080549870; Leader's Guide, product number 0805498699.

Notes

[1]Keith Miller, *Sin: Overcoming the Ultimate Deadly Addiction* (San Francisco: Harper and Row, Publishers, 1987), 27.

APPENDIX A

Confidential Moral Inventory —We have filled in some portions of the exercises as examples.

How My Childhood Shaped Me

Shame I Felt from the Actions of Others (Cleansing, Day 1)

Describe the Shame	Effect on my Attitudes	Effect on My Behavior
example: my mother's drug addiction	example: I believed people looked down on me.	example: I avoided any situation where others might reject me.

How My Childhood Shaped Me

Hurts, Humiliations, Horrors[1] (Honesty, Day 1)

What and When	How it Affected Me
example: My father came to my football game drunk.	example: I learned to feel worried when things were going too well.

My Relationship with God

Ways I Have Disobeyed God Repeatedly (Cleansing, Day 2)

example: made my preoccupation with other relationships more important than Him

_____

_____

_____

_____

_____

_____

Ways I Have Developed a Positive Relationship with God

example: I have been pretty consistent in my prayer life.

_____

_____

_____

_____

_____

_____

Ways I Have Tried to Play God

example: I have tried to control others' lives instead of letting God take charge.

_____

_____

_____

_____

_____

_____

My Relationship with God

Ways I Have Substituted Compliance for Obedience in my Relationship with God (Honesty, Day 2)

example: I attended church because I wanted others to think highly of me and not necesarily to hear what God has to say to me.

_____

_____

_____

_____

_____

_____

Ways I Have Substituted Ritualism and Moralism for Worship and Morality

Write about ritual versus worship in your life.

ex.: I'm scrupulous about attending every church event but seldom worship when there.

_____

_____

_____

_____

_____

Write about moralism and morality in your life.

ex.: I'm quick to tell others what they have done wrong and seldom truly show love and compassion for them.

_____

_____

_____

_____

_____

_____

My Relationships with People

Identify Your Resentments (Cleansing, Day 3)

Make a list of things you strongly resent. Rate each resentment on a scale of 1 to 10, with 10 being a burning resentment. Name the person toward whom you are resentful if appropriate.

example: I resent my mother because she doesn't affirm me.—8

1. _____

_____

2. _____

_____

3. _____

_____

4. _____

_____

5. _____

_____

6. _____

_____

7. _____

_____

8. _____

_____

9. _____

_____

10. _____

_____

How do you believe you deal with resentments? _____

_____

_____

My Relationships with People

Identifying How I Deal with Conflict (Honesty, Day 3)

List four people with whom you have had major conflicts. Indicate the cause of the conflict and how you dealt with it.

Conflict with:	Cause:	How I dealt with it:
1. ex.: my best friend, Jane	ex.: I was jealous of her	ex.: stopped speaking to her
2. _____	_____	_____
3. _____	_____	_____
4. _____	_____	_____

What patterns do you see in the way you deal with conflicts in relationships?

❑ Deny the conflict exists
❑ Run away
❑ Place all blame on the other person
❑ Seek outside help

❑ Talk about it
❑ Compromise
❑ Always assume it was my fault
❑ Other

Do any of the following models describe your approach to conflict?

❑ **Dove**
 I want peace at any price.
❑ **Hawk**
 It's your fault.
❑ **Owl**
 Let's be reasonable.
❑ **Ostrich**[2]
 What conflict?

❑ **Puppy Dog**
 I'll make everybody happy.
❑ **Rabbit**
 I've got to run.
❑ **Skunk**
 Don't criticize me for that when you did _____ to me.

Write three statements which outline how you deal with conflicts with other people.

1. _____

_____

2. _____

_____

3. _____

_____

My Relationships with People

Parents (Honesty, Day 3)

List any unresolved issues or resentments. What was your part in these issues?

❑ Addictive behaviors of mine which have hurt my parents.

example: my addiction to speeding, resulting in traffic tickets and accidents. This cost them a lot of money and worry.

_____

_____

❑ Controlling attitudes of mine which have hurt my parents.

_____

_____

❑ Misplaced priorities of mine which have hurt my parents.

_____

_____

❑ Absences of mine which have hurt my parents.

_____

_____

❑ Verbal statements of mine which have hurt my parents.

_____

_____

❑ Broken commitments of mine which have hurt my parents.

_____

_____

❑ Positive behaviors of mine which strengthened my relationship with my parents. _____

_____

My Relationships with People

Authority Figures (Honesty, Day 3)

List any unresolved issues or resentments. What was your part in these issues?

❑ Addictive behaviors of mine which have hurt authority figures.

example: My addiction to alcohol caused me to miss many days of work and hurt my boss when I caused our office to be behind in a project.

_____

_____

❑ Controlling attitudes of mine which have hurt authority figures.

_____

_____

❑ Misplaced priorities of mine which have hurt authority figures.

_____

_____

❑ Absences of mine which have hurt authority figures.

_____

_____

❑ Verbal statements of mine which have hurt authority figures.

_____

_____

❑ Broken commitments of mine which have hurt authority figures.

_____

_____

❑ Positive behaviors of mine which strengthened my relationship with authority figures. _____

_____

My Relationships with People

Marriage (Honesty, Day 3)

If you are married or have been married previously, think about your relationship to your spouse or ex-spouse.

List three ongoing issues in the relationship.

example: my refusal to discipline our children

1. _____

2. _____

3. _____

What have you contributed to any tensions present in the marriage?

❑ Addictive behaviors of mine which have hurt my spouse.

_____

❑ Controlling attitudes of mine which have hurt my spouse.

_____

❑ Misplaced priorities of mine which have hurt my spouse.

_____

❑ Absences of mine which have hurt my spouse.

_____

❑ Verbal statements of mine which have hurt my spouse.

_____

❑ Broken commitments of mine which have hurt my spouse.

_____

❑ Positive behaviors of mine which strengthened my relationship with my spouse.

_____

❑ Intangibles which I have given my spouse.

_____

My Relationships with People

Children (If you are a parent) (Honesty, Day 3)

No parent is perfect. No parent meets all of a child's needs, but have you hurt your child in any of these areas?

❑ Addictive behaviors of mine which have hurt my child(ren).

  example : I wanted to please my children rather than set boundaries for them.

  _____

  _____

❑ Controlling attitudes of mine which have hurt my child(ren).

  _____

❑ Misplaced priorities of mine which have hurt my child(ren).

  _____

❑ Abusive behavior of mine which has hurt my child(ren).

  _____

❑ Absences of mine which have hurt my child(ren).

  _____

❑ Verbal statements of mine which have hurt my child(ren).

  _____

❑ Broken commitments of mine which have hurt my child(ren).

  _____

❑ Negative parenting patterns from my family of origin which I have not continued.

  _____

❑ Positive behaviors of mine which strengthened my relationship with my child(ren).

  _____

❑ Intangibles which I have given my child(ren).

  _____

My Relationships with People

Friends (Honesty, Day 3)

❑ Addictive behaviors of mine which have hurt my friends.

_____

❑ Controlling attitudes of mine which have hurt my friends.

_____

❑ Misplaced priorities of mine which have hurt my friends.

_____

❑ Abusive behavior of mine which has hurt my friends.

_____

❑ Absences of mine which have hurt my friends.

_____

❑ Verbal statements of mine which have hurt my friends.

_____

❑ Broken commitments of mine which have hurt my friends.

_____

❑ Positive things I have done for my friends.

_____

❑ Commitments of mine which have strengthened my friends.

_____

My Relationships with People

Evaluating My Relationships with People (Honesty, Day 3)

After completing the evaluations, write a paragraph which describes how you relate to people.

_____

_____

_____

_____

_____

_____

_____

_____

_____

What are some areas of your relationships where you need to be forgiven?

_____

_____

_____

_____

_____

Can you think of people to whom you need to make amends?

_____

_____

_____

_____

Self-Destructive Traits

Self-Destructive Behaviors (Honesty, Day 4)

Below describe behaviors that are self destructive.

Behavior _____

_____

How does this behavior hurt your spritual life? _____

_____

_____

How does this behavior hurt your relationships? _____

_____

_____

How does this behavior harm your body? _____

_____

What do you gain from this behavior? _____

_____

Why do you continue with this behavior? _____

_____

Do you believe that God can help you to overcome the self-destructive behaviors in your life?

_____

Some self-destructive patterns which I have changed are: _____

_____

_____

Some disciplines I follow are: _____

_____

_____

Are you being honest with yourself? _____

Affirmations

Positive Habits (Cleansing, Day 4)

example: regular physical exercise

_____

_____

_____

_____

_____

_____

Positive character traits (Cleansing, Day 5)

example: truthfulness

_____

_____

_____

_____

_____

_____

Positive gifts from my family of origin[3]

example: my family taught me the importance of believing in God.

_____

_____

_____

_____

_____

_____

Affirmations

Positive talents, ability, and gifts[4] (Cleansing, Day 5)

example: ability to speak in front of others

_____

_____

_____

_____

_____

_____

Positive permissions[5]

example: permission to have fun instead of working constantly

_____

_____

_____

_____

_____

_____

Positive Recovery Processes[6]

example: I am committed to stop trying to control everyone and let God take over.

_____

_____

_____

_____

_____

_____

Additions

What statements would you add to your moral inventory? (Confession, Day 1)

_____

_____

_____

_____

_____

_____

_____

_____

_____

Notes

[1]David A. Seamands, *Healing of Memories* (Wheaton: Victor Books, 1985), 80, 84, 87.

[2]Gary Chapman, *Communication and Intimacy Couple's Guide* (Nashville: Convention Press, 1992), 17.

[3]Dr. Robert Hemfelt and Dr. Richard Fowler, *Serenity: A Companion for Twelve Step Recovery* (Nashville: Thomas Nelson, 1990), 42.

[4]Ibid., 43.

[5]Ibid.

[6]Ibid.

APPENDIX B

Confidential Reconciliation Worksheet

Example
A person I have harmed is: *Mike Smith*

I hurt this person by: *Breaking off a friendship because he got a promotion at work and I did not.*

Do I need to talk to this person about what happened? *In this case I need to talk to Mike about what happened. I know he knows about it, and it needs to be resolved.*

I need to tell this person: *I am sorry for the way I acted. I was jealous.*

A way that I could make amends is: *Send him a gift or a birthday card.*

Report on your contact with this person: *I had lunch with Mike. I told him I was sorry. Our friendship has been renewed. I have added him to my birthday card list.*

Use this format for Turning Point Seven:

A person I have harmed is: _____

I hurt this person by: _____

_____

Do I need to talk to this person about what happened? _____

_____

I need to tell this person: _____

_____

A way that I could make amends is: _____

_____

Report on your contact with this person: _____

_____

_____

_____

APPENDIX C

Confidential Self-Care Plan

To Continue My Recovery Process, I Need to be Aware of:
My Basic Needs: (list below)

Physical: _____

Emotional: _____

Spiritual: _____

Other: _____

To Continue My Recovery Process, I Plan to Do the Following:
Daily (Ideas: daily journal, affirmations, prayer, reading)

_____

Weekly (Ideas: support group meetings, worship services, Bible study group, time off, recreation/hobbies)

_____

As Necessary (Ideas: recovery workshops, conferences, vacation time)

_____

Use the following questions as necessary to help evaluate your ongoing progress in recovery:

This week I have done the following to take care of some of my basic needs:

_____

_____

Some of my basic needs that seem to be chronically unmet are:

_____

_____

For what am I thankful?

_____

_____

Am I experiencing brokenness in some area of my life? If yes, what?

_____

_____

What do I need to surrender?

_____

_____

How am I doing with compulsive behaviors?

_____

_____

Am I engaging in rebellious or compliant behavior? Describe.

_____

_____

Do I need to initiate the Inward Cycle—Honesty, Confession, Cleansing?

_____

_____

What is something I have done in the last week to express trust toward another person?

_____

_____

Do I need to work on the Upward Cycle—Openness, Asking, Empowering?

_____

_____

How am I doing on obedience? Check the areas listed below:

- ❑ Put God first.
- ❑ Put God in a place all by Himself.
- ❑ Honor the name of God.
- ❑ Set aside a special day to honor God each week
- ❑ Honor your parents.
- ❑ Treat human life as sacred.
- ❑ Honor marriage vows—yours and those of other people.
- ❑ Respect other people's property.
- ❑ Tell the truth.
- ❑ Find and appreciate the good in what is yours rather than focusing your desires on what other people have.

Have I hurt someone in the last week? What do I need to do about it?

_____

_____

Am I letting selected safe people get close to me emotionally? Am I building walls or bridges?

_____

_____

In checking my boundaries—physical, sexual, emotional, spiritual—what areas need work?

_____

_____

Do I need to work on the Outward Cycle—Vulnerability, Sharing, Intimacy?

_____

_____

CYCLES of RECOVERY

Brokenness

Turning Point One:
I admit my powerlessness in the face of my painful past and my current compulsions. I am ready to believe that God is truly more powerful than I am and that he can restore me to spiritual and emotional wholeness.

Surrender

Turning Point Two:
I surrender control of my life to God.

CLEANSING

Honesty

Turning Point Three:
I will take an honest moral inventory of my life.

The Inward Cycle

Confession

Turning Point Four:
I will share my moral inventory with another trusted person.

EMPOWERING

Openness

Turning Point Five:
I am ready to let God change the way I think and act.

The Upward Cycle

Asking

Turning Point Six:
I ask God to remove the defects in my character.

INTIMACY

Vulnerability

Turning Point Seven:
I am willing to share my struggles and weaknesses with selected safe people. I will ask forgiveness of the persons I have harmed.

The Outward Cycle

Sharing

Turning Point Eight:
I will share my feelings and my failures with selected safe people.

Turning Point Nine: With God's help I will keep working on my recovery.